D1121111

INTRODUCTION

to LIBRARIANSHIP

third edition

Jean Key Gates
University of South Florida

Neal-Schuman Publishers
New York   London

Published by Neal-Schuman Publishers, Inc.
23 Leonard Street
New York, NY 10013

Copyright © 1990 Jean Key Gates

All rights reserved. Reproduction of this book, in whole or in part, without written permission of the publisher is prohibited.

Printed and bound in the United States of America

Library of Congress Cataloging-in-Publication Data
Gates, Jean Key.
    Introduction to librarianship/by Jean Key Gates. -- 3rd ed.
        p.   cm.
    Includes bibliographical references (p.
    Includes index.
    ISBN 1-55570-065-9
    1. Library science.   2. Libraries.   I. Title.
Z665.G32   1990
021--dc20   90-6185
                                                            CIP

Contents

Preface

The purpose of this third edition of *Introduction to Librarianship*—like that of its predecessors—is to set forth some of the fundamental elements of librarianship in sufficient detail to help the student acquire a foundation of historical background; an understanding of major library objectives, services, and needs; and an appreciation of librarianship as a profession and a career in preparation for the complex and specialized concepts and problems to be dealt with in later courses, studies, and investigations.

In an introductory course, it is not possible to cover all aspects of this broad and rapidly expanding field. Certain topics which the author considers important have, of necessity, been omitted, and topics which the reader might consider important may also have been omitted or treated inadequately. *Introduction to Librarianship* or a course by a similar title must be supplemented by instructor and student with readings from the literature as well as with illustrative materials.

Areas which have been included in this edition are the history of libraries; the place of the library in society; types of libraries and library services; the library profession; current trends, issues, and problems;

and some important library leaders. The degree of emphasis on each of these aspects will vary from school to school, depending upon the objectives of the institution of which it is a part; the purposes of the course; the available teaching materials, facilities, and resources; the academic level of the students; the methods of instruction; and other factors. Thus, one school will give particular attention to the public library; another to the school library; another to the historical development of libraries, books, and printing; still another to the library as an essential educational, social, cultural, or utilitarian agency; and so on. It is the aim of *Introduction to Librarianship* to present a broad view of the field as well as to provide adequate references that will enable the student, teacher, or interested lay person to pursue a given topic to greater lengths. A serious effort has been made to document dates, statistics, and other hard-to-find items of information.

The material is organized into three parts: history of libraries, librarianship as a profession, and types of libraries and services. Trends, issues, and problems are discussed with the topics to which they relate rather than as separate topics; library leaders are introduced throughout the text apropos of their particular contribution or interest, or in bibliographical references; and federal legislation is presented in the appropriate chapters. Numerous cross references throughout the text and a detailed index provide easy access to all discussions.

Introduction to Librarianship is designed to provide a body of basic material for an introductory course in librarianship, whatever the title of the course may be. In addition, it can be used to supplement other courses in library science in such specific areas as the history of books and libraries, administration, and the various types of libraries and library service. For new library science students, *Introduction to Librarianship* provides material which will help them to develop the basic understanding and appreciation needed in their newly chosen career and to lay the foundation for future courses. For students with some background of study and experience in library science, it is hoped that the book will serve as a review and a helpful summary of the field and introduce them to a sampling of recent developments, problems, trends, experiments, and new materials.

I am greatly indebted to the authors, publishers, and holders of copyrights for their kind permission to use their material.

I would like to express my appreciation to my professional colleagues, especially to Dr. Alice Smith, for their encouragement and
suggestions; and to my own students as well as to students in other
library schools whose reactions to the first two editions of *Introduction to
Librarianship* have aided me in preparing this third edition.

I am grateful to my friends and my family for their continuing
interest and support.

Jean Key Gates
Professor Emeritus
School of Library and Information Science
University of South Florida

Prologue

As early as 1374, according to *The Oxford English Dictionary*, the word "library" was used in English in the sense of being a place where books were kept for "reading, study, or reference." By the nineteenth century, a library was also "a building, room, or set of rooms containing a collection of books for the use of the public or some portion of it, or the members of a society; . . . a public institution or establishment charged with the care of a collection of books."[1] In time, the concepts of circulation and administration of the collection of books were added to the definition.[2] Thus the word "library" has long been established in our language.

As a word, library is in almost everybody's vocabulary and as an institution, it is a part of almost everybody's experience—its meaning for each person depending upon the nature and extent of that experience. For most people, the addition of a descriptive word, such as "public," "school," or "college," calls to mind some particular characteristics of the type of library described—such as size, location, purpose, and accessibility. Thus, although a library is a building or an institution for the custody, circulation, and administration of a collection of books (and other materials), there are definitely established *kinds* of libraries.

The library has inspired some of our most munificent philanthropy and magnificent language. It is frequently referred to as "the heart of the institution"; it has been called "the mind of society. . . the only effective

1

repository of . . . the racial memory";[3] "a live depository of the cultural past and sustainer of the intellectual activity that anticipates the future."[4] The library is the only agency devoted solely to the purpose of collecting, preserving, making available, transmitting, and securing the widest and most effective use of the record of civilization by the society of which it is part.

The library, however, does not function alone; "a library, above all, is a human enterprise and it depends ultimately upon the skilled minds and talents of librarians if it is to perform its proper role in our changing society."[5]

To the lexicographer, the librarian was for many generations "one who has the care or charge of a library"[6]—a definition strongly suggesting a "keeper," one who watches and guards. While these have often been the functions of librarians, they have not been the only characteristics. In *Webster's Third New International Dictionary*, a librarian is defined as "a specialist in the care and management of a library," but this definition is somewhat diluted by the second meaning: "one whose vocation is working with library books (as by cataloguing)."[7] *The Random House Dictionary of the English Language* adds to the definitions the phrase "trained in library science."[8]

One might reasonably expect that the persons who have the "care, or charge, or management" of "the heart of an institution" or the "mind of society" would merit a definition indicative of the extent of their preparation, function, and performance. Some progress has been made in this direction, but, for whatever reason, the word "librarian" does not yet carry with it an indication of the kind and amount of education and other preparation required nor the number and variety of responsibilities. Unlike a teacher, for example, who may be elementary, secondary, college, or kindergarten, to most laymen a librarian is a librarian. Few people outside the profession know what is required in the way of education; what a librarian *can* or *should* do; or what the differences are in the preparation for and the activities in the several types of libraries. Not understanding what a library really is and what its management requires, nor that a librarian is educated for this specific function, the public has too often been satisfied with a "collection of books" and a "keeper" to whom they have given the name librarian. Librarianship may be the only profession in which the professional title is not reserved wholly for the professionals.

The suffix "-ship" denotes condition, office, or profession, and in general, dictionaries define librarianship as being the office, duties, or profession of librarian. It has remained for those who are librarians to define and explain the office, duties, and profession.

In 1933, when books were the main items in a library's collection, Dr. Pierce Butler of the University of Chicago Graduate Library School said that "the basic elements of librarianship consist in the accumulation of knowledge by society and its continuous transmission to the living generation so far as these processes are performed through the instrumentality of graphic records" and that "the fundamental phenomenon of librarianship . . . is the transmission of the accumulated experience of society to its individual members through the instrumentality of the book."[9] About three decades later, another library educator, Dr. Carl White, in discussing the bases of librarianship, wrote that modern librarianship is concerned with assuring the continuance and full use of the power to retain, organize, and use the accumulated heritage of all generations of all mankind in all its forms—the written word being only one.[10]

Librarianship embraces all fields of human knowledge and all forms in which it is recorded. It is made up of the people to whom the collection, preservation, use, and transmission of information and knowledge are entrusted and the programs, activities, and services which they devise to carry out these tasks. It is concerned with their preparation—their education, skills, abilities, attitudes, resources, and professional growth—and with the quality of their performance. It is concerned also with the needs of the societies they serve, their plans and efforts to meet these needs, and the results of these activities.

This book is about these three subjects: libraries, librarians, and librarianship.[11] It offers indications and suggestions about what they have been, what they are now, what they should be, and what they may become. It does not exhaust these subjects; it only introduces them.

NOTES

1. Sir James Augustus Henry Murray *et al.*, eds., *The Oxford English Dictionary*, being a corrected reissue, with an introduction, supplement, and bibliography, of *A New English Dictionary on Historical Principles* (12 vols. and supplement; London: Oxford University Press, 1933). By permission of the Clarendon Press, Oxford.
2. *Webster's New International Dictionary of the English Language* (2d ed.; Springfield, Mass.: G. & C. Merriam Co., Publishers, 1959).
3. Frank G. Jennings, "Carpe Diem," *Library Journal*, 92 (February 1, 1967): 533.
4. Ralph W. Conant, "Sociological and Institutional Changes in American Life: Their Implications for the Library," *ALA Bulletin*, 61 (May 1967): 528.

5. Francis Keppel, "Libraries: Future Unlimited," *ALA Bulletin*, 58 (December 1964): 994.
6. *Webster's New International Dictionary, op. cit.*
7. *Webster's Third New International Dictionary of the English Language* (Springfield, Mass.: G. & C. Merriam Co., Publishers, 1966).
8. *The Random House Dictionary of the English Language* (New York: Random House, Inc., 1966), p. 826. Library science is defined as "the study of the organization and administration of a library and of its technical, informational, and reference services." Reprinted from *The Random House Dictionary of the English Language* © Copyright 1966, by Random House, Inc.
9. Pierce Butler, *An Introduction to Library Science* (Chicago: University of Chicago Press, 1933), pp. 29, 84.
10. Carl M. White, ed., *Bases of Modern Librarianship* (New York: The Macmillan Co., 1964), pp. 10, 11.
11. These terms are used in their broadest sense. The American Library Association's statement of policy regarding library manpower, adopted in 1970, uses the term libraries to include the concept of media centers, learning centers, educational resources centers, and information, documentation, and referral centers. In that statement, the term librarianship encompasses the relevant concepts of information science and documentation. "Library Education and Manpower, A Statement of Policy Adopted by the Council of the American Library Association, June 30, 1970" (Chicago: American Library Association, 1970). The title was changed in 1976 to "Library Education and Personnel Utilization."

PART ONE

The Story of Libraries

The library became an indispensable agency of civilized society when the need arose for a place to keep written records of whatever sort in whatever form, so that they could be protected and preserved, used when needed, and handed on. No one plan can describe the form, nature, purposes, and services of the library throughout history since they have been determined by the needs of the people who have produced and used "the book" in its multiple forms—from the clay tablet to the original scientific report, the magnetic tape and disc, the videotape and cassette, and the various microforms of today.

The story of libraries reflects the social, economic, cultural, and educational needs to which libraries have responded and also demonstrates that the conditions which affected societies also affected the development of their libraries. Libraries have seemed to prosper:

1. In societies of political and cultural maturity which recognize the necessity of preserving, transmitting, and enlarging the body of knowledge;
2. During periods when individuals have both the leisure and the means to plan and pursue cultural and intellectual activities;
3. In periods of intellectual creativity and scholarly activity, when large and varied collections of materials are required for study and research;
4. When there is large societal emphasis on self-improvement and a well-informed citizenry;

5. During revivals of learning which center around and depend upon accumulations of graphic materials and access to them;
6. In areas with concentrated population and especially in an urban environment which can provide the leadership, the financial means to support libraries, and the cultural and intellectual interest to stimulate their use;
7. When economic prosperity provides sizable individual and corporate wealth and encourages philanthropic giving;
8. In times when, as in recent decades, economic growth and national power and status are considered to be dependent upon the wide dissemination and use of information and knowledge.

The following brief historical overview, which traces the development of libraries from the earliest times up to the twentieth century, is designed to present selected facts and describe certain movements, events, and conditions which created the need for the library and determined its character and direction, or conditions which discouraged its development and perhaps caused it to disappear.

1

Antiquity

Scholars commonly believe that civilization had its beginnings in the fertile valleys of the Tigris and Euphrates rivers. Aided by a favorable climate, rich farming lands, and their growing skills as farmers, people gradually became able to live generation after generation in the same place. Nomadic tribal settlements became towns; towns grew into cities. Governmental, economic, social, and religious institutions developed in the cities; trade, commerce, and industry expanded; and technological inventions and discoveries multiplied. In the complex organized life of the cities around 3500 B.C.,[1] writing was invented, primarily as a tool for dealing with the practical day-by-day economic, social, and administrative affairs of the community.

THE FERTILE CRESCENT

On the basis of their present knowledge, scholars believe that the Sumerians were the first people to develop a widely usable writing system. The earliest written documents are in the Sumerian language, and since 1877, when the French began the first successful excavation at a Sumerian site, the ancient city of Lagash (Telloh), a large store of Sumerian written material has been accumulated. Kramer notes "that more than ninety-five percent of all the Sumerian tablets are economic in character"[2]—tallies, accounts, and records relating to personal property and temple business. Sir Leonard Woolley emphasizes the fact that the early Sumerian pictograms "denote things, but that is all; they cannot make statements, and they cannot convey thought."[3] The Sumerians, however, were able to make the needed transition from the pictogram to the hieroglyph to the phonetic sign, so that "some time before the end of the third millennium B.C. the Sumerian men of letters actually wrote down—on clay tablets, prisms, and cylinders—many of their literary creations which until then had been current in oral form only."[4]

Thus the tool of writing, at first crude and pictographic in character, turned out to have highly significant consequences, in time being modified and molded into a phonetic system which served the Sumerians as an instrument for recording their social, political, and philosophical thinking; for maintaining the accounts of schools and social reforms; and for preserving the form and content of their hymns, prayers, rituals, sacred legends, and magic formulas. By 2700 B.C., the Sumerians had established temple, private, and government libraries in which their varied writings could be preserved and used.

Their neighbors were quick to adopt not necessarily the Sumerian system of writing, but the Sumerian idea of writing. There arose a number of scripts which, although they differed completely in form from the Sumerian, were indebted to it for the basic conception that a written sign might represent not a thing but a sound.[5] For example, Sumerian culture, including religious beliefs and practices and the Sumerian script, was readily taken over and assimilated by the Babylonians. These Semitic conquerors adapted the Sumerian script to the needs of their own language, so that in time "the Babylonian language written in the cuneiform script became the recognized diplomatic language of the middle east."[6]

Much of our knowledge of Babylonian civilization comes from the tablets of the Library of Borsippa, which were copied and then preserved in the library of King Ashurbanipal of Assyria (r. 668-626 B.C.). His library embraced all branches of learning and his reign marks the golden age of Assyrian art and literature. Through his efforts, the wisdom of the Babylonian past was brought "en masse" to his library at Nineveh.[7] The library contained thousands of tablets, tagged for identification and arranged by subject or type in alcoves, with a list of the contents of each alcove painted or carved on the entrance to serve as a catalog. It is believed that this library was open for the use of the king's subjects.

As a vehicle for conveying thought, the Babylonian cuneiform[8] system represented a revolutionary advance over the primitive pictographic form. It was, however, such an intricate system of ideographs and syllabic signs that the literate Babylonian or Assyrian had to spend years of study in its mastery. Beginning about the second millennium B.C., various peoples on the Asiatic mainland were attempting to work out new forms of writing. The main role in developing a more usable form of writing was played by the Phoenician inhabitants of the Syrian coast whose commercial activities had created the need for a simpler script to use in keeping their business records. The Phoenician alphabet of 22 consonants was more manageable than the cuneiform system because its signs were definite in their meaning and could be easily memorized so that "a man could become literate in a matter of weeks."[9]

ANTIQUITY—EGYPT

The civilization of ancient Egypt flourished simultaneously with that of Sumer. The earliest written texts date from the last quarter of the fourth millennium B.C., as do those of Sumer, but the style of writing developed by the Egyptian scribes to suit their needs and language was hieroglyphic—a name deriving from two Greek words meaning "sacred" and "to carve." The chief purpose of their writing was to provide lasting and impressive inscriptions suitable for monuments, for writing was believed to glorify kings, and the inscriptions on monuments and on the walls of the temples were meant to impress the world. Since most of the people were illiterate, the style of writing was more or less pictorial. This elaborate, pictorial, hieroglyphic style was not practical for writing manuscripts, and a cursive style called hieratic was devised for everyday use; eventually a popular script called demotic evolved.

The invention of a flexible writing material, made from the pith of the papyrus plant and known from ca. 3200 B.C., greatly advanced the progress of writing.[10] The form of the Egyptian book was the roll, and the instruments for writing were a brushlike pen and ink. While the hieroglyphs continued in use for the sacred carvings on monuments and in tombs and for inscriptions on temples, the hieratic script was used largely for religious purposes. Few people outside the priestly class were literate, and it was in the temple schools that scribes received their training. Examples of official literature as well as religious, philosophical, historical, and scientific writing survive.

Our knowledge of Egyptian libraries is scant,[11] but there are references to temple libraries and records of a library which belonged to Khufu, a monarch of the Fourth Dynasty, and another to Khafre, the builder of the second pyramid. At Edfu, the library was a small chamber in the temple on the wall of which was a list of all the works given to the priests. The only library of any significance of which we have a record was that founded by Rameses II at Thebes about 1250 B.C. This library, in which the King took great pride, is believed to have had 20,000 books[12] and was called "a place of Healing for the Soul."[13]

GREECE

In the early part of the second millennium B.C., Crete became the center of a highly developed civilization which spread to the mainland of Greece and, before the end of the fifteenth century B.C., throughout the entire Aegean area. The Cretans developed the art of writing from a pictographic system to a cursive form, Linear A, and by the fifteenth century B.C. to a system now called Linear B.[14] Many scholars believe that the language of the Linear B tablets is an early form of Greek which was spoken by the Mycenaeans who occupied Knossos ca. 1460 B.C. and eventually overthrew the Minoan Kingdom. The Mycenaeans adopted the Minoan Linear B script and improved and simplified it, but their invention was short-lived since after 1200 B.C. the Mycenaean world ceased to exist and the script disappeared.[15] A period of illiteracy is believed to have existed from the time of the disappearance of the Linear B script until the time when the Greeks adopted the consonantal 22-letter alphabet of the Phoenicians; "thus the introduction of the alphabetic script in the eighth century (most probably about the middle of the century) may be regarded as representing a new birth of literacy in Greece."[16]

Early uses of the alphabetic script were for inscriptions of a practical nature, though there are some examples of verses written on pottery. Of the seventh and sixth centuries B.C., only fragments of literature remain. Transmission of literature continued to be oral—poets and rhapsodes recited their works to an audience—but by the fifth century oral tradition declined and by the end of the last decade of the fifth century, books became common and private libraries existed. Athenaeus refers to the libraries of Euripides and others in the fifth century when the civilization of ancient Greece reached its golden age under Pericles—a time which saw the spread of reading as a pastime and the development of a book trade.[17] Aristotle (384-322 B.C.) is said to have been the first person to collect, preserve, and use the culture of the past.[18]

The most important libraries of ancient Greece were established during the Hellenistic Age—a period which was characterized by the spread of Greek culture and learning through the conquests of Alexander and his successors, the creation of new Greek cities, and the development of monarchal governments. These libraries were located at Alexandria in Egypt and in the kingdom of Pergamum in Asia Minor.

The new city of Alexandria, established at the direction of Alexander by Ptolemy Soter in 332 B.C., was destined to become not only one of the world's most splendid cities but also the intellectual and literary center of the Hellenistic world. In the Royal Greek Center of the city, Ptolemy I (305-283 B.C.) founded the Museum, an academy of scholars under royal patronage, consecrated to the Muses and dedicated to learning. An essential part of the Museum was the library (called the Museion or the Brucheion) and its aim was to collect all Greek texts as well as manuscripts in all languages from all parts of the known world and to provide facilities for writing and copying books.

Demetrius of Phalerum, who had been largely influential in establishing both the Museum and its library, was given the task of building the collection. Manuscripts were acquired in every way possible—by private purchase or force, honestly or otherwise—and under his administration the holdings grew to 200,000 rolls. The library was greatly enlarged and enriched by succeeding Ptolemies, and by the middle of the first century B.C., it contained more than 700,000 rolls. A second library, the Serapeum, was established by Ptolemy III in the Temple of Serapis in another section of Alexandria. To this library was allocated a collection of 42,800 carefully selected rolls; the collection was gradually enlarged until it reached more than 100,000 rolls.

The vast holdings of the two libraries were classified and organized, and, in addition, two other important tasks were carried out: all texts were edited, arranged into convenient form,[19] and provided with commentaries; and a comprehensive bibliography of Greek literature was compiled.

All the librarians of Alexandria were scholars—poets, critics, or grammarians. Zenodotus, said to be the first librarian and the first editor of the Homeric and other poems,[20] is given credit for dividing the *Iliad* and *Odyssey* into 24 books each. Aristophanes of Byzantium, who systematized accentuation and punctuation, produced the first collected edition of Pindar. The poet Callimachus was given the responsibility for compiling a bibliography of Greek literature, and he is said to have made lists of authors and their works which included brief biographies, dates of the production of certain dramas, and the number of lines in each work. His *Tables of All Those Who Were Eminent in Any Kind of Literature and of Their Writings* (the *Pinakes*) is claimed to have filled 120 volumes in which the works cataloged were arranged by categories: drama, legislation, history, poetry, oratory, rhetoric, and miscellaneous.[21] "The scholars of Alexandria were . . . the earliest examples of the professional scholar and they deserve the gratitude of the modern world for criticizing and classifying the literature of the golden age of Greece and handing it down to posterity."[22]

Although there is not complete agreement regarding the fate of the Alexandrian libraries, some historians date the destruction of the Museion from Julius Caesar's campaign in Alexandria in 47 B.C. and that of the Serapeum from the reign of Theodosius the Great (379-395), whose edicts against paganism resulted in the destruction of many pagan temples.

In northwest Asia Minor, Pergamum, like Alexandria, became a great center of learning and literary activity. In the second century B.C., Eumenes II founded a library, and, following the example of the Ptolemies, he assiduously searched the Hellenic world for manuscripts. Both cities and individuals were prevailed upon to part with their written treasures. Copies were made when originals were not obtainable, and for this copying program great quantities of papyrus were imported from Egypt. Jealous of this rival library and hoping to halt its growth, Ptolemy VII—then King of Egypt—forbade the export of papyrus to Pergamum. Of necessity, a new writing material, called parchment, was developed in Pergamum, making it possible to continue the copying of manuscripts, and the holdings of the Pergamene library reached a total of 200,000 rolls.[23] Crates of Mallos, known for his criticism of Homer, became head of the school and librarian at Pergamum and was probably responsible for making a classified listing of works in the library.[24]

Pergamum's great library remained in active use for nearly a hundred years. It is believed that Antony gave it to Cleopatra[25] (the last of the Ptolemies) and that she, in turn, added it to the collection of the Serapeum in Alexandria, making Alexandria again the site of the largest library in the world.

ROME

Rome had felt the influence of Greek culture since the beginning of the period of Greek colonization in Italy (ca. 760 B.C.) and, finally, with the conquest of Greece in 146 B.C., Rome inherited the achievements of Greece in philosophy, art, literature, music, theater, and everyday life. Romans read and studied Greek literature, philosophy, and science; sent their sons to Athens to be educated; and, at times, spoke Greek.

Private libraries became an important feature of Roman civilization when generals began to bring back entire libraries as spoils of war from their campaigns in Greece. For example, Sulla captured Athens in 86 B.C. and with it, the library of Aristotle.[26] Another collection which had been brought back by Lucullus 23 years earlier was the basis of his library, which, according to Plutarch, he opened to all Greeks.[27]

From the time of Cicero (106-43 B.C.), who had a library in each of his villas, private libraries were a necessity since the educated man required both Greek and Latin works. Manuscripts were sought eagerly in Rome and Athens for the libraries of wealthy collectors; and private libraries became so fashionable, numerous, and large by the middle of the first century that Seneca spoke out against the collecting of books "not for the sake of learning, but to make a show."[28] The great demand for books stimulated book production, and multiple copies were made by dictating the text to a roomful of slaves. Bookstores occupied prominent places on the busiest streets and often were the meeting places for scholars.

By the time of Julius Caesar, Greek influences—especially from Alexandria and Pergamum—were widely in evidence, particularly in the growing appreciation of literature. With the prospect of an extended period of peace after long years of building a strong national life, it was possible to give attention to cultivating the minds and talents of the people. Caesar wanted to found Greek and Latin libraries and open them to the public. His libraries would preserve books and records, serve as a means of instructing the people, and add to the cultural influence already being exerted by the private libraries, bookshops, and schools; and the nucleus of their collections would be the historical and political archives. Marcus Terentius Varro was to organize and manage them. Although these plans were interrupted by Caesar's death, they were carried out by Asinius Pollio in the reign of Augustus, who began the imperial custom of establishing libraries by founding the Palatine Library in the Temple of Apollo with both Greek and Latin collections. Later a second library, the Octavian, was set up in a temple dedicated to Juno and Jupiter.

The period from A.D. 96 to 180 has been called the high point of ancient civilization. During this time of peace, prosperity, and order, not only the accumulated inheritance of art, letters, philosophy, and the science of government was handed down from generation to generation, but new literary production was encouraged. More than 25 public libraries flourished in Rome in the second century.[29] The Ulpian Library in Rome, a scholarly collection housed in two structures—one for Greek and one for Latin works—was founded by Trajan.[30] Among ancient libraries, it was second in importance only to those of Alexandria and Pergamum. The library founded by Emperor Hadrian (r. A.D. 117-138) in the Temple of Olympeium in Athens was known widely for the magnificence of its building and the quality of its collection.

As a significant part of Rome's civilizing process, libraries spread throughout the Empire to important towns and cities in Italy, Greece, Asia Minor, Cyprus, and Africa. Typical of these was the one established by Emperor Trajan (r. A.D. 98-117) at Timgad in North Africa. There were private libraries in the provinces also. In the excavation of Herculaneum, which had been covered with volcanic ash in the eruption of Mt. Vesuvius in A.D. 79, a library was found in what is now called the "Villa of the Papyri." The Celsus Library in Ephesus was built in A.D. 135.

At the height of the Roman Empire, a new book form came into prominence. The roll, inconvenient to write on and to read and difficult to consult quickly, was superseded by the codex, in which parchment sheets were fastened and bound together as in a modern book.

The transition from the roll to the codex has been called the "most momentous development in the history of the book until the invention of printing."[31] The physical origin of the codex dates back to the writing tablet, which was made of two or more pieces of wax-coated wood held together by a strong clasp or a string—one of the oldest forms of writing materials known to the Greeks. However, the use of the word codex for book dates only from the second half of the third century. The codex form was used universally by Christians in the second century and by the fourth century, it became the dominant form used for all literature— pagan and Christian.

The codex was cheap, convenient, and saved space. It accommodated more text on a given amount of papyrus than the roll: the average content of the codex was said to be perhaps six times that of the roll.[32] It could be consulted easily—a feature of major usefulness in legal works and in Christian writings. The physical form, with title and list of contents provided a means of control over the text, making difficult any additions or substitutions.[33] In addition, the codex form of a book greatly improved its chances for survival, a factor of extreme importance in long works like the Homeric poems.[34] The use of parchment in codexes, which further improved the chances for survival, also made possible larger pages than using papyrus, thus providing room for illustrations or for the marginal notes and commentaries now so important to scholars.

By the third century, the body of Christian literature had materially increased and Christian libraries had been established in many places throughout the Empire. Two important Christian centers for learning were at Alexandria, dating from about A.D. 180, and at Caesarea, where a notable library was assembled; in the western provinces, Carthage, in Africa, became the first center of Christian scholarship and libraries.

During the third century, barbarian invaders succeeded in making considerable inroads into the Roman Empire. Civil strife, combined with the attacks of Germanic tribes to the north and pressure from the Persian kings to the east, threatened to disrupt the Empire and resulted in the loss of entire provinces. However, before the end of the century, Emperor Diocletian (284-305) had begun the task of restoring the strength and power of the imperial government and of returning the Empire to its early greatness. As a part of his plan to secure efficient administrative control over the Empire, he divided it into eastern and western spheres and established a system by which he was "supreme commander of the East with a colleague, Maximian, to govern the Western provinces."[35] In 303, Diocletian instituted a persecution against the Christians which raged until 313, when Constantine—who had openly accepted Christianity—issued the Edict of Milan giving Christians religious freedom and restoring their property and their civil rights. During the ten-year persecution, many churches with their libraries were razed and great numbers of books were burned.

Constantine the Great became Emperor of both the Eastern and the Western Roman Empire in 324, at which time he chose a new capital, Byzantium (which he called Constantinople), made it the seat of his government in 330, and named Christianity the state religion. Moving the capital from Rome to Constantinople was to have far-reaching cultural as well as political and religious significance. As the major center of Greek learning and scholarship, Constantinople became the source of civilization to both Eastern and Western Europe.

Constantine began the establishment of the imperial library and emphasized the collecting of Latin works, since Latin was the official language until about the sixth century. His successors enriched the library by the addition of Christian and pagan works, both Latin and Greek, and employed scribes to copy manuscripts. By the fifth century, the imperial library had about 120,000 volumes, the largest book collection in Europe.[36] During that century, Theodosius II, a serious scholar and an ardent book collector, founded the University of Constantinople, which became the most important center of learning in the Empire.

The church was the Empire's most important institution in its early days and bishops, monks, and priests were more prominent than secular scholars and writers. Church buildings multiplied and, as a consequence of the requirement that each bishop have a library, ecclesiastical libraries and monastic collections were established widely.

During the fourth and fifth centuries, invasions by barbarian tribes into the western parts of the Empire continued with increasing frequency. Britain, Gaul, Spain, and North Africa were conquered, and in 476 the western part of the Roman Empire fell to the invaders. At this very time, however, the eastern part—called the Byzantine Empire—was entering a period of vitality and progress which was to last almost a thousand years.[37]

In Rome and other urban centers in Italy during the sixth century, classical culture was kept alive, secular letters were cultivated, and some literature was produced. The most notable scholar and writer in Italy during this century was Boethius, whose works included theological and philosophical writings and Latin translations of the works of Aristotle with commentaries. From these translations and commentaries the Western world derived its knowledge of Aristotle for the next six centuries.[38]

A final attempt to restore the former bounds of the Roman Empire and to reestablish one absolute emperor was made by Justinian, who, as emperor of the Byzantine Empire (527-565), directed all his efforts toward these goals and succeeded in recovering Italy, North Africa, and parts of Spain. In both territorial expansion and the revival of cultural activities, some of the former grandeur of the old Roman Empire was recovered. The age of Justinian produced a culture which covered almost every branch of learning in some degree; it is especially noteworthy for its contributions in mathematics, science, law, architecture, and art.

NOTES

1. M. E. L. Mallowan, "Civilized Life Begins . . . ," *The Dawn of Civilization*, ed. Stuart Piggott (New York: McGraw-Hill Book Co., 1961), p. 83.
2. Samuel Noah Kramer, *Sumerian Mythology, A Study of Spiritual and Literary Achievement in the Third Millennium, B.C.* (Rev. ed.; New York: Harper Torchbooks, Harper and Row, Publishers, Inc., 1961), p. 10.
3. Sir Leonard Woolley, *History of Mankind, Cultural and Scientific Development*, Vol. I, Part 2: *The Beginnings of Civilization* (New York: Mentor Books, New American Library of World Literature, Inc., 1965), p. 364.

4. Samuel Noah Kramer, *History Begins at Sumer* (Indian Hills, Colo.: Falcon Wing's Press, 1956), p. xix.

5. Woolley, *op. cit.*, p. 364.

6. *Ibid.*, p. 383. *See also* Ernst Posner, *Archives of the Ancient World* (Cambridge, Mass.: Harvard University Press, 1972), p. 73.

7. A. T. Olmstead, *History of Assyria* (Chicago: University of Chicago Press, 1951), p. 490. Olmstead also describes the manner in which Ashurbanipal collected materials for his library. Sir Austen Henry Layard discovered the library of King Ashurbanipal together with the ruins of ancient Nineveh in the 1840s. Some 25,000 tablets were found in the ruins.

8. The key to cuneiform writing is the Behistun inscription which is located on the side of a mountain in Iran. Written in three languages (Old Persian, Elamite, and Accadian), it was deciphered by Sir Henry Rawlinson ca. 1846.

9. Woolley, *op. cit.*, pp. 387 ff.

10. In order to make a papyrus sheet, the marrow of papyrus stalks was cut into thin strips and laid flat, side by side, one layer crossways over the other. The two layers were treated with a gum solution, pressed, pounded, and smoothed until the surface was suitable for writing, and then sized to resist the ink.

11. *See* Ernst Posner, *Archives of the Ancient World* (Cambridge, Mass.: Harvard Univ. Press, 1972), p. 86, regarding Egyptian libraries.

12. C. L. Nichols, *The Library of Rameses the Great* (Cambridge: Cambridge University Press, 1909), p. 30.

13. *Ibid.*, p. 10.

14. In 1900, Sir Arthur Evans made his first discovery of clay tablets in Linear B stored in the Palace of Knossos. In 1939, over 500 tablets were found at Pylos; many more have been found at Pylos since World War II and at Mycenae also from 1952 on. *See* M. S. F. Hood, "The Home of the Heroes: The Aegean Before the Greeks," Piggott, *op. cit.*, pp. 216, 220. *See also* Rudolf Pfeiffer, *History of Classical Scholarship from the Beginnings to the End of the Hellenistic Age* (Oxford: At the Clarendon Press, 1968), p. 20.

15. Woolley, *op. cit.*, pp. 385-386, *passim*.

16. Alan J. B. Wace and Frank H. Stubbins, eds., *A Companion to Homer* (London: Macmillan and Co., Ltd. 1963), pp. 217, 552, *passim*. Scholars are not in agreement regarding the date of the adoption of the Greek alphabet. Suggested dates range from as early as the fourteenth century B.C. to the end of the eighth century B.C. *Ibid.*, p. 554.

17. Athenaeus, *The Deipnosophists* (Cambridge, Mass.: Harvard University Press, 1951). I, 11.

18. The fate of his library is told by Strabo, who relates that Aristotle left his library to Theophrastus, who willed it to Neleus, who, in turn, took it to Scepsis and bequeathed it to his heirs. Later, when the Attalid kings of Pergamum were gathering manuscripts for their library, the descendants of Neleus hid the books underground in a kind of trench, where they remained until, much later, they were sold to Apellicon of Teos for a large sum of money. It was the library of Apellicon, including that of Aristotle, which Sulla confiscated when he captured Athens in 86 B.C. *See The Geography of Strabo*, with an English translation by Horace Leonard Jones ("The

Loeb Classical Library"; Cambridge, Mass.: Harvard University Press, 1960), VI, 111, 113.

19. *See* James T. Shotwell, *The Story of Ancient History* (New York: Columbia University Press, 1939), pp. 55-56.

20. Pfeiffer, Rudolph, *History of Classical Scholarship from the Beginnings to the End of the Hellenistic Age* (Oxford: At the Clarendon Press, 1968), p. 105, 106.

21. Frederick William Hall, *A Companion to Classical Texts* (Oxford: Clarendon Press, 1913), p. 32.

22. Sir John Edwin Sandys, *A History of Classical Scholarship*, Vol. I: *From the Sixth Century B.C. to the End of the Middle Ages* (3d ed.; Cambridge: Cambridge University Press, 1921), p. 144.

23. Parchment was the skin of animals, principally that of the sheep or calf, prepared for writing. Although this kind of writing material had been known to the Greeks for some time, it had not been used widely, since papyrus was cheaper and easier to write on. During the reign of Eumenes II, parchment was developed and improved. It eventually displaced papyrus and continued to be the chief writing material until the invention of printing.

24. Crates also served as envoy to the Roman Senate. While in Rome he suffered an accident, and during the period of his recovery, he gave many lectures on Greek literature and many recitations. He is said to have been the first to introduce the Romans to the scholarly study of literature. Sandys, *op. cit.*, p. 159.

25. *Plutarch's Lives of Illustrious Men,* corrected from the Greek and revised by A. H. Clough (Boston: Little, Brown and Company, 1930), p. 674.

26. *See* p. 11 and 17, footnote 18.

27. *Ibid.*, p. 367.

28. Seneca, "De Tranquillitate Animi," in Seneca, *Moral Essays*, with an English translation by John W. Basore ("The Loeb Classical Library"; Cambridge, Mass.: Harvard University Press, 1958), pp. 247, 249.

29. F. R. Cowell, "The Greece and Rome of Everyday," *The Birth of Western Civilization: Greece and Rome*, ed. Michael Grant (New York: McGraw-Hill Book Co., 1964), p. 205.

30. The Roman Empire reached its greatest extent about A.D. 117 under Trajan.

31. C. H. Roberts, and T. C. Skeat, *The Birth of the Codex* (London: published for the British Academy by the Oxford University Press, 1987), p. 1. *See also* C. H. Roberts, "The Codex," *Proceedings of The British Academy* 40 (1954): 169.

32. Roberts and Skeat, *op. cit.*, p. 76; Roberts, *op. cit.*, p. 202.

33. Roberts, *op. cit.*, p. 200. *See also* L. D. Reynolds and N. G. Wilson, *Scribes and Scholars, A Guide to the Transmission of Greek and Latin Literature* (London: Oxford University Press, 1968), pp. 29-31.

34. Wace and Stubbins, *op. cit.*, p. 225.

35. Michael Gough, "From the Ancient to the Medieval World: A Bridge of Faith," *The Birth of Western Civilization*, ed. Michael Grant (New York: McGraw-Hill Book Company, 1964), p. 329.

36. James Westfall Thompson, *The Medieval Library* (New York: Hafner Publishing Co. Inc., 1957), p. 313.

37. *See* pp. 29-30.

38. M. L. W. Laistner, *Thought and Letters in Western Europe A.D. 500 to 900* (Rev. ed.; Ithaca, N.Y.: Cornell Paperbacks, Cornell University Press, 1957), p. 87.

2

The Early Middle Ages

The restored Empire came apart under Justinian's successors, and as the sixth century advanced, the West again fell victim to the invading barbarians. Centralized control in Western Europe came to an end except for that of the papal state of Rome. Learning and literature continued to decline, leaving the monasteries as the only repositories of culture and education in Western Europe.

WESTERN MONASTICISM

Christian monasticism, which had originated in Egypt in the last years of the third century, was introduced into the West by Athanasius and greatly advanced by the efforts of St. Martin, who founded religious settlements in Poitiers and later at Tours. Monastic foundations quickly multiplied in other parts of Gaul and in Italy since the monasteries offered a life of stability and security in contrast to the disorder and confusion of the barbarian conquests that brought an end to the Western Roman Empire. Looked upon as the refuge of holy men, the monasteries were often spared in war and frequently received gifts of land and such special privileges as exemption from taxes.

Of particular importance in the story of Western monasticism is St. Benedict, who founded several religious communities near Subiaco in Italy and a larger monastery at Monte Cassino (ca. 529) and who formulated a rule for the guidance of his monks which was eventually adopted by most monasteries in the West. This Benedictine Rule was made up of moral and religious precepts and specific rules of conduct and organization, including devotional reading. Although this reading requirement suggests the existence of a library, the only kinds of mental activities encouraged in the early monasteries were those contributing directly to spiritual growth. It was not until the last half of the sixth century that the monastery became a center for all studies and for the preservation of all writings, both religious and secular. These important developments began with Cassiodorus.

A contemporary of Boethius and a distinguished official under three Ostrogothic kings, Cassiodorus had wanted to establish in Rome a center for the study and teaching of Christian literature comparable to those in which pagan literature had been taught. However, this desire was not fulfilled; and when, upon his retirement, he established the monastic community of Vivarium (ca. 540 or 553), he made it a center for religious studies based on the Bible and recommended to the monks the reading and studying of secular as well as Christian authors in order to better understand the Scriptures. To support his program of studies, he set up a great library, giving his personal collection to the monastery and adding manuscripts of the great literature of the past—Greek and Latin, pagan and Christian—which he collected from many parts of the world. The library was further enlarged and enriched by the products of the scriptorium which he established for the copying of Christian and secular literature and the translating of Greek authors into Latin. As patron, editor, and writer, he set high standards of achievement. His zeal in bringing together a large and diversified library assured the preservation of much ancient writing, both sacred and profane, which otherwise would have perished in those disturbed days.[1]

In other parts of the West, continuous wars and invasions created conditions highly unfavorable to cultural activities, but in Spain the scholarly writings of Isidore, Bishop of Seville (d. 636), on a wide range of subjects indicate the breadth of his reading and reveal the extent of the library at Seville. His most extensive work, the *Etymologiae*, an encyclopedia of the arts and sciences containing much of the learning of the ancient world, became a standard reference work found in most monastic libraries.

Although Cassiodorus may be regarded as "the inaugurator of the learned, compiling, commenting, and transcribing functions of monasticism,"[2] the preservation and transmission of learning in the widest sense—literature, history, rhetoric, grammar, and astronomy as well as the Scriptures and the writings of the Church Fathers—began in northwestern Europe in the period of monastic expansion during the first half of the seventh century.

Ireland and Britain

Unconquered by the Romans, Ireland's tribal, agricultural society was virtually undisturbed by outside forces until the Norsemen came late in the eighth century. In 431, a bishop was sent from Rome to organize a church, and the following year Patrick arrived on his historic Christianizing mission.

In the sixth century numerous monasteries came into existence,[3] including Clonard, Clonmacnois, and Bangor, and all monasteries encouraged learning. Although Latin was the language of the church, the Irish vernacular continued to be used in ordinary speech and for written composition. Manuscripts of the Bible and of theological works and writings of secular authors had been brought into the country during the fifth and sixth centuries. Schools in the larger monasteries attracted many students and, from the seventh century, many foreign students. The Scriptures, writings of the Church Fathers, Latin classics, mathematics, and astronomy were studied. The Scriptures were in Latin and Greek, and from Ireland, the pure classical Latin was carried back to the continent of Europe.

In the scriptoria of the Irish monasteries, a national script and a national art evolved and the first great development of manuscript books was begun. These books were characterized by superb calligraphy and illumination[4] and fine workmanship. In fact, manuscript art attained an eminence never surpassed, reaching its height in the *Book of Kells*, a manuscript of the Gospels written in the eighth century and representing Irish calligraphy and illumination at its best; it is believed to be the most richly decorated manuscript ever produced by an Irish scriptorium.[5]

Irish monks were characterized by their asceticism, their zeal for learning, and their missionary spirit. They became the greatest missionaries of the early Middle Ages, taking the Gospel and their learning and art to Scotland, northern England, and Europe, and establishing many monastic centers in which learning was kept alive.

Foremost among the missionaries was St. Columba who founded several monasteries in Ireland, including Durrow and Kells, and then went to the coast of north Britain, where at Iona (ca. 565) he established a monastery with a scriptorium and a library. From Iona, Irish missionaries went to northern Britain to found at Lindisfarne in Northumbria (ca. 634) the first of a series of monastic houses. Lindisfarne became the center for intellectual activity on the east coast. Throughout Northumbria churches and religious houses were established, and in their schools Irish teachers taught English boys not only the rudiments of knowledge but also advanced learning.[6] The monastery at Iona and her dependent houses were famous for their illuminated books, notably the Book of Durrow, a copy of the Latin Gospels; and the Lindisfarne Gospels, a copy of the Vulgate text, which is the greatest surviving example of Northumbrian book production in the period of Celtic influence.

From the monastery at Bangor, another Irish monk, Columban, took Irish Christianity to the Continent; in northern France he founded a number of monasteries, including Luxeuil, which became the greatest monastery of the time and an important writing center. His last monastery, founded in 614 at Bobbio in the Apennines, had a library and an active scriptorium. Columban's disciples founded the Abbey of Corbie in France and the monastery of St. Gall in Switzerland, which became great writing centers in the eighth and ninth centuries. Bobbio, Corbie, and St. Gall maintained close relations with Luxeuil and continued to be strongly influenced by Irish tradition and practices.

Irish monks, teachers, and pilgrims took not only the Scriptures and the lives of the saints with them to the Continent, but also their own Latin writings on theology and on the learned disciplines taught in their schools; many of these were masterpieces of illumination. These writings are known almost exclusively from copies preserved on the Continent and later in England, since great numbers of manuscripts were lost when the Vikings invaded Ireland in the eighth century and destroyed churches and monasteries and with them their libraries and schools.[7]

During the period of Irish missionary and cultural activity in Scotland and northern Britain and on the Continent, the church at Rome sent a mission to southern England, and in 597 the monk Augustine landed at Kent, where he founded the church at Canterbury. After 597, there were continuous relations between Britain and Italy, and pilgrims and travelers often brought back books and manuscripts. In the next century, under Theodore and Hadrian (ca. 669), the school at Canterbury became an educational center, attracting great numbers of students. Both Greek and Latin were taught, and the library, enriched by manuscripts which

Theodore and Hadrian brought from Rome, had Greek and Latin works as well as many theological and secular works that had not formerly been known in Britain.[8]

In the eighth century, Benedict Biscop founded the joint monasteries of Wearmouth and Jarrow in Northumbria. On numerous trips to Rome, he made a point of securing great numbers of books to enrich the library, a practice that was continued by his successors. This great collection of books made possible the literary work of Bede, the most learned theologian and most widely read and comprehensive author of the early Middle Ages.

Like the Irish church, the English church sent missionaries to the Continent. Most eminent was Boniface, called the Apostle to Germany, who was instrumental in the formation of many monasteries. Fulda, his greatest monastery, founded in the eighth century, became a center of learning and literature in Germany. Its library was strengthened by gifts of manuscripts from England as well as by copies made in its scriptorium.

For more than a century and a half after Cassiodorus, the Irish, first alone and later with the Anglo-Saxons, were the chief transmitters and preservers of learning in the West and the "decisive cultural factor throughout the territory of the future Carolingian Empire."[9]

THE CAROLINGIAN RENAISSANCE

At the mid-point between ancient and modern history stands the commanding figure of Charles the Great. The centuries of the Middle Ages which precede him record the decadence and final extinction of ancient institutions, while the nearly equal number of centuries which follow up to the time of the Renaissance and Reformation record the preparation for modern history. Thus, as finisher of the old order of things and beginner of the new, he is the central secular personage in that vast stretch of time between antiquity and the modern world, which we call the Middle Ages.[10]

The reign of Charles the Great (Charlemagne, 768-814) was marked by his efforts to raise the educational and cultural level of all his subjects, which brought a period of educational and cultural growth and a revival of sacred and profane studies to Western Europe. Giving first attention to improving the education of the clergy, on whom his educational program would depend, Charlemagne then extended his interest to "all who were able to learn according to the capacity of each individual."[11]

Alcuin, master of the school at York in Northumbria and renowned throughout Britain for his teaching, was chosen by Charlemagne to direct his educational program. In 782, Alcuin became head of the Palace School in Aachen and began the task of establishing educational centers and of disseminating learning throughout the Frankish empire. Under his leadership, schools were founded, educational reforms were introduced, and grants for the purpose of establishing schools were made to the clergy, who were instructed to educate both the sons of freemen and those of servile origin. In his *Mind of the Middle Ages,* Henry Osborn Taylor refers to this period as "the schoolday of the Middle Ages," pointing out that "the whole period was at school . . . at school to the Church Fathers, at school to the transmitters of antique culture."[12]

Scriptoria were established in the monasteries and in many cathedrals; a library became a necessary part of religious institutions; and a carefully planned system of selecting, collecting, and copying scholarly literature, both religious and secular, was begun.[13] Correct Latin for literary purposes was revived, and authentic copies of the best texts were made. A new style of writing, the Caroline minuscule, was developed. This style was adopted everywhere for manuscripts written in Latin and was copied centuries later in metal types by the early printers to print the Latin classics.

When Alcuin retired from the Palace School to the monastery of St. Martin at Tours, one of the oldest and wealthiest in the kingdom, he set about making it a center of learning by introducing the study of the liberal arts,[14] which he had introduced at York and later emphasized at the Palace School. To support his program of studies, he sent to York to obtain the scholarly works which he had used while master of the school there; the York library was one of the most famous in Christendom and was reputed to contain whatever learning there was at that time.

In addition to his program of instruction, Alcuin supervised the copying of manuscripts in the scriptorium, giving careful attention to punctuation, spelling, and style of writing. These works served as models for copyists for many generations.

> Perceiving that the precious treasure of knowledge was then hidden in a few books, he [Alcuin] made it his care to transmit to future ages copies undisfigured by slips of the pen or mistakes of the understanding. . . .Thus, in every way that lay within his power, he endeavored to put the fortunes of learning for the times that should succeed him in a position of advantage, safeguarded by an abundance of truthfully transcribed books, interpreted by teachers of his own training, sheltered within the church, and defended by the civil power.[15]

This revival of learning, sponsored by Charlemagne and inspired and directed by Alcuin, is called the Carolingian Renaissance. Out of the renewed educational activity had come new interest in all learning. Even after the partial collapse of Charlemagne's empire, interest in education and the cultivation of letters continued. "It was due to the efforts of the Carolingian scholars that the Latin past was salvaged at all . . . anything that reached the eighth century has survived for our use today."[16]

The Carolingian Renaissance did not extend beyond the Frankish empire, but a century later King Alfred (871-899) tried to do for his kingdom of Wessex what Charlemagne had done in the Frankish empire. He brought foreign scholars to Wessex to reintroduce learning on a broad scale and organized a school attached to his household in which his own sons, the sons of noblemen, and even those from humble families were taught to read both Latin and the vernacular. Since only a few men could read Latin but many could read the vernacular, Alfred's educational plans included translating Latin works into the vernacular, and he himself undertook the translation of several works. During the latter part of the ninth and throughout the tenth century, Wessex was the cultural center of England, with schools, monasteries, and scriptoria.

THE SCRIPTORIA

The story of the libraries in which manuscripts were preserved during this period cannot be separated from the story of the scriptoria[17] in which manuscripts were copied; both libraries and scriptoria are a part of the story of Western monasticism.

Every monastery of any importance made some provision for copying manuscripts, usually a scriptorium. Logically, the most productive scriptoria were in monasteries and cathedrals with sizable libraries. Library catalogs of the later eighth and ninth centuries show that most of the major monastic foundations acquired large collections of manuscripts. From the time of Charlemagne, the practice of copying both religious works and Latin classics was diligently followed. The scriptorium of a large monastery or abbey would have a number of scribes: some did ordinary copying while others who were specially trained in calligraphy or in illumination made the beautiful books for which the period is renowned. Manuscript art attracted the best artists of the period, and in addition to the scribes living in the monastery, secular scribes were often brought in for special tasks. In many monasteries, multiple copies of an author or a particular work were made and some

were distributed to other monasteries. "It was the universal multiplica-
tion of copies in the century 750-850 that enabled scholarship to survive
the disasters[18] of the following century and hand on a legacy to the
future."[19]

The seventh- and eighth-century scriptoria in Ireland, Britain, and
on the Continent have already been noted. Some of these scriptoria
became increasingly active in the ninth century, notably Bobbio, Corbie,
St. Gall, and Tours, and their libraries grew correspondingly, having
large collections of both sacred and secular literature. There were many
other scriptoria in the monasteries and cathedrals of Europe, and the
frequent references to the borrowing and lending of manuscripts for
copying reveal that there were close working relationships among them.

Although some scriptoria declined in the tenth century, others, like
St. Gall and Fleury, became more productive. The borrowing and lending
of manuscripts continued, and the many extant manuscripts copied in
the tenth century attest to the activity of the scriptoria and their role in
the transmission of Carolingian culture.

NOTES

1. Laistner, M.L.W., *Thought and Letters in Western Europe, A.D. 500 to 900* (Rev.
   ed.; Ithaca, N.Y.: Cornell Paperbacks, Cornell University Press, 1957),
   p. 102.
2. Henry Osborn Taylor, *The Mediaeval Mind, A History of the Development of
   Thought and Emotion in the Middle Ages* (4th ed.; Cambridge, Mass.: Harvard University Press, 1925), I, 94.
3. Ludwig Bieler, *Ireland, Harbinger of the Middle Ages* (London: Oxford University Press, 1963), p. 24. *See* map showing the major monasteries.
4. Illumination was the adornment of manuscripts, using ornamental letters,
   scrolls, or miniatures (small paintings) in color. The principal colors were
   red, blue, and gold; purple, yellow, and green were also used.
5. Bieler, *op. cit.*, p. 134.
6. John Godfrey, *The Church in Anglo-Saxon England* (Cambridge: Cambridge
   University Press, 1962), p. 106.
7. Bieler, *op. cit.*, p. 110.
8. Laistner, *op. cit.*, p. 151.
9. Bieler, *op. cit.*, p. 104. *See also* map on p. VIII showing the most important
   centers of Irish-Christian influence.
10. Andrew Fleming West, *Alcuin and the Rise of Christian Schools* ("The Great
    Educators"; New York: Charles Scribner's Sons, 1892), p. 1.
11. "Letter of Charlemagne to Abbot Baugulf, 780-800," *Basic Documents in Medi-
    eval History*, ed. Norton Downs (Princeton, N.J.: Anvil Books, D. Van
    Nostrand Co., Inc., 1959), p. 32.
12. Taylor, *op. cit.*, pp. 103, 214.

13. According to Einhard, Charlemagne commanded that at his death the books which he had collected in his library in great numbers be sold for fair prices and the money given to the poor. Einhard, *The Life of Charlemagne,* with a foreword by Sidney Painter (Ann Arbor, Mich.: Ann Arbor Paperbacks, University of Michigan Press, 1960), p. 66.

14. The subjects believed to ensure a liberal education were the *trivium*: grammar, rhetoric, and dialectic; and the *quadrivium*: arithmetic, music, geometry, and astronomy. (Laistner, *op. cit.,* pp. 40-41.)

15. West, *op. cit.,* pp. 122, 123.

16. Philip Grierson, "Charlemagne and the Carolingian Achievement," *Dawn of European Civilization*, ed. David Talbot Rice (New York: McGraw-Hill Book Company, 1966), pp. 294, 295.

17. *See* James Westfall Thompson, *The Medieval Library* (New York: Hafner Publishing Co., Inc. 1957). p. 313, pp. 594-612, and Laistner, *op. cit.,* pp. 225-237, for discussions of the scriptoria of this period.

18. *See* the Viking Invasions, p. 22.

19. Grierson, *op. cit.,* p. 295.

3

The Middle Ages: A.D. 850 to 1200

The breakdown of Charlemagne's empire was hastened by invasions from all sides, and the pieces out of which he and his predecessors had put together their empire fell apart along old geographical and tribal lines. From the ninth and tenth to the twelfth and thirteenth centuries, the personal relationships which existed between the fighting and landholding classes and their subjugated peasantry formed the basis of the social and political system of feudalism. Although it had existed in the Frankish kingdom since the eighth century and had been encouraged by Charlemagne, feudalism did not become widespread until the beginning of the tenth century when the need for protection against barbarian invaders became urgent. In this time of almost continuous warfare, the monastery once again became the retreat of literature and learning in Western Europe. In the East, however, the Byzantine Empire was flourishing.

THE BYZANTINE EMPIRE

The Byzantine Empire was wealthy and thickly populated by people whose heritage of civilization went back to the time of the invention of writing. Politically, intellectually, and culturally mature, enriched by Greek and Oriental learning, and influenced by the Roman tradition in government, it did not experience any "dark ages." For more than 11 centuries, Constantinople survived the attacks of barbarians and the encroachments of the Arabs and became in the eighth, ninth, and tenth centuries the "most stable and cultured power in the world, and on its existence hung the future of civilisation."[1]

From the middle of the seventh to the middle of the ninth centuries, very little secular literature was produced. The controversy growing out of iconoclasm (a ban on the representation of Christ or the saints which lasted for over a century) resulted in the closing of the University of Constantinople and of some schools. Numerous monasteries were shut down and their properties confiscated; as a result, many Greek monks sought refuge in Italy, taking with them their language and culture. Thus the learning of the East was made known in the West. During this period, illumination was not used in Bibles or religious works, but abstract letters and patterns were introduced into the copying of certain kinds of manuscripts.

By the second half of the ninth century, the religious controversies were settled and the University of Constantinople was reopened, becoming a center for the study of ancient Greek works. The revival of interest in learning sparked great literary activity; and during the next three centuries, ancient Greek texts were copied, commentaries were written, compilations and digests of Greek literature were made, and encyclopedias and lexicons were produced. While these works show little new or original thought, they are of inestimable value to the classical scholar and the cultural historian.

> The peculiar, indispensable service of Byzantine literature was the preservation of the language, philology, and archaeology of Greece. It is impossible to see how our knowledge of ancient literature or civilisation could have been recovered if Constantinople had not nursed through the early Middle Ages the vast accumulations of Greek learning in the schools of Alexandria, Athens, and Asia Minor; . . . if indefatigable copyists had not toiled in multiplying the texts of ancient Greece. . . . It is no paradox that their very merit to us is that they were never either original or brilliant. Their genius indeed would have been our loss. Dunces and pedants as they were, they servilely repeated the words of the immortals. Had they not done so, the immortals would have died long ago.[2]

THE ARABS

Toward the end of the sixth century, a new Oriental religion and a new political power arose in Arabia under the Prophet Mohammed. His followers, called Muslims, were a militant religious power. Bent upon world conquest, they began raiding the Byzantine Empire, and although during the seventh century they conquered most of Syria, Babylonia, Mesopotamia, Persia, and Egypt, Constantinople was able to withstand their attacks. Moving westward, the Arabs overran parts of Africa and Spain, but their attempts to invade the Frankish kingdom were checked at Tours in 732. Within two centuries, they acquired an empire extending from Spain on the Atlantic to the boundaries of China. Although the Arabs were great conquerors, it was in their role of "adapters, preservers, and spreaders of civilization" that they contributed to the story of libraries. It was largely through them that mathematical and scientific knowledge was transmitted to Europe.

During the eighth and ninth centuries, when the study and production of secular literature were at a standstill in Constantinople, Bagdad became the center of Greek studies. As Bagdad grew into a great city, physicians and scholars gathered there to translate Greek medical, scientific, and philosophical works into Arabic, sometimes from Syriac or Aramaic versions rather than from the original Greek. The height of this translation movement was reached under the Abbasid Al-Mamum, who established in 830 "a house of wisdom," an institution of learning that combined the functions of library, academy, and translation bureau. Scholars were able to go to Asia Minor and Constantinople for materials, for although hostilities existed between the Muslim and Byzantine Empires, trade and travel between them were only sporadically interrupted. Emphasis was placed on the study of medicine, mathematics, and natural science; and on the works of Plato, Aristotle, Hippocrates, and Galen which were translated into Arabic. The period of translation, lasting roughly for a century and ending about 850, was followed by one of original works on astrology, alchemy, and magic.

Under the Abbasids, Bagdad rivaled Constantinople as a center of cultural activities, boasting many colleges and more than a hundred booksellers. In the course of their military conquests, the Arabs had learned the Chinese secret of papermaking, and paper was manufactured in Bagdad in the eighth century, when the Western world was still using parchment and even papyrus. Papermaking remained under the almost exclusive control of the Muslims for the next five centuries and the technique was taken by them to various parts of their empire. Since paper was cheap, plentiful, and easier to write on than parchment or papyrus, book production increased tremendously and great libraries were assembled in the mosques and colleges. In the library of Shiraz, founded in the last half of the tenth century, books were listed in catalogs, arranged in cases, and administered by a regular staff.[3] In the eleventh century, the library of the caliph of Cairo is said to have contained some 150,000 books.[4]

When Arab culture moved to the western part of the Muslim Empire, many Arabic translations of Greek works were taken to Spain, where Spanish Muslim rulers continued the practice of patronizing scholars and founding schools and libraries. The library at Cordova, which was the center of a brilliant culture in the tenth century, contained 400,000 books.[5] In the libraries of Cordova, Toledo, and Seville, the Greek classics which had been translated from Syriac into Arabic were preserved until the scholars of the twelfth century came to render them into Latin and take them to the new universities in Europe.

THE CRUSADES

The capture of Jerusalem in 1078 by the Seljuk Turks, the ruling element in the Muslim world, led to the Crusades, which began as religious wars aimed at the recovery of holy places captured by unbelievers. The First Crusade, launched in 1095 by Pope Urban to aid the Byzantines in taking back Jerusalem, resulted in the city's recovery in 1099. Many other Crusades covered a period of more than two centuries.

The name and idea of the Crusades were eventually extended to expeditions other than the religious wars against the Mohammedans in the East. Such a campaign was the Fourth Crusade, directed against Egypt but diverted to Constantinople, which the Crusaders captured and sacked in 1204. There was a great loss of literary works by fire and in the destruction and loss of libraries during the capture of the city, but many manuscripts were dispersed. From that time on, Greek works, including the original texts of Aristotle, found their way to Western Europe in increasing numbers.

The Crusades stimulated trade, brought goods and money into circulation, and created new activity and enterprise, and as a result, towns grew up around castles and monasteries or along waterways. The lot of the peasants gradually improved, resulting eventually in their emancipation. By the twelfth century, some towns had achieved self-government and others had won a measure of freedom. The merchant class became important and, for mutual support and protection, formed guilds. Artisans and craftsmen followed the example of the merchants, and guilds became an important part of the social, political, economic, and industrial life of the time.

From the viewpoint of the student of librarianship, the most significant result of the Crusades was that twelfth-century Europe was brought into touch with the highly developed civilization of the East and exposed to new ideas, new knowledge, and new literature.

RISE OF THE UNIVERSITIES[6]

The economic and social changes resulting from the rise of towns, the expansion of trade and industry, and the growth of municipal institutions and individual freedom were accompanied by comparable developments and advances in art, literature, education, science, and thought.

The intellectual darkness of the century following the breakup of Charlemagne's empire was brightened by the cathedral school at Rheims and the teaching of Gerbert, the greatest scholar of the tenth century in Western Europe. Through his influence, cathedral schools were established in other French towns in the eleventh century and teaching again became important in a number of monasteries. Although the amount of knowledge then available was scant, there was a marked growth of interest in, and eagerness for, learning. The first notable increase in knowledge was in the field of medicine, when Salerno, already known throughout Europe as a school of medicine, began to receive Latin translations of the Arabic versions of Greek medical works. Early in the following century, the study of Roman law was revived at Bologna.

From the middle of the twelfth century, Spain was the center of translation from Arabic into Latin of Greek works of science, philosophy, medicine, and geography which the Arabs had preserved, as well as of recent works by the Arabs themselves. These Latin translations were transmitted to the scholars of twelfth- and thirteenth-century Europe and to the newly-established universities, thus increasing the knowledge and outlook of the learned world and further stimulating intellectual curiosity.

Exposure to Latin grammar and other basic subjects in the cathedral schools, the development of writing in the language of the masses, and more favorable social and economic conditions accelerated the enthusiasm for learning. Many students wandered from place to place to pursue more advanced studies with individual teacher-scholars. In time, a sufficient number of teachers and students congregated regularly in certain locations forming the nuclei of institutions of higher learning. In the beginning, these institutions did not own land or permanent buildings, but gradually teachers united into faculties according to their areas of scholarship and were empowered either by religious or civil authority to grant degrees. The universities of Bologna, Paris, and Oxford are examples of permanent institutions of higher education which grew out of the wanderings of students and the instruction of individual teachers. The first universities in Italy, France, and England were followed by those in Spain and other countries of Western Europe, and by the close of the Middle Ages there were about 80 universities in Europe.[7]

Control over education and books, now passed from the monasteries to the secular clergy and the universities. Book dealers (*stationarii*), appointed or controlled by the university to guarantee authenticity of texts, stocked correct editions of books used for instruction and rented them to students. As long as students could rent texts, there was little need for libraries. However, as the number of students increased, the universities were forced to establish libraries, and in time, gifts of books for student use were made by individuals. One of the most important academic libraries was given by Robert de Sorbon to the college which he founded in Paris in the thirteenth century for students of theology and which became a part of the University of Paris.

Eventually, every college in a university had its own library. The more important books were chained to the desks, but in some libraries the chains were lengthened so that the student could take a book to a nearby table while studying.

DEVELOPMENT OF VERNACULAR LANGUAGES AND LITERATURE

In the new society created by the social, economic, and cultural changes of the eleventh, twelfth, and thirteenth centuries, not only were there the scholars and students, but also the knights and lords of the feudal aristocracy, the townsmen, the Germanic and Norse invaders, and the Celts and Romans, most of whom neither spoke nor understood Latin. These people, too, felt a new interest in learning, but literature intended for their use had to be written in the language of their daily life. France became the center of this vernacular literary activity, producing the *chansons de geste*, the *Fabliaux*, and the poetry of the troubadours and the trouvères. Other examples of vernacular literature were the English epic poem, *Beowulf*, the *Eddas* of Iceland, the German *Nibelungenlied*, and Spain's *El Cid*. Medieval literature reached its height in Italy in the *Commedia (Divine Comedy)* of Dante, who wrote in Latin but also in Italian, thus establishing the vernacular Italian as a language suitable for literary expression.

NOTES

1. Frederic Harrison, *Byzantine History in the Early Middle Ages*, The Rede Lecture Delivered in the Senate House, Cambridge, June 12, 1900 (London: Macmillan & Co., Ltd., 1900), p. 11. By permission of Macmillan & Co., Ltd.
2. *Ibid.*, pp. 36-37.
3. Philip K. Hitti, *The Near East in History: A 5000 Year Story* (New York: D. Van Nostrand Co., Inc., 1961), p. 271.
4. Douglas C. McMurtrie, *The Book, the Story of Printing & Bookmaking* (New York: Oxford University Press, 1943), p. 67.
5. R. H. Pinder-Wilson, "Islam and the Tide of Arab Conquest," *Dawn of European Civilization*, ed. David Talbot Rice (New York: McGraw-Hill Book Co., 1966), p. 62.
6. *See* Richard Hunt, "The Sum of Knowledge: Universities and Learning," *The Flowering of the Middle Ages*, ed. Joan Evans (New York: McGraw-Hill Book Co., 1966), pp. 179-202.
7. Rashdall Hastings, *The Universities of Europe in the Middle Ages*, ed. F. M. Powicke and A. B. Emden (New ed., 3 vols., London: Oxford University Press, 1936), I, xxiv.

4

The Late Middle Ages

Had not the forces of war and nature intervened, the collecting of books and founding of libraries might normally have been the result of the social, economic, cultural, and educational progress made in the thirteenth century with its accompanying interest in reading and production of literary materials. As it turned out, the Hundred Years War and the Black Death made the fourteenth century one of the most calamitous in all history. It is estimated that the Black Death alone killed one-third to one-half of the population of England and Europe. Homes and families were blotted out, agriculture ceased because of lack of tenants or lords and overseers, there were no master craftsmen in many guilds, trade diminished, few monks were left in the monasteries, and schools closed. Prices rose, taxes were increased to pay for the cost of the war, and peasants in both France and England revolted against the burden of taxation.

During this period, only royalty, nobility, the church, and the universities could afford books. Charles V of France (r. 1364-1380), known widely for his patronage of art and literature, built a large library which became the basis of the French Royal Library. In spite of the deprivation of the times, his brother Jean, Duke of Berry, built 20 castles and surrounded his luxurious court with the most illustrious artists of his time. His passion for collecting books resulted in one of the most varied manuscript collections in history, numbering among its treasures the handsomely illuminated Book of Hours.[1] The first large private library in England, estimated at 1,000 volumes, was collected during this period of war and suffering by Richard de Bury, Bishop of Durham. His library was dispersed, but his *Philobiblon*,[2] one of the first books about books, reveals his extravagant love of books and some of his methods of collecting them.

The fourteenth century was as disastrous for the Byzantine Empire as it was for Western Europe. The steadily advancing armies of the Ottoman Turks frightened many Byzantine Greeks into fleeing Constantinople and seeking shelter in Italy. Taking with them manuscripts of the ancient writers, they were welcomed by Italian scholars, who encouraged them to open schools for the study of both Greek and Latin.

Constantinople, which had been menaced for more than a century by the Ottoman Turks, finally yielded to them in 1453, and the Byzantine Empire came to an end. One scholar pays tribute to Constantinople's contribution to culture by saying that:

> The capital of the Eastern empire had ... proved strong enough to stand for centuries as the bulwark of Europe against the barbarians of the East, thus sheltering the nascent nations of the West, while they slowly attained the fulness of their maturity, and, at the same time, keeping the treasures of the old Greek literature in a place of safety, until those nations were sufficiently civilised to receive them.[3]

It cannot be said that the fall of Constantinople caused the Renaissance, but it is clear that it did aid greatly the revival of learning begun by Petrarch, Boccaccio, and others by dispersing to Europe many works of Greek and Latin literature.

THE ITALIAN RENAISSANCE

Petrarch (fl. 1304-1374) is credited with "preparing the soil of Italy for the reception of Greek culture" because he was the first to recognize the intellectual and cultural value of ancient Latin and Greek literature. Called the Father of Humanism,[4] Petrarch added to medieval culture a worshipful appreciation of the ancient classics. He searched neglected libraries in monasteries for old manuscripts, and many long-lost ancient Latin works were recovered, including the writings of Cicero, Quintilian, Plautus, and Lucretius. Petrarch had the idea of bequeathing his library to the Republic of Venice as the nucleus of a future public library, but his wish was never carried out. His books were dispersed—some to Paris, others scattered over various parts of western Europe.[5]

Boccaccio was influenced by Petrarch to study the Latin classics, and he learned Greek in order to be able to read the Greek authors. Continuing the search for manuscripts, Boccaccio visited many monasteries, made copies of ancient works, and became a student of Tacitus, whose *Histories* he is believed to have found in Monte Cassino.[6] Foremost in the quest for ancient manuscripts was Poggio Bracciolini, whose searches of monasteries at Cluny, St. Gall,[7] and throughout France and Germany yielded many works of early Latin literature. The decline of monastic life following the rise of towns and universities had led to gross neglect of the libraries. Precious manuscripts were left unprotected from dust, dirt, and the elements; in some monasteries pages were torn out of manuscripts or portions were cut out and sold. Boccaccio is said to have wept over the condition of manuscripts in Monte Cassino, and Poggio found many manuscripts exposed to the dampness of the church towers at St. Gall.

The Renaissance in Italy, also called the Age of Humanism, was characterized by the eager and unceasing search for the manuscripts of ancient Greek and Latin authors, the intense yearning and effort to read and understand them, the aim to imitate and reproduce their style and form, and the acquisition of great libraries in which to preserve and use them. "It was an age of accumulation, of uncritical and indiscriminate enthusiasm. Manuscripts were worshiped. . . . The good, the bad, and the indifferent received an almost equal homage. Criticism had not yet begun."[8]

Florence became the center of the Italian Renaissance. For over a century, the Medici were its greatest patrons and led the rich middle class in sponsoring the most brilliant development of culture since the Golden Age of Greece. Cosimo de' Medici, who ruled until 1464, was an enthusiastic patron of manuscript collectors, copyists, and Humanists. He sent his agents throughout the known world to find classic works and was successful in bringing together most of the Latin classics. He established the library of San Marco and from his own collection founded the great Medici Library, now housed in the Laurentian Library in Florence. His grandson Lorenzo, a generous patron of the arts, writer, and lover of learning, continued the search for manuscripts, greatly enriched the Medici Library, and established the great Florentine library of Greek and Latin classics.

After the sack of Rome in 1527,[9] when many collections of manuscripts were destroyed or scattered and many artists and scholars perished or were forced into exile, the center of the Renaissance moved to northern Europe, where a new medium for transmitting knowledge was then being developed, a medium which would make the learning of the ancients—and all learning—easily available to all men.

NOTES

1. *The Belles Heures of Jean, Duke of Berry, Prince of France*, with an intro. by James J. Rorimer (New York: The Cloisters, The Metropolitan Museum of Art, 1958), *passim.*
2. Richard de Bury [Richard Aungerville], *The Philobiblon* (Berkeley, Calif.: University of California Press, 1948).
3. Sir John Edwin Sandys, *A History of Classical Scholarship*, Vol. I: *From the Sixth Century B.C. to the End of the Middle Ages* (3d ed.; Cambridge: Cambridge University Press, 1921), p. 439.
4. Humanism stressed the study of the "more human letters" of the Greek and Latin writers in contrast with the theological letters of the medieval scholars.
5. Rudolph Pfeiffer, *History of Classical Scholarship from 1300 to 1850* (Oxford: Clarendon Press, 1976), pp. 12-13.
6. *See* p. 20.
7. *See* p. 22, 26.
8. John Addington Symonds, *Renaissance in Italy: The Age of the Despots* (New York: Henry Holt and Co., 1888), p. 21.
9. Although this was a period of intellectual and artistic supremacy for Italy, it was, politically, a period of civil strife. Italy was a divided country; there were wars among the several states and also with France, Germany, and Spain; and Rome was sacked by the mercenaries of Charles V of Spain.

5

Printing with Movable Type

> While we gratefully recall the preservation of Latin manuscripts in the mediaeval monasteries of the West, as well as the recovery of lost Classics by the humanists of the fourteenth and fifteenth centuries, and the transference to Italy of the treasures of Greek literature from the libraries of the East, we are bound to remember that all this would have been of little permanent avail, but for the invention of the art of printing.[1]

The zeal for learning engendered by the Renaissance brought about a demand for books which could no longer be satisfied by handwritten copies. The need for a new and faster medium for transmitting thought and knowledge was immediate and urgent. A kind of printing had been known since the time when the Babylonians and Egyptians used metal or wooden seals to print on soft clay or wax. As early as the fifth century, the Chinese printed short mottoes and charms from seals on which the characters to be printed were carved in relief. The full-page woodcut, printed from a wooden block on which the text and illustrations had been carved, was the next step in printing, and by A.D. 868 the Chinese had produced a complete book, *The Diamond Sutra*, in this manner. Woodcut printing in Europe, however, was delayed until the fourteenth century.

Movable type, made first of clay and then of tin, also originated in China, but was never used extensively by the Chinese. It is likely that

Europeans had heard of printing and may have seen samples of it during the Crusades.

The materials required for printing—a cheap and plentiful substance on which to print, an ink that would adhere to metal surfaces and transfer to paper, a press to bring paper and metal into contact with each other, and a general knowledge of metal technology—were all available by the second quarter of the fifteenth century. To Johann Gutenberg is given the credit for combining these materials and supplying the necessary technological skill which resulted in the invention of printing with movable type. This event of incalculable significance in the cultural history of mankind occurred between 1440 and 1450 in the vicinity of Mainz, Germany.

The first piece of printing which bears a date (1454) was a papal indulgence. The 42-line Bible, commonly called the Gutenberg Bible and generally regarded as the first printed book in Europe, was completed not more than two years later. By the end of the century, printing had been carried to all parts of Europe. Of the fifteenth-century German centers of printing, Nürnberg was the most important, and Anton Koberger its greatest printer. His most elaborate publication was the *Liber Chronicarum*, 1493, with 1800 woodcut illustrations. The first book printed in the English language was the *Recuyell of the Histories of Troy*, printed between 1474 and 1476 by William Caxton, who learned the art of printing in order to print his own translation of this work.

About one-half of the books printed in the fifteenth century were religious works: the Bible, works of the church Fathers, manuals for priests, and religious tracts. Other publications included encyclopedias, pamphlets, calendars, epistles, handbills, and some books on mathematics and astronomy. Printed books which can be dated before the year 1501 are called incunabula.

Venice, already important for trade and commerce, became a major center of printing by the beginning of the sixteenth century. Here Nicolas Jenson became the world's first great type designer, including Greek type, and Aldus Manutius began the publication of pocket editions of the Latin and Greek classics. By 1515, all the principal Greek classics had been printed in this scholarly, compact, and inexpensive format and were easily available to all who wanted to own them.

The most important library of the fifteenth century was the Vatican Library. While still a priest, Pope Nicholas V (1447-1455) drew up a plan for a library for Cosimo de' Medici, aided in the search for manuscripts, and copied manuscripts himself. When he became Pope, he added his own library to the approximately 350 manuscripts which then constituted the Vatican Library and began the task of collecting the works of classical authors. With his librarian, Tortelli, Pope Nicholas V planned the complete translation of Greek literature into Latin, employing many copyists. In the Vatican Library, classical, Humanist, scholastic, and patristic works stood side by side. Pope Sixtus IV continued the work of Pope Nicholas V and also opened a part of the library to the public.

The Duke of Urbino had an outstanding private library which contained copies of all the Latin and Greek authors then discovered—all "written by hand because the Duke would have been ashamed to possess a single printed book."[2]

Renowned contributors to the art of printing and to the spread of the Renaissance in sixteenth-century France were 1) Robert Estienne and his son, Henri, who published the Greek and Latin classics and Latin, Greek, and Hebrew dictionaries; 2) Claude Garamond, designer of Roman typefaces; and 3) Geofroy Tory, printer to the king, scholar, spelling reformer, type designer, and wood engraver.

Antwerp was notable in this century for the work of Christopher Plantin, whose 22 presses produced religious, classical, scientific, and medical works and the works of contemporary French authors. His most important publication was the Polyglot Bible, 1568-1573.

By the beginning of the sixteenth century, vernacular works outnumbered Latin ones in all countries. Interest in education had been stimulated by the intellectual activity of the Renaissance and the religious upheaval which resulted in the Protestant Reformation. Among all classes of society, except the very lowest, there was an intense desire to read.

The invention of printing with movable type resulted in an inestimable increase in the supply of books, a greater diffusion of knowledge, the dissemination of classical literature, the flowering of national literature, the development of literary criticism, and the rise of publishing as a business. Libraries increased in number and in size; and learning, formerly confined to monasteries or universities, was now within reach of any person who wished to pursue it.

Francis I, King of France and patron of the arts, aided the development of the Renaissance in his country by giving protection and encouragement to authors and scholars and by founding chairs of Latin, Greek, and Hebrew which formed the nucleus of the Collège de France. He assembled the various royal libraries at Fontainebleau; appointed Guillaume Budé, learned scholar and one of the first French Humanists, as Royal Librarian; and added to the library by acquiring Greek and Oriental manuscripts and requiring (in 1537) that one copy of every Greek book published in France be given to the Royal Library.

The most important private libraries in France were those of Jean Grolier (3000 volumes) and Jacques Auguste de Thou (8000 printed works and 1000 manuscripts).

In Germany, the efforts to make Latin and Italian literature available to more people by translating it in the vernacular encouraged reading and the practice of book collecting by individuals.

THE PROTESTANT REFORMATION

As the sixteenth century advanced, Humanism slowly but steadily declined and the study of Latin and Greek gradually gave way to theological and moral discussions. As a result religious differences between Catholics and Protestants, and among Protestants themselves, received most of the intellectual emphasis of the time. The Protestant Reformation, begun in 1517 to reform certain doctrines and practices in the Roman Catholic Church, resulted in the establishment of various Protestant denominations in central and northwest Europe.

During this period of religious upheaval and controversy, many monastic libraries disappeared and others were scattered or destroyed, but in some places, libraries passed from Catholic to Protestant ownership with little change.

Martin Luther encouraged the building of good libraries, and library buildings and municipal libraries in Germany date from this period. There were also many church and private libraries. It has been said that Germany in the sixteenth century "was saturated with books."[3]

Libraries in England suffered more than those of any other country in the sixteenth century when Henry VIII dissolved the monasteries, 1535-1539, and appropriated their wealth for himself and his favorites. The contents of many libraries were lost, some books were sold, and others were exported. Fortunately, some were saved by the abbots, who took them to their new posts. Sir Robert Bruce Cotton, collector of manuscripts and coins, saved many works from the dissolved monasteries, including the Lindisfarne Gospels.

In Spain, an important library was established by Philip II in the monastery of San Lorenzo Del Escorial outside Madrid with his own private collection of almost 2000 volumes. It was enriched by gifts of Greek, Latin, and Arabic works, by "choice items" which the king's learned representatives brought back from Italy, Germany, and Flanders, and by the writings of eminent scholars of the time. The library was housed in a building reportedly as magnificent as its collections.[4]

NOTES

1. Sir John Edwin Sandys, *A History of Classical Scholarship,* Vol. II: *From the End of the Revival of Learning to the End of the Eighteenth Century* . . . (Cambridge: Cambridge University Press, 1908), p. 95.
2. Sandys, *op. cit.,* II, p. 96.
3. Alfred Hessel, *History of Libraries,* trans. Reuben Peiss (2d ed.; New York: Scarecrow Press, Inc., 1955), p. 55.
4. John W. Montgomery (trans.), *A Seventeenth-Century View of European Libraries: Lomeier's De Bibliothecis, Chapter X* (Berkeley, Calif.: University of California Press, 1962), pp. 58-60.

6

The Seventeenth Century to the Twentieth Century

The Renaissance, with its artistic and literary achievement, also laid the foundations for the scientific revolution of the seventeenth century. Humanists had gradually developed a critical approach to the study and comparison of ancient manuscripts and to the interpretation of the history of the ancient past. In the revival of learning, scientific as well as philosophical, literary, and artistic works were recovered, stimulating the study of astronomy, mathematics, medicine, and physics. The discovery of America and the new routes to the East led to the scientific construction of maps. The printing press, itself a scientific achievement, provided the medium for quickly disseminating all knowledge.

Led by Galileo, Kepler, Francis Bacon, and Descartes, the new scientific era focused attention on the bases of science and on the scientific method. By the end of the seventeenth century, the decline in the power of the clergy was seen in the secularization of society, the emphasis on reason over faith, and the questioning, rather than the uncritical acceptance, of authority. It was a period of exploration, territorial expansion, and colonization. The first permanent English Colonies in America were established during the first three decades of this century.

The general spirit of inquiry and research, which was dependent upon access to materials of all kinds, stimulated the formation of libraries made up of printed works as well as hand-written manuscripts. One analyst of the times has noted that "certainly, in any listing of the factors which, at that critical period in European history contributed to a settled order in things of the mind, to the overthrow of superstition and the growth of tolerance, libraries will have to be ranked high."[1]

Some of the great national libraries[2] were founded during the seventeenth century: the Prussian State Library in Berlin (1659), the Kongelige Bibliotek in Copenhagen (1661), and the National Library of Scotland (1682).

In 1622, under Louis XIII, the first catalog of the Bibliothèque du Roi (the French Royal Library) was drawn up by Nicolas Rigault,[3] and in the reign of Louis XIV, under the direction of Colbert, the library almost doubled in size. Cardinal Mazarin's library in Paris was collected and arranged by Gabriel Naudé in 1642. Its collection soon numbered 40,000 volumes and it was open to all who wanted to go there and study.

In 1598, Sir Thomas Bodley began the work of rebuilding the library at Oxford and opened it in 1602 with 2000 volumes. He later persuaded the Stationers' Company to deposit in the library a free copy of every book published in England and he himself left a considerable legacy of land and property to it.

That libraries were an important part of seventeenth-century life can be seen in the statement of Johannes Lomeier that "one may scarcely find any moderately famous city, scarcely any community, gymnasium, university or monastery where a library has not been set apart for the public use of the studious."[4]

The scientific spirit of the age was reflected in writings on the history, planning, organization, and administration of libraries and on the classification and arrangement of materials. In 1602, Justus Lipsius published his *De Bibliothecis Syntagma*, described as "the foundation of all modern histories of libraries."[5] Of the numerous treatises written on the systematic organization of libraries, the earliest was Naudé's *Advis Pour Dresser Une Bibliothèque*, published in 1627, in which he discussed the reasons for establishing a library; the size, quality, and arrangement of the collection; the kind of building required; and the library's basic purpose.[6]

John Durie, Keeper of the Royal Library, made the first contribution to library economy in England in 1650 with his *The Reformed Librarie Keeper*, in which he outlined a plan for expanding the Royal Library into a "truly national collection"; and in 1697 Richard Bentley added to the literature of libraries his *Proposal for Building a Royal Library.*

Principles which should govern the development of a large scholarly research library were set forth by Leibniz, who administered the library of Wolfenbüttal in Germany. Still valid, his principles included firm financial support with regular appropriations, continuing and systematic acquisition of all major works of learning, and classification of all works for greater accessibility.[7]

The interest in research extended to all fields of knowledge and was reflected in the diversity of the great libraries of the time and in the national institutions and societies which were organized to pursue research and to provide the necessary materials. A notable example was the Royal Society in London, founded in 1662 as a cooperative endeavor of scientists, historians, and philosophers.

The appearance of the parish library in the late seventeenth century attested to the importance the Anglican Church attached to the continuing education of its ministers. Established by Reverend Thomas Bray and others in England, it was designed to aid the rural Anglican clergy in carrying out its educational, as well as spiritual, mission.[8]

EIGHTEENTH AND NINETEENTH CENTURIES

The scientific thought and progress of the seventeenth century gathered momentum in the eighteenth century, bringing greater advances in both pure and applied sciences and leading to the mechanical inventions and technological achievements which resulted in the industrial revolution and the rise of the working class.

With the French Revolution in 1789, church libraries became national property and the libraries of the émigrés were confiscated. Great numbers of books were taken from their owners and placed in the *"dépôts littéraires,"* which had been established to receive them. Many books were assigned to university libraries, but the largest share was given to the French Royal Library, which became national property and was renamed La Bibliothèque Nationale. By the time of the Revolution, the library was open not only to scholars,[9] but also to the public on two days a week for five hours. During the Revolution, a regulation of 25 Fructidor, An IV (11 September 1796) opened the library every day for four hours.[10] The governments after the Revolution were as interested in the growth of the Bibliothèque Nationale as were the sovereigns of the Ancien Régime, and through governmental appropriations, legal deposit, gifts, and legacies, the library continued to grow. The publication of catalogs, begun in 1622, continued, and in 1897 the *Catalogue Général des Livres Imprimés: Auteurs* was begun.

During both the eighteenth and nineteenth centuries, national libraries were established throughout Europe: La Biblioteca Nazionale Centrale in Florence, the Kungliga Biblioteket in Stockholm, the Koninklijke Bibliotheek in The Hague, the Universitetsbiblioteket in Oslo, La Bibliothèque Royale de Belgique in Brussels, Ethnike Bibliotheke tes Hellados in Athens, La Biblioteca Nacional in Madrid, The National Library of Ireland in Dublin, and La Bibliothèque Nationale Suisse in Bern.

Of the many private libraries that were established, the most famous one of this period in England, and the only one to survive in its original state, was that of Samuel Pepys, with its 3000 volumes arranged in 11 carved mahogany cases.

Many large libraries, rich in materials for research, were also assembled. Edward Gibbon owned a library of nearly 7000 volumes, which he systematically collected in order to write *The Decline and Fall of the Roman Empire*. Sir Hans Sloane's library numbered more than 40,000 printed works and 3,576 manuscripts, including all fields of knowledge; and the libraries of Robert and Edward Harley, Earls of Oxford, contained thousands of printed books and pamphlets and several thousand manuscripts.

The Sloan and Harleian collections and that of Sir Robert Cotton, together with the Royal Library which had existed from the reign of Henry VII, formed the foundation of the British Museum, incorporated in 1753. Other collections of the royal family, famous collections from many sources, and books provided by the copyright deposit law added to the size and importance of the Museum's holdings. Under the direction of Sir Anthony Panizzi, who became Keeper of the Printed Books in 1837, the British Museum became an institution for the "diffusion of culture" and a national library in the sense that it preserved all English books and most of the important foreign literature. Panizzi made sure of a large and regular yearly budget, reorganized the library, designed its new building, which included a reading room separate from the rooms used for shelving, and began the complete revision of the catalog. By 1870, the holdings had reached a million volumes.

In the eighteenth century, the habit of reading became fashionable for women, spread to the lowest social classes, and gained widespread popularity for instruction, political purposes, and recreation. Bookshops, newspapers, magazines, pamphlets, coffeehouses, book clubs, and learned societies and institutions served some of the intellectual, literary, and social needs of the people. To meet all the new demands for books from people who were unable to buy them, a new kind of library was developed: the lending or circulating library, begun by booksellers who loaned books on payment of a small fee. A commercial enterprise, the lending library was more concerned with making money for its owner than with the education of its readers. Its chief item was the novel, and most of its patrons were women. The first lending libraries were opened in Edinburgh in 1726 and in London in the 1730s. In 1804, the three largest lending libraries in Dresden had a combined stock of 60,000 volumes, and by the end of the eighteenth century, lending libraries had become a common feature of every town in Western Europe.[11]

The mechanization of industry following the industrial revolution created many problems relating to the training and welfare of apprentices. In 1800 when George Birkbeck, a Scottish teacher of philosophy, started classes and a library for the mechanics' apprentices, his example was followed by others. Mechanics' institutes were organized in the industrial centers and in London to provide elementary instruction and lectures for the benefit of apprentices who needed to improve their technical knowledge. Libraries were organized as a further aid to the self-education of the apprentices and for moral betterment as well as recreation. Members managed these libraries and financed them through their subscriptions, together with gifts from wealthy individuals. By the middle of the century, mechanics' institutes and libraries had spread throughout England, providing help and encouragement to the laboring class.[12]

In 1850, the English Parliament passed the first Public Libraries Act, allowing local councils to organize libraries and support them by taxation, but limiting the amount that could be spent for that purpose. The first public library in England was established at Manchester with Edward Edwards as librarian. Edwards, who had been influential in securing the passage of the Public Libraries Act, set forth some general principles of library service which have been followed ever since: library service must be given freely to any citizen who wants to use it; library service is a local responsibility and the cost is borne collectively by all who pay taxes whether they use it or not; and books of all kinds and on all aspects of a question should be included in the collection. During the first 20 years of the Public Libraries Act, only 35 new libraries were established.[13] With the passage of the 1870 Education Act and the organization of the Library Association in 1877 for the purpose of encouraging the establishment of public libraries, the public library movement was greatly accelerated.

The closing years of the nineteenth century were characterized by the expansion of public library service in Great Britain, the Scandinavian countries, and Germany and by the growth of all established libraries throughout Europe, especially the great national and university libraries.

NOTES

1. John W. Montgomery (trans.), *A Seventeenth-Century View of European Libraries: Lomeier's De Biblothecis, Chapter X* (Berkeley, Calif.: University of California Press, 1962), p. 11.
2. One of the functions of a national library is to collect and preserve for future generations the written production of that country.
3. La Bibliothèque Nationale ("La Documentation Francaise Illustrée," No. 50; Paris: La Direction de la Documentation, 1951), p. 15.
4. Montgomery, *op. cit.*, p. 12.
5. Raymond Irwin, *The Origins of the English Library* (London: George Allen & Unwin Ltd., 1958), p. 182.
6. Gabriel Naudé, *Advice on Establishing a Library*, with an intro. by Archer Taylor (Berkeley: University of California Press, 1950), p. 74. Regarding purpose, he remarked that "in vain does he strive to carry out the preceding suggestions or go to any great expense for books who does not intend to devote them to the public use and never to withhold them from the humblest of those who may reap benefit thereby. . . ."
7. Alfred Hessel, *History of Libraries*, trans. Reuben Peiss (2nd ed.; New York: Scarecrow Press, Inc., 1955) p. 72. *See also* Ernest Maass, "Leibnitz' Contribution to Librarianship," *College and Research Libraries*, IV (June 1943), pp. 245-249.
8. *See* also p. 56-57.
9. As early as 1720, the library (then the French Royal Library) was open to scholars of all nations on days and hours regulated by the librarian and open to the public on one day each week for two hours. *La Bibliothèque Nationale, op. cit.*, p. 8.
10. *Ibid.* Fructidor was the twelfth month of the Republican Calendar.
11. S. H. Steinberg, *Five Hundred Years of Printing* (2d ed.; Baltimore: Penguin Books, Inc., 1961), pp. 259, 260.
12. *See also* p. 61.
13. Lionel McColvin, "The British Public Library," Carl M. White, ed., *Bases of Modern Librarianship* (New York: The Macmillan Co., 1964), pp. 57-67, *passim.*

7

America—Through The Early Nineteenth Century

One of the early achievements of the Renaissance was the discovery of America.[1] Its colonization was the result of more than a century of such Renaissance influences as the spread of learning, the religious unrest following the Reformation, the growth of trade and commerce, the emergence of capitalism, the rise of the middle class, and scientific study and technological invention.

The English colonists came to the New World for various reasons: to secure religious freedom, to acquire land, to develop trade, for self-enrichment, or for the glory of England. While they shared the same political, social, and intellectual heritage, the society developed by the colonists took several forms, depending on the part of the New World in which it grew. Land was the principal resource in every colony, but the basis on which it was acquired and distributed was a determining factor in a colony's growth and development. For example, in the Chesapeake Colonies (Virginia and Maryland) land was given directly to individuals and additional holdings were acquired through head-rights for each servant or slave. Great estates were acquired, and land-owners settled along the waterways and at some distance from each other, rather than in villages. Communication was difficult, methods of transportation were slow, and in this society of widely scattered farmers, the maintenance of churches and schools was impossible. The family became the social and economic unit. Itinerant clergymen ministered to religious needs and schoolmasters imported from England attended to the educational needs of the plantation family. The Southern Colonies (Georgia and the Carolinas), also based on large grants of land, developed a plantation system of agriculture with a few staple products and a society which was comparable to that of Virginia and Maryland. From 1670, these colonies were strongly affected by the introduction and use of slaves.

In Massachusetts Bay and the other New England colonies, land was distributed in townships. A community was created within the township; outside the community—but within the township—lands were allotted for farming and grazing. Even though individuals were given titles to land, "the essence of the system was the preservation of a community."[2] The population was homogeneous, the town was the center of life, and the church and school were easily accessible to all. When the Massachusetts Bay Colony expanded, it was in group migrations along the coast, and communication and trade between settlements were maintained. "New England can properly be called a section as early as the middle of the seventeenth century, whereas the Chesapeake colonies cannot be properly called a section until very late in the eighteenth or early in the nineteenth century."[3]

In the Middle Atlantic Colonies, a cosmopolitan society developed. New Netherland began as a trading post, and commerce, its chief activity, attracted a heterogeneous population. A landed aristocracy was established under the Dutch patroon system, but land was looked upon primarily as an investment; the vocations were business, law, and other professions. From the beginning, Pennsylvania included non-English-speaking peoples since the Dutch and Swedish colonies, which had been established earlier, became a part of William Penn's Colony in 1628. In these colonies, emphasis was on ethnic or religious groups rather than on the community as a whole.

In spite of the differences in their social and political structure, the early colonists resembled each other as well as their English contemporaries in attitudes, ambitions, and characteristics, and particularly in their interest in learning.

EARLY COLONIAL PERIOD

Books were among the valued possessions which all the early settlers brought to America or imported as necessities as soon as they were settled. Since the literary tastes and special needs of the settlers influenced their choice of books, the Puritans brought with them, and later imported, more religious works than did the Southern planters. Even so, there tended to be a similarity in the titles in all the Colonies. Theological and moral works were most numerous, but there were also textbooks for self-instruction; handbooks on medicine, law, and farming; dictionaries and encyclopedias; and some historical, political, scientific, and classical works. These books constituted the collections of the first libraries in America, and although they were the private libraries of individuals, they were often shared with friends and neighbors.

The size of these libraries varied. Captain John Smith is said to have owned two books; Miles Standish, 50; Governor Bradford, 80; John Harvard, more than 300; and Elder William Brewster, 400. John Winthrop, Jr., Governor of Connecticut, had the largest scientific library in the colonies—over 1000 volumes—which were used freely by his neighbors. Even though a printing press was in operation in Massachusetts as early as 1639, books had to be imported from England and the Continent for many generations.

The importance of learning to the colonists is revealed in their early efforts to establish colleges, in which books and libraries were a significant part. Almost as soon as the Jamestown Colony was settled, steps were taken to establish a college for the colonists and Indians at Henrico, Virginia. The London Company granted 15,000 acres of land toward the endowment of the College, and more than 100 colonists were settled on the land. At the request of King James I, the English churches contributed £1500 pounds to aid in erecting churches and schools. Other gifts came from many sources, including a library valued at 10 marks given to the college by Master Thomas Burgrave. The Indian massacre of 1622 put an end to the plans for Henrico College, and not until the last decade of the century did the Virginia colonists make another effort to establish an institution of higher education.

Efforts to found a college in the Massachusetts Bay Colony proved to be more successful than those in Virginia. In 1636, the General Court voted £400 toward the establishment of a college or school. Two years later the college became a reality when John Harvard willed half of his property and his complete library of more than 300 volumes to this college. The founding of Harvard is described in "New England's First Fruits, 1643":

> After God had carried us safe to *New England*, and wee had builded our houses, provided necessaries for our liveli-hood, rear'd convenient places for Gods worship, and setled the Civill Government: One of the next things we longed for, and looked after was to advance *Learning* and perpetuate it to Posterity; dreading to leave an illiterate Ministery to the Churches, when our present Ministers shall lie in the Dust. And as wee were thinking and consulting how to effect this great Work; it pleased God to stir up the heart of one Mr. *Harvard* (a godly Gentleman, and a lover of Learning, there living amongst us) to give the one halfe of his Estate (it being in all about 1700.*1*.) towards the erecting of a Colledge: and all his Library: after him another gave 300.*1*. others after them cast in more, and the publique hand of the State added the rest: the Colledge was, by common consent, appointed to be at *Cambridge* (a place very pleasant and accommodate) and is called (according to the name of the first founder) *Harvard Colledge*.[4]

In 1693 the Virginia colonists successfully established the second colonial college, the College of William and Mary; and in 1701 Yale College was founded in Connecticut, and 11 ministers, meeting for that purpose, gave a number of books toward its founding.

Provisions for what may be called the first public library[5] in the colonies were made in the will of Captain Robert Keayne of Boston (d. March 23, 1655/56), who gave £300 for a public building in Boston which was to include a room for a library. Captain Keayne gave certain of his own books to begin the collection and authorized his wife and son to give others. The building, called the Town House, was erected, and the library served the people for almost a century.[6]

Toward the end of the seventeenth century, another kind of library— already well known in England[7]—made its appearance in the American Colonies. When Rev. Thomas Bray was appointed by the Anglican Church in 1696 as Commissary for the Colony of Maryland to work toward the establishment of the Anglican Church there, he immediately proposed a system of parochial libraries for the colonies similar to those he had established in England for the rural Anglican clergy. With the approval and aid of the Anglican Church, he collected money and books for these libraries before he sailed for Maryland on December 16, 1699. Rev. Bray remained in Maryland only a few months, but through his Society for Promoting Christian Knowledge and its branch, the Society for Propagating the Gospel in Foreign Parts, he established libraries in the English Colonies from Massachusetts to South Carolina. His society is said to have been responsible for founding 39 libraries with more than

34,000 volumes.[8] These libraries were of three kinds: 1) parochial, for the sole use of the minister; 2) provincial, for the use of all types of readers; and 3) layman's, containing books to be "lent or given at the discretion of the Minister." The largest of the provincial libraries, the Annapolitan Library at Annapolis, Maryland, had a collection which totalled 1,095 volumes.

PRE-REVOLUTIONARY PERIOD

Through travel and correspondence, the American colonists were acquainted with the spirit of scientific inquiry which characterized the Age of Enlightenment in Europe.[9] William Byrd II of Virginia and other Americans who were members of the Royal Society of London shared a common desire for wider knowledge in all areas of thought. Their need to have access to a broad range of materials for study and research led to their acquisition of large private libraries. Cotton Mather of Boston owned between 3000 and 4000 volumes before his death in 1728; Thomas Prince, Minister of the Old South Church in Boston, collected 1400 volumes; James Logan of Philadelphia acquired more than 2000 volumes, especially rich in both classical and scientific works; William Byrd II's library had reached 3600 titles at his death in 1744; and William Fitzhugh, Robert Carter, Ralph Wormeley, and other Southern gentlemen assembled large and valuable collections. All these libraries included not only religious works, but also titles in natural science and history and a number of Greek and Roman classics.

Social Libraries

Interest in learning was not confined to the wealthy, even though they alone had the means for acquiring large libraries. The desire for self-improvement, a characteristic of the American colonists, led to the establishment of the social library, which grew out of the social club idea. Benjamin Franklin, a native Bostonian, had lived in London as a journeyman printer and became familiar with the English social club as an organization for the encouragement of intellectual and cultural, as well as social, life. In 1727, Franklin and some of his friends in Philadelphia formed a club for "mutual improvement" which they called the Junto— also sometimes known as the Leathern Apron Club because the members worked at "lowly jobs" during the day. The club members met on Friday evenings for discussions and debates, activities calling for the use of many books. Franklin tells of his plan for meeting this need:

> About this Time [1730] our Club Meeting, not at a Tavern, but in a little Room of Mr. Grace's set apart for that Purpose; a Proposition was made by me that since our Books were often referr'd to in our Disquisitions upon the Queries, it might be convenient to us to have them all together where we met, that upon Occasion they might be consulted; and by thus clubbing our Books to a common Library, we should, while we lik'd to keep them together, have each of us the Advantage of using the Books of all the other Members which would be nearly as beneficial as if each owned the whole. It was lik'd and agreed to, and we fill'd one End of the Room with such Books as we could best spare. The Number was not so great as we expected; and tho' they had been of great Use, yet some Inconveniences occurring for want of due Care of them, the Collection after about a Year was separated, and each took his Books home again.[10]

Franklin was not discouraged by the failure of his plan for providing the books his club needed. In fact, failure stimulated him to produce another plan:

> And now [1731] I set on foot my first Project of a public Nature, that for a Subscription Library. I drew up the Proposals, got them put into Form by our great Scrivener Brockden, and by the help of my Friends in the Junto, procur'd Fifty Subscribers of 40s. each to begin with and 10s. a Year for 50 Years, the Term our Company was to continue. We afterwards obtain'd a Charter, the Company being increas'd to 100. This was the Mother of all the N American Subscription Libraries now so numerous.[11]

Any "civil gentleman" was allowed to peruse the books in the library, but only subscribers could borrow them.

In this manner was begun the social library, a voluntary association of individuals who contributed to a common fund to be used for the purchase of books which every member had the right to use but whose ownership was retained by the group. It provided a means of self-education and self-improvement, of promoting useful learning, and of affording profitable recreation and social life for the members.

Social libraries spread rapidly. In 1733, the Book Company of Durham, Connecticut, was established, and in 1747 the Redwood Library was founded in Newport, Rhode Island. By the middle of the century, New England had at least a dozen social libraries.

The Southern Colonies produced only two social libraries of prominence before the Revolution. In 1748, seventeen young men in Charleston, South Carolina, associated themselves for the purpose of raising a small fund to collect new magazines and pamphlets published in England. Before the close of the year, they took the name Library Society and arranged to buy books as well as pamphlets and magazines. The library suffered greatly during the Revolution. Many books were lost, but those that were saved, together with the few added from time to time, formed the nucleus of the present library of Charleston which was organized in 1790.

The only other social library known to have existed south of Philadelphia prior to the Revolution was the one attached to the Winyaw Indigo Society in Georgetown, South Carolina. Formed about 1740 by the planters of the Georgetown District, this society was originally a social club which met once a month to discuss the latest news from London on the culture of indigo, the staple product of the county. The society was chartered in 1755, and out of the initiation fees and annual subscriptions, which were paid in indigo, a library was acquired and a charity school for the poor—attended by all classes—was established. For more than a hundred years, this was the chief school for all the county lying between Charleston and the North Carolina line. Both the school and the library were destroyed in the Civil War.

The New York Society Library, incorporated in 1754 and first called The City Library, was formed by a group of men who "clubbed together" for the purpose and raised in a few days nearly £600 for 700 volumes of "well-chosen" books. These volumes were deposited in the city hall along with the remnants of two other collections: one, a small library presented in 1700 by Rev. John Sharp; and the other, a gift in 1729 from the Society for Propagating the Gospel in Foreign Parts. A charter was granted in 1772 under the name New York Society Library.

The importance of the social library in the years before the Revolution was pointed out by Franklin in his *Autobiography:*

> It [the subscription library] is become a great thing itself, and continually increasing. These Libraries have improv'd the general Conversation of the Americans, made the Common Tradesmen and Farmers as intelligent as most Gentlemen from other Countries, and perhaps have contributed in some degree to the Stand so generally made throughout the Colonies in Defence of their Privileges.[12]

Further evidence of the contributions of the social library to the cultural life of the colonists is given by Rev. Jacob Duché:[13]

> You would be astounded . . . at the general taste for books, which prevails among all orders and ranks of people in this city. The librarian of the Philadelphia Library Company assured me that for one person of distinction and fortune, there were twenty tradesmen that frequented this library. . . . But such is the prevailing taste for books of every kind that almost every man is a reader; and by pronouncing sentence, right or

wrong, upon the various publications that come in his way, puts himself upon a level, in point of knowledge with their several authors.

The Philadelphia Library Company suffered little from the Revolutionary War, and both the members of the Continental Congress and British Army officers who occupied the city from 1777 to 1778 used the library.[14] Other social libraries, however, suffered greatly; some were lost completely; others were forced to suspend operation during the war.

POST-REVOLUTIONARY PERIOD

At the time of the Revolution, libraries reflected the existing cultural interests and attitudes of the public, offering works on the political, economic, and social issues of the time as well as literary, historical, scientific, and theological works. They were either connected directly with institutions of higher learning or were the outgrowth of associations of persons who had common tastes and interests. After the Revolution, the growth of the social library was greatly accelerated and new forms appeared. Some were organized for a particular purpose, such as the athenaeum; others were designed to meet the special needs or reading interests of a particular clientele, such as the mechanics' apprentices, mercantile clerks, factory and mill workers, and members of the Young Men's Christian Association.

The Athenaeum

Before the nineteenth century, few libraries had a reading room; in general, books were taken out of the library for use. An increasing interest in magazines, newspapers, and pamphlets—both American and foreign—led to a movement to establish, and maintain by subscription, reading rooms where members could have access at all times to periodical publications. Out of this movement came the form of social library called the athenaeum.[15] In 1807, the Boston Athenaeum opened as the Anthology Reading-Room and Library, an affiliate of the magazine *The Monthly Anthology*. The first department to be opened was a reading room, and the second, the library, was to contain outstanding scholarly works in all languages, especially those which could not be obtained easily in America. The Philadelphia Athenaeum was incorporated "for the promotion of literature" on April 5, 1815, and within a decade athenaeums were established in Brunswick, Salem, and Portland, Maine; in the New York Society Library; and in Frankfort, Kentucky.

Mechanics' Apprentices' Libraries

The growth of manufacturing in the nineteenth century greatly increased the demand for apprentices and brought many problems regarding their behavior and welfare. Boys became apprentices as early as thirteen years of age, and many came from rural sections to the city, where they lived in rooming houses which offered neither supervision nor means of recreation or self-improvement.

William Wood, a Boston merchant, believed that much could be done for the welfare of apprentices through libraries and set about getting subscriptions, books, and a place to keep the books. In 1820, the Mechanics' Apprentices' Library was established in Boston through his philanthropy, and other libraries for mechanics' apprentices were organized, through the aid and encouragement of educators, religious leaders, social reformers, and philanthropists.

Apprentices' libraries were established in other cities and included some for girls. Courses, sponsored debates, and other educational activities were offered by some of these libraries. In many cities, apprentices were given access, without cost or at reduced rates, to libraries which were formed by mechanics' institutes. These institutes, here as in England,[16] were designed to help apprentices train for the new factory system brought about by the industrial revolution. The mechanics' institutes were a form of adult education, offering not only library materials, but also lectures and evening study courses.

Mercantile Libraries

America was quickly becoming an industrial nation in the early nineteenth century as a result of the increasing trade and commerce brought by the steamboat and railroad, and those who made up the mercantile community were very important in the new commercial society. Unfortunately, however, the mercantile class did not have the educational background which their growing social importance demanded. This was particularly true of many of the mercantile clerks, who, like the mechanics' apprentices, were quite young—sixteen years of age or under—and had come to the cities from rural sections where their educational opportunities had been meager. They, too, had to live in dreary boarding houses, and had few, if any, opportunities for self-improvement.

Soon after he had organized the apprentices' libraries, William Wood began a companion movement to provide libraries for the "young gentleman employed by the merchants," and in 1820 the Boston Mercantile Library was established. Similar libraries were organized in New York (1820) and in Philadelphia (1821).[17]

In contrast to the libraries for mechanics' apprentices, which were provided and administered free of charge to the users by interested citizens, the ones for mercantile clerks were established by the young clerks themselves and were supported and administered by them for their intellectual improvement and wholesome recreation. In general, each library had a school or an educational department which offered classes in bookkeeping, arithmetic, writing, and debating, and some of them provided gymnasiums, museums, and exhibitions. In addition to materials of practical importance in trade and commerce, the library collections contained literature, biography, history, travel, and popular reading matter.

Other Types of Social Libraries

Factory or mill libraries were established by some of the larger manufacturers in New England and the Middle states for the use of employees and their families, but in most cases the employees were required to contribute to the upkeep of these libraries. In addition to books, lecture halls and facilities were provided for the cultural improvement of the workers. One of the best-known of this type was the Pacific Mills Library in Lawrence, Massachusetts.

The Young Men's Christian Association libraries, which were organized as a means of self-improvement for members, at first emphasized books of a religious and moral nature; later on, history, travel, and biography were added. This type of social library did not develop until the middle of the nineteenth century when the first one opened in Boston in 1851.

Forms and Contributions of Social Libraries

Two basic forms of the social library developed during its most active period of more than a century: 1) proprietary, or joint-stock, based on ownership of shares in the property of the library; and 2) subscription, or association, based on payment of an annual or other fee or subscription.[18] Only shareholders had library privileges in proprietary libraries, but all who paid a fee could use the subscription libraries.

The collections of social libraries were at first strongly theological and moral in content. In time, they emphasized history, biography, literature, and travel, and by the second decade of the nineteenth century, they included a number of scientific materials. In varying degrees, they reached every level of literate society, revealing, and to a certain extent satisfying, the desire and need of each class for educational and cultural improvement. Even so, the social library as a type of service agency inevitably declined because it served only those who could pay and was always in need of financial aid since there were too few subscribers and too few gifts to provide adequate support. Only one social library had more than 100 members; most of them had between 25 and 50. Many social libraries suffered from the competition of the circulating libraries.[19] The final results were that some social libraries disappeared completely shortly after the death of their founder; some became parts of other existing libraries; some formed the nucleus of the public libraries which followed; and some are still in existence today.

As an important factor in the evolution of the American public library, the social library cannot be overlooked. Its contributions lay not only in the influence it exerted upon the society which was to create and support the public library, but also in the fact that it pointed up, negatively by its inadequacies and affirmatively by its contributions to literate society, the overwhelming need for libraries serving all people.

Circulating or Lending Libraries

Circulating or lending libraries originated and became numerous in Scotland in the eighteenth century, and then spread to England and the Continent.[20] The first attempts to open circulating libraries in the American colonies, however, met with short-lived success. William Rind of Annapolis began a circulating library in 1762, but it was abandoned two years later; John Mein opened one in Boston in 1765 which functioned only until about 1770. After the Revolution, circulating libraries operated successfully in connection with bookshops, general stores, and other kinds of shops, and before the end of the eighteenth century, a bookseller and a circulating library were operating as far west as Pittsburgh.

The circulating libraries were strictly business enterprises based on payment for the use of books, either a rental fee per book borrowed or a quarterly or annual subscription. Consequently, their chief purpose of making money for the owner greatly influenced and limited the kinds of reading materials offered. In general, and with varying degrees of effectiveness, the social libraries provided for the needs of those who had a real interest in good literature and for those seeking moral, intellectual, or vocational self-improvement; while the circulating libraries arose in answer to the desire for popular reading materials, with collections reflecting popular reading tastes. Catering to the recreation and entertainment needs of their clients, the circulating library in America, as in England,[21] featured the novel. In addition to fiction, many of these libraries offered drama, history, and travel. Although they filled an immediate need for certain kinds of reading materials, the contribution of the circulating libraries to American library development was negligible.

NOTES

1. *See* p. 47.
2. Clarence L. Ver Steeg, *The Formative Years: 1607-1763* ("The Making of America Series"; New York: Hill and Wang, Inc., 1964), p. 55.
3. *Ibid.*, p. 52.
4. "New England's First Fruits, 1643," reprinted in Samuel Eliot Morison, *The Founding of Harvard College* (Cambridge, Mass.: Harvard University Press, 1935), p. 432. This selection is found also in *American Higher Education, A Documentary History*, ed. Richard Hofstadter and Wilson Smith (Chicago: The University of Chicago Press, 1961), I, 6.
5. The term "public library" is used here in the sense that it was open to the public and it was not supported by taxes levied for that purpose.
6. Jesse H. Shera, *Foundations of the Public Library: The Origins of the Public Library Movement in New England 1629-1855* (Chicago: The University of Chicago Press, 1949), pp. 19-24, *passim*.
7. *See* p. 49.
8. Edgar L. Pennington, *The Reverend Thomas Bray* ("The Church Historical Society Publication," No. VII; Philadelphia, 1934), p. 14. *See also* Bernard C. Steiner, "Rev. Thomas Bray and His American Libraries," *The American Historical Review*, II (1896), pp. 59-75.
9. See pp. 47, 49.
10. *The Autobiography of Benjamin Franklin*, ed. W. Labaree *et al.* (New Haven, Conn.: Yale University Press, 1964), p. 130.
11. *Ibid.*
12. *Ibid.*, pp. 130-131.
13. Jacob Duché, *Observations on a Variety of Subjects, Literary, Moral and Religious* . . . (Philadelphia: Printed by John Dunlap, 1764), pp. 10-11. (Microfilm.)
14. Today, the Library Company of Philadelphia is open to the public for research and interlibrary loan.
15. The Athenaeum in Greek antiquity was the temple of Athena, in which professors taught their students, and orators and poets rehearsed their compositions. The meaning evolved to that of a building or institution in which books, periodicals, and newspapers are provided for use. In 1822, it referred to a literary clubroom, reading room, and library in such an institution in Manchester, England. It assumed this meaning in America.
16. *See* p. 51.

17. U.S., Bureau of Education, *Public Libraries in the United States of America, Their History, Condition and Management, Special Report*, Part I (Washington, D.C., U.S. Government Printing Office, 1876), pp. 928, 963. By 1875, there were 15 mercantile libraries located in 11 states. *Ibid.*, pp. 800-801.
18. Carleton Bruns Joeckel, *The Government of the American Public Library* (Chicago: The University of Chicago Press, 1935), p. 2.
19. Oliver Garceau, *The Public Library in the Political Process: A Report of the Public Library Inquiry* . . . (New York: Columbia University Press, 1949), pp. 19-20, 21.
20. *See* p. 51.
21. Garceau, op. cit., pp. 19-20, 21.

8

America—the Nineteenth Century

The period following the Revolution was a time of extraordinary political, economic, and social change, characterized by 1) a developing sense of nationalism; 2) westward expansion and the building of towns and cities along the Ohio, the Mississippi, and the Great Lakes; 3) widespread interest in formal education and in self-education and self-improvement; and 4) the accumulation of great individual wealth. All these developments were accompanied by the establishment of libraries.

INFLUENCE OF NATIONALISM

The spirit of nationalism can be seen in the growing interest in history, particularly American history, and in the desire to preserve it. Historical societies and museums were established for this purpose, and the collection and preservation of historical materials was a major concern of the Library of Congress—established to serve the federal government—as well as of the state and territorial libraries.

Historical Societies

Of the historical societies which were formed to collect and preserve the materials of American history, the earliest were the Massachusetts Historical Society, organized in 1791 and incorporated in 1794; the New York Historical Society in 1804; and the New Hampshire Historical Society in 1823. Other states, as well as associations and groups within the states, also formed historical societies, some of them emphasizing the collection of materials important only in the history of that state or locality. By the last quarter of the century, there were 51 historical libraries in 24 states.[1]

The Library of Congress

The library needs of the Continental Congress were met by the "chance researches of its members and the gratuitous use of books tendered them by the Library Company of Philadelphia,"[2] but the new Capital city, Washington, did not have any library facilities, and a library had to be organized to provide books and information to meet the needs of the National Congress. The Library of Congress was authorized in 1800, and on April 24 of that year, Congress made the first appropriation ($5000) for books and for "fitting up a suitable apartment for containing them and placing them therein." Two years later, an act providing for the organization of the Library of Congress placed the facility in the Capitol building, set up regulations for operating the library, and established the office of librarian. When the Capitol was burned by the British Army in 1814, the Library of Congress was lost. Former President Jefferson's private library of 6,487 volumes purchased for $23,950 then formed the basis for a new congressional library. Another fire in 1851 destroyed all but 20,000 volumes out of the 55,000-volume collection. The library was rebuilt out of fireproof materials, and from that time it entered upon a period of continuous growth. It was greatly strengthened by the acquisition in 1866 of the Smithsonian Institution's scientific collection of some 40,000 volumes and the Peter Force historical collection of 60,000 volumes the following year.[3]

State and Territorial Libraries

It was more than 30 years after the Constitution went into effect in 1789 before the states began to establish libraries to serve the state governments. In the older states, collections of laws and legislative proceedings had been preserved in one or more legislative libraries.

Records of the state of Pennsylvania show that there was a library at its capital as early as 1777, though the state library was not officially established until 1816. In 1811, Massachusetts initiated the system of the annual exchange of statutes between the states, and it was these documents which constituted the basic collections of state libraries. By 1876, every state and territory had a governmental library whose purposes were 1) to collect and preserve complete sets of all publications of the state or territory and, as far as possible, of the several states and territories; and 2) to collect works in American history, especially of the state or territory.

WESTWARD EXPANSION

As settlers moved west, they took with them the culture and ideas to which they had become accustomed in their former homes. Schools were soon established, and books were accessible through general merchants, whose stocks included dictionaries, grammars, spelling books, arithmetics, devotional books, and handbooks. Peddlers carried books and pamphlets to the outlying parts of the settlements, and before the close of the eighteenth century, some subscription libraries were started. The "coonskin library," so named because the subscribers paid their fees in coonskins, was begun in 1803 in Ames Township, Ohio. It is estimated that there were probably a dozen subscription libraries in Ohio before 1812.[4] In the Far West, the gold rush brought a great influx of population to California. Many of these persons were well educated, and by the middle of the century, there were 50 printers in San Francisco, at least three social libraries, and many private libraries.

EDUCATIONAL INFLUENCES

The belief of our early national leaders that knowledge is necessary to good government grew in the early decades of the nineteenth century to a widespread belief that universal literacy is necessary in a democracy.

School District Libraries

In his message to the legislature in 1827, Governor Dewitt Clinton of New York recommended the formation of school district libraries.[5] In 1835, the New York legislature passed a law permitting the voters in any school district to levy a tax of $20 to begin a library and $10 each succeeding year to provide for its growth. Few districts, however, voted the necessary tax. Three years later, legislation was enacted authorizing the state to distribute among its school districts a total of $55,000 a year to buy books for libraries, and requiring each school district to raise by taxation, for the same purpose, an amount equal to that received from the state. Some districts were so small that their share of the money was negligible, but even so, by 1853 school district libraries in New York contained more than 1,604,210 volumes.[6] Unfortunately, school districts began to use the appropriations for other purposes.[7] By 1875 only about one-half of the state appropriation was spent on libraries, and the number of volumes decreased by almost 50 percent.

The concept of the school district library found wide favor, and before 1850, nine states had followed the example of New York and 12 other states and territories had made similar provisions by 1876.

Most of these libraries were ineffective. In analyzing the reasons for their eventual failure, Garceau[8] points out that the school districts were artificially created by state planners and did not follow local patterns of cultural loyalties and intellectual needs. The libraries served too small an area, were inadequately housed, poorly supervised by school trustees, and badly managed by elected librarians.

The Tax-Supported Free Public Library

Free town libraries date from Captain Robert Keayne's gift to Boston in the mid-seventeenth century.[9] They were usually established by gifts from affluent citizens or from other philanthropy. In 1803, Caleb Bingham, a Boston bookseller, founded the Bingham Library for Youth in his hometown of Salisbury, Connecticut, with a gift of 150 books—the first free library for children and young people. The vote of the citizens of the town in 1810 to give financial support to this library is believed to be the first time a municipal governing body contributed financial aid to public library service.[10] However, Peterborough, New Hampshire is given the distinction of having established the first free town library when, in 1833, the citizens voted to use for a town library funds distributed by the state for free schools and other educational purposes; and they voted to maintain it by an annual appropriation.

As worthy as Peterborough's effort was, the concept of a fully tax-supported free library open for use by all who might need it was not yet established among the tax-paying public. As Scudder pointed out, "The idea of a free public library could hardly find general acceptance until the idea of free public education had become familiar to men's minds."[11] Therefore, the educational revolution of the second quarter of the nineteenth century led by Horace Mann and Henry Barnard, which resulted in the beginning of our American system of free public education, provided a strong stimulus to the public library idea. Both Mann and Barnard supported the school district public libraries and saw the library as an essential contributor to the educational program of the school, an invaluable aid in continuing education and in self-improvement, and an indispensable part of the cultural life of the people.

The second quarter of the nineteenth century was a period of scholarly and literary activity and accomplishment. Interest in American history, first seen in the establishment of historical and state libraries for its preservation, spread to the study of American history and then to the history of other countries. Historical research and investigation reached a high point in the writings of Prescott, Motley, and Parkman, in spite of the fact that the dearth of materials for research in America made it necessary for historians and scholars to go to Europe and England to carry on their investigations—a fact emphatically pointed out by those who worked for the establishment of publicly-supported libraries. American literature reached its peak in the middle half of the century in the works of Hawthorne, Longfellow, Emerson, Lowell, Whittier, and Holmes.

The period brought many changes in education that eventually led to free, universal, secular elementary and secondary schools. Elementary education was removed from the control of religious, charitable, and other private groups; tuition fees were abolished; and the principle of taxation for the support of schools was established. The demand for practical education to meet the needs of an industrial society resulted in the addition of vocational subjects to the course of study offered by the academies. The belief in universal educational opportunity gained widespread support, leading in 1852 to the passage by Massachusetts of the first compulsory school attendance law.

As early as 1826, George Ticknor, a trustee of the Boston Athenaeum, realized that social libraries could no longer meet the growing needs of scholars and laymen for library materials and proposed that all libraries in the city of Boston be united with the Boston Athenaeum and that their facilities be made freely available to the public. This particular plan did not materialize, but Ticknor's efforts on behalf of a public library did not cease. In 1841, Nicolas Marie Alexandre Vattemare, a French actor and ventriloquist, gave new impetus to the idea of a free public library when he presented to the city of Boston a proposal for international exchanges of books. The people of Boston saw this proposal as a means of achieving international goodwill, but a library was needed before such exchanges could be effected.

Although the idea of a free public library was well received, little would have been accomplished had it not been for the continuous efforts of civic-minded citizens, notably George Ticknor and Edward Everett. Both men believed that in a democracy education must be provided equally for all people and they saw the public library as a means of self-education and continuing education after high school. Financial support was offered in 1847 by Mayor Josiah Quincy in the amount of $5000 for books if the city would provide an equal amount. The following year, the state legislature gave the city of Boston permission to levy taxes to support a library, and by 1852 the Boston Public Library was organized. When it was opened to the public in 1854, the free, public, tax-supported library became a part of American life.

The historical significance of the Boston Public Library cannot be measured, for it established the precedent for free, publicly-supported library service to all citizens and set an example both in administrative organization and in objectives for other public libraries to follow.[12]

During the period in which the Boston Public Library was taking form, the State Legislature of New Hampshire passed permissive legislation (1849) enabling towns to levy taxes for the support of libraries. Massachusetts passed permissive legislation for the entire state in 1851, and other states followed: Maine, 1854; Vermont, 1865; Rhode Island and Connecticut, 1867; and New York, 1872. The pattern of state legislation then, as now, was permissive—not mandatory—and thus the levying of taxes for the establishment of libraries has always depended upon local interest and initiative.

The public library developed where there was a concentrated and homogeneous population with more than average education and cultural background; where there were leaders who had a deep sense of civic responsibility; and where there was adequate taxable wealth to support it. Before the Civil War, public libraries flourished in the northeastern section of the country; after the Civil War, they had their greatest growth in the West and North.

College Libraries

Before the Revolution, nine colleges were founded in the Colonies, each one modeled after Oxford and Cambridge and shaped by aristocratic tradition to serve the aristocratic elements of colonial society. After the Revolution, "a commitment to the republic became the guiding obligation of the American college,"[13] and in the course of westward expansion, the college as a distinctive American institution evolved, "shaped and adapted to the peculiar needs of an advancing people."[14]

Before the Civil War, more than 500 colleges (182 of them became permanent) and 21 state universities were founded. Of these, only Yale and Harvard had library collections numbering as many as 50,000 volumes by 1850. The Land Grant College Act of 1862 gave added impetus to the establishment of institutions of higher education, and by 1875, there were 312 college libraries with a total of 1,949,105 volumes.[15]

Since the colleges of the period emphasized textbook teaching and discouraged wide reading, their libraries were open chiefly for the occasional loan of a book to a professor or student or for the perusal of recent periodicals. Upperclassmen could use the library under certain conditions, but, in general, freshmen and sophomores were not permitted this privilege. Literary societies formed an important part of college life, and each society had its own library which provided materials needed for the debates and discussions sponsored by the society and for recreational reading. The society library often had a larger collection than the college library and always offered a wider variety of materials. In time, many of the literary society libraries were merged with the college libraries.

State Library Commissions

Although the Tenth Amendment to the Constitution gave to the states all powers not reserved to the federal government and was interpreted as authorizing the states to establish school systems, it was not until 1837, when Massachusetts established a state board of education, that a state moved in this direction. By 1875 nearly all the states required local administrative units to tax themselves for the support of the public schools, and by 1880 every Northern state had established a state educational system. As schools improved and public high schools became common, the states began to take an interest in providing the means of continuing education after high school by aiding public library development.

In 1875, Rhode Island gave the state board of education the right to grant sums to existing libraries. Massachusetts established the first state library commission in 1890, followed by New Hampshire in 1891. Other commissions came into existence during the next decade, all for the purpose of extending library service within the state. Financial aid was provided by the states for the founding of libraries; boxes of books were sent to libraries; and traveling libraries—small collections of books to be sent from place to place to circulate freely—were initiated in a number of states.

County Libraries

The scattered population and uneven distribution of wealth in some of the states called for a type of library organization which could provide service to rural areas. The county was the logical governmental unit to provide this service. In 1898, two county libraries were incorporated and both were opened in 1901—the County Library in Van Wert, Ohio preceding the Washington County Free Library in Maryland by a few months.[16] Under the leadership of Mary L. Titcomb, the Washington County Free Library initiated a book-wagon service in 1907.[17]

Influence of Philanthropy

The tremendous industrial and commercial growth of the United States in the nineteenth century resulted in relative prosperity for the country as a whole and in the accumulation of great fortunes by certain individuals. Among the philanthropic enterprises of these individuals was the endowment of libraries. Endowed libraries—sometimes called patronymic libraries—were fully supported by private funds but were opened to the public on conditions specified by the donor.

Three endowed libraries which were established in New York City in the latter half of the century are of major historical and cultural importance. John Jacob Astor, one of the first of the great fortune makers, bequeathed $400,000 for the founding of a library for the public, and the Astor Library was organized in 1848 "for the advancement of useful knowledge." The Lenox Library, founded in 1870 by James Lenox, was "dedicated to history, literature and the fine arts." The third library was the gift of Samuel Jones Tilden, who, at his death in 1886, left about two million dollars and 15,000 books for the establishment of a library under the Tilden Trust "to serve the interests of science and popular education." These three libraries—the Astor, the Lenox, and the Tilden Trust—were consolidated in 1895 to form the New York Public Library, an institution which continues to be supported by both public funds and private philanthropy and which is the nation's outstanding public library.[18]

Other endowed libraries which were established before the end of the century and during the first quarter of the twentieth century are the Peabody Institute of Baltimore, established in 1857 and opened to the public in 1866; the Newberry Library, Chicago, 1887; the John Crerar

Library, Chicago, 1894; the Henry E. Huntington Library, San Marino, California, 1919; and the Pierpont Morgan Library, New York City, 1924.

City libraries, in particular, were aided during the last quarter of the nineteenth century by the gifts of Andrew Carnegie. From 1881 to 1898, Carnegie provided funds for 14 municipal libraries. During the year 1899, his gifts totaled approximately four million dollars and were made to more than 30 libraries or localities in the United States. "These gifts made the endowment of libraries the most striking feature of the library year 1899, supplemented as they were by gifts from other benefactors."[19] By 1917, Carnegie public library buildings numbered 1,681 and his contributions for these buildings exceeded 41 million dollars.[20]

LIBRARIANS' CONFERENCE OF 1853

By 1853 there were about 700 libraries in the United States—mercantile, society, school, and college—with total collections estimated at about two million volumes, but with no single collection numbering as many as 100,000 volumes.[21]

Generally speaking, by mid-century librarians as a group had not made any significant contribution to library development in America. Leadership had been provided by educators, scholars, authors, religious leaders, and civic-minded citizens, but in 1853 practicing librarians made a public effort on behalf of library advancement.

On May 15, 1853, an invitation was sent by Charles C. Jewett, librarian of the Smithsonian Institution, Charles E. Norton, publisher and bookseller, and others to librarians and persons interested in bibliography "to meet in convention at New York on Thursday the Fifteenth day of September, for the purpose of conferring together upon the means of advancing the prosperity and usefulness of public libraries and for the suggestion and discussion of topics of importance to book collectors and readers."[22] In response to the invitation, 82 men—librarians, educators, authors, and clergy—met in New York to share experiences, give attention to common problems and ways of solving them, and offer suggestions regarding the establishment of popular libraries. One of the most important decisions made was to organize a permanent association of librarians at the next meeting. Unfortunately, the next meeting was never called because the War between the States and the long period of Reconstruction occupied the attention of the country for the next quarter of a century. While the measurable results of the meeting were few, the convention deserves attention as the first effort toward the organization of librarians as a group.

LIBRARIANS' CONFERENCE OF 1876

Almost a quarter of a century later, another meeting of librarians was called to be held in Philadelphia during the Centennial Exposition of 1876. By that time, according to the U.S. Bureau of Education's published special report, *Public Libraries in the United States of America, Their History, Condition, and Management,*[23] there were 3,682 libraries of all kinds in the United States, a noticeable growing interest in library work, and a consequent increasing demand for librarians. At this meeting, the American Library Association was organized "to promote the library interests of the country."[24]

The year 1876 was of great significance for libraries and librarians with such events as the founding of *The American Library Journal* by F. Leypoldt, and the publication of Melvil Dewey's *A Classification and Subject Index for Cataloguing and Arranging the Books and Pamphlets of a Library* and C. A. Cutter's *Rules for Making a Dictionary Catalogue.*[25] The first formal library school program was opened at Columbia College by Melvil Dewey in 1887, and before the close of the century, four other programs for the training of librarians were established.

At the close of the nineteenth century in the United States, there was a developing interest in all libraries, in the extension of library services on local, county, state, and national levels, and in the training of persons for library positions.

NOTES

1. U.S., Bureau of Education, *Public Libraries in the United States of America, Their History, Condition, and Management, Special Report,* Part I (Washington, D.C., U.S. Government Printing Office, 1876), pp. 798-799.
2. Ainsworth R. Spofford, "The Library of Congress, or National Library," *Ibid.,* p. 253.
3. *See also* pp. 114-116.
4. Louis B. Wright, *Culture on the Moving Frontier* (Bloomington, Ind.: Indiana University Press, 1955), p. 118.
5. Oliver Garceau, *The Public Library in the Political Process: A Report of the Public Library Inquiry* . . . (New York: Columbia University Press, 1949), p. 25, states that these were "adult collections for adult readers and were not necessarily housed in school buildings."
6. U.S., Bureau of Education, *op cit.,* p. 40.

7. In 1843, authority had been given to school districts to pay for school apparatus from the library fund, and later they were allowed to use the money for teachers' salaries rather than for library purposes, if they chose.

8. Garceau, *op. cit.*, p. 25.

9. *See* p. 56.

10. Jesse H. Shera, *Foundations of the Public Library: The Origins of the Public Library Movement in New England 1629–1855* (Chicago: The University of Chicago Press, 1949), p. 160.

11. Horace E. Scudder, "Public Libraries a Hundred Years Ago," U.S., Bureau of Education, *op. cit.*, p. 1E.

12. Walter Muir Whitehill, *Boston Public Library, A Centennial History* (Cambridge, Mass.: Harvard University Press, 1956), pp. 27-34.

13. Frederick Rudolph, *The American College and University: A History* (New York: Alfred A. Knopf, Inc., 1962), p. 61.

14. Donald G. Tewksbury, *The Founding of American Colleges and Universities Before the Civil War* (New York: Bureau of Publications, Teachers College, Columbia University, 1932), p. 1.

15. U.S., Bureau of Education, *op. cit.*, pp. 798-799.

16. Mary Lemist Titcomb, *Story of the Washington County Free Library* (Hagerstown, Md.: n.d.), p. 7. The county library type of organization was particularly suited to the Southern states.

17. *Ibid.*, p. 14. *See also* pp. 129-131.

18. New York Public Library, *The Many Faces of the Library: Its History, Its Services, Its Future* (New York: The New York Public Library, n.d.), *passim.*

19. *Library Journal*, 25 (January 1900): 3.

20. Florence Anderson, *Carnegie Corporation Library Programs, 1911-1961* (New York: Carnegie Corporation of New York, 1963), pp. 4, 25.

21. George B. Utley, *The Librarians' Conference of 1853: A Chapter in American Library History*, ed. G. H. Doane (Chicago: American Library Association, 1951), pp. 113-114.

22. *Norton's Literary and Educational Register for 1854* (New York: Charles B. Norton, 1854), p. 49.

23. U.S., Bureau of Education, *op. cit.*, pp. 798-801, *passim.*

24. *The American Library Journal*, 1 (March 1877): 253.

25. This publication constituted Part II of U.S., Bureau of Education, *op. cit.*

PART TWO

Librarianship as a Profession

> Professionalization seeks to clothe a given area with standards of excellence, to establish rules of conduct, to develop a sense of responsibility, to set criteria for recruitment and training, to ensure a measure of protection for members, to establish collective control over the area, and to elevate it to a position of dignity and social standing in the society.[1]

One of the recurring questions about librarianship concerns its professional status. Discussions of the topic, among both librarians and non-librarians, usually involve an examination of the essential elements of a profession as delineated by students of this subject and an analysis of the extent to which librarianship possesses these elements. A sampling of the definitions of a profession will reveal some of the ingredients which are usually used as bases of comparison.

1. *The Oxford English Dictionary* defines a profession as "a vocation in which a professed knowledge of some department of learning or science is used in its application to the affairs of others or in the practice of an art founded upon it."[2]
2. *A Dictionary of the Social Sciences* says that "the term professions denotes occupations which demand a highly specialized knowledge and skill acquired at least in part by courses of a more or less theoretical nature and not by practice alone, tested by some form of examination either at a university or some other authorized institution, and conveying to the persons

who possess them considerable authority in relation to 'clients.' . . . At present the term usually denotes certain occupations whose members give service rather than engage in the production and distribution of goods. . . ."[3]
3. The eminent social scientists, A. M. Carr-Saunders and P. A. Wilson, writing on the subject of professions, said "we recognize a profession as a vocation founded upon a prolonged and specialized intellectual training which enables a particular service to be rendered."[4] In another work, they pointed out that "special competence, acquired as the result of intellectual training, is the chief distinguishing feature of the professions."[5]

Among the essential elements of a profession which are generally agreed upon by analysts of the subject are:[6]

1. A systematic theory which delineates and supports the skills that characterize the profession;
2. A level of authority which comes from extensive education in the systematic theory;
3. Community sanction and approval of this authority as expressed in the conferring on the profession of such powers as accreditation, formulation of standards of performance, and establishment of rules for admission into the profession;
4. A code of ethics which regulates relations of professional persons with clients and colleagues;
5. A professional culture sustained by formal associations, consisting of its values, norms, and symbols and having at its center the career concept;
6. A service orientation.

Other elements sometimes added are monetary or honorary awards for work achievements, the degree of recognition by people outside librarianship, the amount of time devoted to the occupation, and whether or not there is a feeling of commitment to a calling.[7] There is no consensus regarding the elements of a profession.

Some of the steps which are often identified as moving an occupation toward full professionalization are: 1) the establishment of formal training within a university; 2) forming local and national associations; 3) achieving control over admission to the profession and over certification and/or licensing; and 4) the adoption of a formal code of ethics.

In checking librarianship against the criteria which have been enumerated, one can see that some steps have been taken toward professionalization. Librarianship is an occupation which demands specialized knowledge and skills which are acquired at least in part by courses of a more or less theoretical nature and are tested by an examination at a university or other authorized institution. Implicit in this requirement for specialized knowledge and skills is the availability of a body of literature to be used in acquiring them; librarianship has produced such a body of literature and is continually adding to it. The persons who satisfactorily complete these courses develop a sense of responsibility for their technique, which they reveal in their concern for the competence and performance of the practitioners as a whole; and they are given considerable authority in formulating standards of performance, in the power of accreditation, and in establishing rules for admission into the profession. Librarianship has professional organizations which promote excellence in the work of the members, influence public sentiment and support, and endeavor to raise it to a position of dignity and social standing. It has at its center the career concept; and from the beginning, it has rendered a service.

In view of these actualities, the student might well assume that there is agreement among librarians that librarianship qualifies as a profession. However, this is not the fact; there is not unanimity of opinion. While acknowledging that librarianship has many of the ingredients that characterize a profession, those who do not believe that it has achieved professional status have questioned, for example, the intellectual content of its knowledge base; the rigor of its educational requirements; the extent of its authority; the strength of its code of ethics; the degree of external recognition which it is accorded; the extent to which its associations promote the economic well-being of members; and the service motivation of librarians.[8]

Every student of librarianship may want to accept the opportunity and assume the responsibility of examining the question, Is librarianship a profession? and should be aware of the ideology, the processes, and the activities by which an occupation moves toward becoming a profession.

It is not the purpose of the chapters in Part Two to attempt to answer this question, but rather to present two of the major steps which librarians have taken toward the professionalization of their occupation and toward making themselves professional people. The two steps to be considered in this section are: 1) the establishment of professional associations which, according to Carr-Saunders and Wilson, usually occurs as soon as a profession emerges, for "a profession can only be said to exist when there are bonds between the practitioners, and these bonds can take but one shape—that of formal association"[9]; and 2) the development of educational programs to provide the specialized intellectual study and training necessary for providing skilled service.

NOTES

1. Herbert Blumer, "Preface," *Professionalization,* eds. Howard M. Vollmer and Donald L. Mills (Englewood Cliffs, N.J.: Prentice-Hall, Inc. 1966) p. xi.
2. *The Oxford English Dictionary,* VIII, 1427. By permission of the Clarendon Press, Oxford.
3. N. Elias, "Professions," *A Dictionary of the Social Sciences,* ed. Julius Gould and William L. Kolb, compiled under the auspices of the United Nations Educational, Scientific and Cultural Organization (New York: The Free Press of Glencoe, 1964), p. 542.
4. A. M. Carr-Saunders and P. A. Wilson, "Professions," *Encyclopaedia of the Social Sciences,* XI-XII (1933): 478.
5. A. M. Carr-Saunders and P. A. Wilson, *The Professions* (London: Oxford University Press, 1933; second impression published by Frank Cass & Co., Ltd., 1964), p. 307. By permission of the Clarendon Press, Oxford.
6. *See* Ernest Greenwood, "Attributes of a Profession," *Social Work,* 2 (July 1957): 44-55. *See also* J. A. Jackson (ed.), *Professions and Professionalization* (Sociological Studies 3; Cambridge: At the University Press, 1970), pp. 155-156; and Wilbert E. Moore and Gerald W. Rosenblum, *The Professions: Roles and Rules* (New York: Russell Sage Foundation, 1970), pp. 5-6.
7. Moore and Rosenblum, *op. cit.,* pp. 5-6.
8. *See* William Goode, "The Librarian: From Occupation to Profession?" *The Library Quarterly,* 31: (October 1961): 306-318 for the views of a nonlibrarian.
9. Carr-Saunders and Wilson, *The Professions, op. cit.,* p. 298.

9

Professional Organizations

It is no simple task to isolate clearly the beginnings of librarianship as a self-conscious occupation. Some library historians date this beginning from the seventeenth century, when writings dealing seriously with major library problems and functions appeared for the first time. After the invention of printing, libraries began to be faced with large numbers of books on all known subjects and in various sizes which had to be added to their traditional collections of handwritten manuscripts and codexes. By the middle of the seventeenth century, library materials included such new forms as periodicals, broadsides, newspapers, news pamphlets, reference books, maps, globes, charts, and printed books in various sizes, as well as the extant collections of handwritten books. Certainly not at any time before, and perhaps not again until the middle of the current century, did the volume and multiplicity of form of recorded knowledge create so many problems of organization and administration for librarians in comparison with what had gone before.

Gabriel Naudé offered guidance for establishing and operating libraries in his *Advis Pour Dresser Une Bibliothèque* by presenting such sound principles of selection, arrangement, and use of materials that they are still considered to be basic in building library collections. Some of the writings of Leibniz, noted mathematician and philosopher, were concerned with systematic acquisition of materials, financial support, and the need for bibliographic access to a library collection through an ordered system of classification. Contributions to the general history of libraries by Justus Lipsius and Johannes Lomeier and to the history of national libraries by Durie and Bentley, as well as the writings of Naudé and Leibniz, constituted a sizable body of what could be considered professional literature.[1]

These writings indicated clearly that special knowledge, techniques, and principles are required in the effective organization and administration of a library. Writings on the classification of knowledge, inventories and catalogs of library collections—both national and private—charters of purpose, and other materials relevant to library organization and operation were produced throughout the seventeenth and eighteenth centuries. It was not, however, until school district libraries and the subsequent public library movement began to take hold in nineteenth-century America that a fruitful self-consciousness regarding the importance and distinctiveness of their activities and purposes emerged among those who were devoting themselves in a practicing or supporting capacity to the establishment and operation of libraries.

EMERGENCE OF THE PROFESSION

In 1853, a group of men—librarians, scholars, teachers, and clergymen—"believing that the knowledge of Books, and the foundation and management of collections of them for public use"[2] could be promoted by consultation among librarians and others interested in bibliographical activities, met in New York for that purpose.[3] This conference brought to the attention of the public the fact that the special distinctive function of the library is to collect, organize, and promote the use of books and that special methods are required in carrying out this function. It also pointed up the need of librarians as a group to confer together and emphasized *service* as the primary motivation and aim of the library. Some library historians date the emergence of the library profession from this convention. Another meeting was planned, but because of unfavorable social and political conditions it was never held.

"Taking the hint from the meeting of 1853, a few library devotees in May 1876 proposed a like gathering in connection with the great Exhibition"[4] in Philadelphia that year and the announcement of such a meeting, to be held in October, was sent to the leading libraries of this country and to the leading librarians abroad.

In the meantime, on September 30, 1876, the first issue of *The American Library Journal* appeared. Published by F. Leypoldt, with Melvil Dewey as managing editor and with 21 leading librarians as associate editors, the new publication was planned as a "journalistic medium of exchanging thought and experience on topics of interest to librarians."[5] It carried the program of the October conference, numerous items of practical interest to librarians, and articles by a number of notable librarians, including Melvil Dewey's now classic statement, "The Profession."[6]

THE AMERICAN LIBRARY ASSOCIATION

On October 4, 1876, a large number of librarians from the United States, Canada, and the United Kingdom convened in Philadelphia and a permanent organization of librarians was effected, with the following officers: Justin Winsor of the Boston Public Library as president; Ainsworth R. Spofford of the Library of Congress, William F. Poole of the Chicago Public Library, and Henry A. Homes of the New York State Library as vice-presidents; and Melvil Dewey as secretary. The object of the newly formed American Library Association, as stated in its constitution, was "to promote the library interests of the country by exchanging views, reaching conclusions, and inducing co-operation in all departments of bibliothecal science and economy; by disposing the public mind to the founding and improving of libraries; and by cultivating good-will among its own members."[7] The February 28, 1877 issue of *The American Library Journal* carried on the title page, "Official Journal of the American Library Association."

Early activities of the association were restricted largely to holding annual meetings and to committee work. It was not until World War I that the ALA gained national prominence and stature as a result of its contribution to the war effort, which included supplying library materials for the armed forces; building, equipping, and operating camp libraries here and abroad; and carrying on a national campaign for magazines and books for these purposes. In its impressive war effort, ALA collected over one million books for the WWI camps.

As early as 1902, the American Library Association received an initial endowment from Andrew Carnegie, and since 1924, the Carnegie Corporation has played a significant role in the development of the association and many of its programs. From 1924 to 1926, the corporation provided $549,000 toward ALA's general support, and in 1926 gave two million dollars as an endowment. Since that time, ALA has been the recipient of many other grants from the Carnegie Corporation for specific purposes, such as the creation and publication of teaching materials to be used in library schools; the preparation of reading courses; making studies of adult education, public library needs, and such library activities as circulation, reference, book selection, and library services for children; and the development of standards for library service.

State and regional associations of librarians appeared soon after ALA was organized: the New York State Library Association in 1909 and within a decade the Pacific Northwest Library Association, followed in 1922 by the Southeastern Library Association and the Southwestern Library Association. At the present time, there are 57 state, regional, and territorial library organizations which are chapters of ALA and 22 library associations which are affiliated with it. ALA works cooperatively with a number of library associations including the Bibliographical Society of America, Special Libraries Association, Library Association (London), Canadian Library Association, International Federation of Library Associations, Association for Library and Information Science Education, and American Society for Information Science.[9]

ALA—Organization

"The mission of the American Library Association is to provide leadership for the development, promotion, and improvement of library and information services and the profession of librarianship in order to enhance learning and to ensure access to information for all."[10]

The organization of ALA is made up of an Executive Board, the central management board; a governing body, the Council, composed of elected representatives of the membership; ALA committees, which are responsible for various areas; 11 divisions, each devoted to a specified area; 15 round tables composed of members who are interested in aspects of librarianship not within the scope of any division; 57 chapters, each one responsible for the promotion of library service within its geographic area; 22 affiliated organizations—national or international—which have purposes similar to those of the ALA; and a headquarters staff under the direction of the Executive Director.[11]

ALA—Activities

All activities of ALA are directed to carrying out its mission and include conducting programs to educate the American public in the important contributions which the library makes to our cultural, social, and educational life; providing leadership in planning for the extension and improvement of library services to all citizens and in securing public and financial support on national, state, and local levels; maintaining a constant watch over the freedom to read; establishing and encouraging the adoption of standards to improve the quality of library service and to ensure the provision of qualified personnel; striving to maintain equal access to materials, facilities, and services; conducting studies and surveys regarding problems, trends, and needs in librarianship for purposes of information and planning; and creating, publishing, and encouraging the publication of professional literature. ALA is receptive to new trends and new knowledge, and encourages the use of the new technologies to improve library and information services. ALANET, the electronic information service developed and managed by ALA, provides electronic newsletters, database services, networking support services, electronic mail, conference schedules, and other services to all types of libraries, publishers, etc.

At the present time (1990), more than 95 awards, grants, and scholarships are available through the ALA awards program. These awards are given in recognition of high achievement in various areas of librarianship to promising students who wish to enter the profession of librarianship or to individuals or groups to conduct special studies. In 1987, a grant of $560,000 was made to the American Library Association by the Carnegie Foundation for a program to "enhance the role of educational videocassettes in libraries." This program includes grants to selected Carnegie libraries for the purchase of videocassettes; recipients match the grant with a TV monitor or educational programming.

Some major activities of ALA are in the fields of intellectual freedom, standards, and legislation.

Intellectual Freedom

Since 1939 the American Library Association has "consciously promoted the concept of man's freedom to seek the truth where and how he will."[12] During that year the "ALA Bill of Rights" was adopted, and in 1940 the Committee on Intellectual Freedom to Safeguard the Rights of Library Users to Freedom of Inquiry—later changed to ALA Intellectual Freedom Committee—was created to recommend necessary steps to safeguard the rights of library users in accordance with the Bill of Rights of the United States and the "Library Bill of Rights." In 1948, the ALA Council adopted the "Library Bill of Rights," amended it in 1951 to include all media of communication collected or used by libraries, and in 1961 broadened it to include the statement that the right of an individual to use libraries should not be denied because of race, religion, national origin, or political views. In 1967 and in 1980, it was further revised to strengthen and clarify its content.[13] This official statement of the American Library Association regarding free inquiry sets forth basic policies which govern librarians in the selection of library materials, their attitude toward the censorship of library materials and the right of library users to free access to ideas and freedom of expression, and their efforts to make library facilities equally available to all groups. The purpose of the "Library Bill of Rights" is not "to protect librarians, but to preserve the right of *every citizen* to read whatever he wishes, forming his own private judgments."[14]

"Access to Resources and Services in the School Library Media Program..." (1986) reaffirms the principles of the "Library Bill of Rights" and guides the school library in the selection of materials.[15] The "Statement on Professional Ethics, 1981" sets forth certain ethical norms regarding the free flow of information.[16] Other statements by ALA regarding its steadfast belief in free access to ideas and its opposition to all attempts to restrict that right are the "Statement on Labeling," presented by the Committee on Intellectual Freedom to the ALA Council in 1951 and adopted at that time; and "Freedom to Read," drawn up in collaboration with the American Book Publishers Council in 1953.[17]

Two intellectual freedom organizations outside ALA, but with which the ALA and its units work closely, are the Freedom to Read Foundation and the LeRoy Merritt Humanitarian Fund.

Standards and Guidelines

Standards are criteria which are established by authority or by general consent as a measure or test of the quantity or quality of a given thing. They point out a condition or degree or level which must be attained if a desired goal is to be realized and are designed to set and maintain a high level of professional performance.

Early standards in librarianship were quantitative, measuring such tangible elements as physical facilities, staff, budgets, and collections. Now they are concerned with the library's functions, purposes, and services and with the material resources needed to carry out the programs. Some standards are established to serve as general guides for those who are developing library programs or an aspect of a program; others are designed to be used for purposes of accreditation. They may set goals, may explain how certain activities should be carried on, or may be actual units of measurement. Standards formulated by national associations to apply to all states must, of course, be general since library development and the conditions affecting it vary from state to state and within a state. Therefore, standards cannot offer the specific quantitative criteria which are often needed by a particular library.

Through its divisions, committees, and other units, ALA has developed standards for all types of libraries, and for graduate programs of education.[18] It has also formulated guidelines for services, personnel utilization, collection development, database services, interlibrary loans, library equipment, and services to special groups. These standards and guidelines have played a significant role in the development of libraries and library services and in the professional growth of librarians.

Legislation: The ALA Washington Office

In the interest of securing federal legislation of benefit to libraries, the ALA Washington Office was opened in 1945. In 1949, it took over the functions of the former ALA National Relations Office and International Relations Office.

The first major piece of library legislation to which the office gave its attention was the Public Library Demonstration Bill which was introduced in 1948 and in 1949, and defeated in 1950.[19] Prior to and following the passage of the Library Services Act in 1956,[20] the legislative activity of the ALA Washington Office increased. Since that time, it has played a highly significant role in the activities which have led to the passage of major federal legislation for libraries. Its ongoing program includes: keeping up with congressional opinion concerning libraries; advising with state and local library officials on library needs; organizing national, state, and local support for favorable legislation as well as against unfavorable legislative action; providing information and witnesses for congressional committees; and reporting regularly to the profession on the status of legislation—both pending and enacted.

Professional Participation

A profession grows in strength, importance, and influence with and through its members; and the principal vehicles for growth are the professional organizations—local, state, and national—which are organized and directed by members to that end. Thus an individual librarian's responsibility extends beyond the boundaries of a job description and library staff membership to include participatory membership in professional organizations and their programs.

There are several ways of participating in a professional organization: enrolling and paying dues to help finance the programs and services of the organization; attending meetings, taking part in programs, and serving on committees; making contributions to professional literature; conducting and reporting the results of studies and research; and supporting and seeking support for the organization's activities. Emphasis on the professional aspects of librarianship and participation in the professional activities within the library and its supporting institution as well as those initiated by local, state, and national organizations help to keep the librarian at a professional level.

NOTES

1. *See* pp. 48-49.
2. *Norton's Literary and Educational Register for 1854* (New York: Charles B. Norton, 1854), p. 49.
3. *See* pp. 75-76.
4. *The American Library Journal*, 1 (September 30, 1876): 13.
5. *Ibid.*
6. *Ibid.*, p. 5. *See* Appendix II, pp. 215-217.
7. *The American Library Journal*, 1 (March 1877): 253.
8. Florence Anderson, *Carnegie Corporation Library Programs, 1911–1961* (New York, Carnegie Corporation of New York, 1963), p. 89.
9. *ALA Handbook of Organization 1987/1988* (Chicago: American Library Association, 1987), p. 1.
10. *Ibid.*
11. *Ibid.* For changes in the names and specific purposes and responsibilities of the divisions, round tables, chapters, affiliated organizations, and offices, see the current issue of the *ALA Handbook of Organization*.
12. David K. Berninghausen, "The History of the ALA Intellectual Freedom Committee," *Wilson Library Bulletin*, 27 (June 1953): 813.
13. *See* Appendix II, p. 219.
14. Berninghausen, *loc. cit.*, p. 817.
15. *See* Appendix II., pp. 220-221.
16. *See* Appendix II., pp. 218.
17. *See* Appendix II., p. 222.
18. The American Library Association accredits only graduate library programs. *See* p. 95, 102 n. Standards formulated by ALA as well as those established by national, state, and regional groups are discussed in the appropriate chapters.
19. *See* pp. 126-127 for a discussion of the Public Library Demonstration Bill.
20. The Library Services Act was amended in 1964 and named the Library Services and Construction Act. *See* pp. 127, 144-145.

10

Library Education

In his annual report for 1869, Justin Winsor, superintendent of the Boston Public Library, spoke about the current status of library education:

> We have no schools of bibliographical or bibliothecal training whose graduates can guide the formation of, and assume management within, the fast increasing libraries of our country; and the demand may perhaps never warrant their establishment: but every library with a fair experience can afford inestimable instruction to another in its novitiate; and there have been no duties of my office to which I have given more hearty attention than those that have led to the granting of what we could from our experience to the representatives of other libraries whether coming with inquiries fitting a collection as large as Cincinnati is to establish or merely seeking such matters as concern the establishment of a village library.[1]

The report on American libraries made by Charles C. Jewett in 1850 had listed 10,640 libraries of one kind and another in the United States,[2] and according to Winsor's own statement 19 years later, libraries were increasing rapidly; yet the demand for persons with special library training to fill positions in these libraries was not great enough to justify the establishment of schools for the preparation of librarians.

The professional development of librarians was not completely neglected, however, since aid and instruction were given by experienced librarians. Additional help was available in library reports, rules, and catalogs and in such publications as *Norton's Literary Gazette* and *Norton's Literary Almanac,* which carried statistical information and news items about American libraries as well as notices of publications of interest to them.

The report of the U.S. Bureau of Education published in 1876, *Public Libraries in the United States of America, Their History, Condition, and Management,* provided many helpful aids for librarians: historical and statistical information, numerous discussions on library economy and management, and as a special bonus, the *Rules for Making a Dictionary Catalogue* by C. A. Cutter. It was soon followed by the publication of *The American Library Journal* which was "intended to cover the entire field of library and bibliographical interests."[3] This journal became the official organ of the newly organized American Library Association. During that same year, Melvil Dewey's publications, *Library Notes* and *A Classification and Subject Index for Cataloging and Arranging the Books and Pamphlets of a Library,* were added to the literature and other aids available to librarians and aspiring librarians for their self-education and improvement.

EARLY TRAINING AGENCIES[4]

Even after the American Library Association had been established for several years, little attention was given to the matter of training librarians. Dewey's proposals to train prospective librarians by apprenticeship and a later proposal to establish a school of library economy were not endorsed by the association, but in 1887 he was successful in opening the first school for librarians, the School of Library Economy at Columbia College. When it was transferred to the New York State Library at Albany in 1889 and became the New York State Library School, Dewey continued as its head. The curriculum developed by Dewey was based on the routine and typical day-by-day activities of a library and thus was essentially technical and clerical in content.

Once the idea of formal library training had taken shape, other training programs for librarians were established: Pratt Institute, 1890; Drexel Institute, 1892; and Armour Institute in Chicago, 1893, which was transferred to the University of Illinois in 1897 and became the University of Illinois Library School. Apprentice classes were conducted in the Los Angeles Public Library in 1891 and later in the public libraries of Denver and Cleveland; summer courses were offered at Amherst College and by some of the state library commissions; and in 1900, a training program for children's librarians was established at the Carnegie Library of Pittsburgh, the first effort to offer training in a particular area of library operations and service.

In the first two decades of the twentieth century, preparatory programs for librarians took several forms: 1) library schools offering one- and two-year programs; 2) colleges giving summer courses only; 3) libraries providing apprentice and in-service training; 4) colleges and normal schools offering courses in bibliography or library economy; 5) institutions of various kinds giving courses by correspondence. All these programs stressed courses in cataloging, book selection, reference work, and classification.[5] The Association of American Library Schools was organized in 1915 to establish and maintain standards of instruction, entrance requirements, and curriculum.

In 1915 a study of selected Carnegie libraries made by Alvin S. Johnson for the Carnegie Corporation showed that many of these libraries were not providing good service because they lacked trained personnel. Johnson recommended that the corporation turn its attention to the preparation of librarians before giving more money for buildings. In 1919, the trustees commissioned C. C. Williamson, head of the Division of Economics and Sociology of the New York Public Library, to conduct a study of library training programs. This study, published in 1923, marks the turning point in education for librarianship.

Prior to the Williamson report, Andrew Carnegie and the Carnegie Corporation had contributed to the training of librarians by making grants for endowment and/or support of the library schools at Western Reserve University and Hampton Institute, the schools operated by the Carnegie Institute in Pittsburgh, the Carnegie Library of Atlanta, and the New York Public Library.

Criticizing the emphasis then being placed on the clerical and routine aspects of library work to the neglect of general education, Williamson pointed out that "no amount of training in library technique can make a successful librarian of a person who lacks a good general education."[6] He described the two types of training required: 1) thorough preparation for professional service, represented by a full college course providing a broad general education and at least one year of graduate study in a library school properly organized to give professional preparation; and 2) training for clerical and routine work by completion of a four-year high school course, followed by a course of instruction designed to provide an understanding of the mechanics and routine operations of a library.

In addition to the need to differentiate between professional and clerical types of library work and to provide the kind of training required for each, Williamson pointed out, among other things, the need for:[7]

1. Standards regarding the scope and content of courses, the accrediting of library schools, and the certification of librarians, and an authoritative body to formulate and enforce them;
2. Entrance requirements based on a college education or its full equivalent, thus placing library schools on the graduate level;
3. Adequate budgets to support library education programs,[8] including higher salaries to attract better qualified faculty and to ensure higher standards of instruction;
4. Provision of textbooks, handbooks, treatises, and other professional literature in all areas of library practice;
5. A better grade of student and the provision of fellowships and scholarships to attract such students;
6. The establishment of the professional library school as a department of a university;
7. Specialized training for certain types of libraries and in certain areas of librarianship;
8. Opportunities for librarians to continue their professional and educational growth.

As a result of the Williamson report, the Carnegie Corporation began a considerable expansion of its library program with emphasis on improving library education, and in 1926 launched a ten-year "Library Service Program."[9] Grants for the endowment and support of existing library schools and for the establishment of a new school for graduate training in librarianship at the University of Chicago totaled more than three million dollars.[10] The University of Chicago was the first graduate library school offering a curriculum leading to the Ph.D. degree.

Between 1928 and 1930, the corporation further promoted the cause of library training with funds for fellowships. After World War II, grants were made by the corporation for specific purposes, such as training in library administration, administering audiovisual materials, developing teaching materials for library schools, and developing a curriculum in librarianship at Western Reserve University.

DEVELOPMENT OF STANDARDS

In 1924 the Board of Education for Librarianship was established by ALA and in 1926, following the recommendations of the Williamson study, it formulated minimum standards[11] for advanced graduate library schools, graduate library schools, junior and senior undergraduate library schools, summer courses, library apprentice and training classes, and the curriculum in school library work. The first list of accredited library schools, which was published in 1925-1926, included 14 schools, of which only six were organized within a college or university. In 1932 the standards for training and apprentice classes and for summer schools not a part of the regular curriculum of accredited schools were discontinued. New qualitative standards, "Minimum Requirements for Library Schools,"[12] adopted by the American Library Association in 1933, recognized three classes of library schools: Type I, first year graduate and advanced graduate work—the master's degree program; Type II, those offering only the first year of graduate work—the second bachelor's degree, the B.L.S.; and Type III, those giving a full year of library science without the degree requirement for admission. The next year, additional standards, "Minimum Requirements for Teacher-Librarian Training Agencies," were formulated to aid institutions in developing programs for teacher-librarians.

When new standards for accrediting library schools were prepared in 1951 by the Board of Education for Librarianship[13] with the assistance of ALA's Library Education Division and the Association of American Library Schools, they provided qualitative bases for evaluating the basic professional program of education for librarianship, consisting of five years of study beyond the secondary school and leading to a master's degree. Since that time, the American Library Association has accredited only this type of program. The 1951 standards were used until 1972, when new standards were adopted.[14] These standards, limited to the evaluation of graduate programs of education leading to the first professional degree, describe the essential features of library education programs which prepare librarians for responsibilities beyond the narrowly local level. They identify these essential components of a graduate program of library education: program goals and objectives, curriculum, faculty, students, governance, administration and financial support, and physical resources and facilities. Accreditation by the American Library Association is not compulsory, and the ALA Committee on Accreditation visits a library school only upon the school's invitation.

Toward the end of the forties, criteria relating to school libraries were added to state and regional accreditation requirements. Concerning the educational preparation of school librarians, the requirements ranged from four semester hours of library science in some states to 24 or more semester hours in others; and to help librarians and teacher-librarians meet these requirements, colleges—chiefly teacher-training and state-supported institutions—added library science courses to their curricula.

In order to provide guidance in the establishment of these programs, the American Library Association formulated "Standards for Library Science Programs in Teacher Education Institutions" in 1952. In 1959 ALA drew up new guidelines, "Standards for Undergraduate Library Science Programs,"[15] to be used for advisory purposes by a library education program engaged in a self-study, by the National Council for the Accreditation of Teacher Education, or by a regional accrediting association engaged in evaluating an institution of higher education offering an undergraduate library science program. In 1970, the Board of Directors of the Library Education Division adopted "Criteria for Programs to Prepare Library Technical Assistants,"[16] a document intended to serve as a guide for planning programs for library technical assistants and for evaluating existing programs.

MAJOR INFLUENCES

In addition to the influence of early library leaders, the Williamson report and other studies, and the standards established from time to time by the Board of Education for Librarianship and its successor, the ALA Committee on Accreditation, contributions to the development of library education have been made—and are being made—by ALA's Library Education Committee, the Association for Library and Information Science Education,[17] the U. S. Department of Education, state departments of education, state library commissions, federal legislation, and philanthropic foundations.

The Library Education Committee of ALA develops and recommends policies related to the training and education of library personnel; identifies needed research; and cooperates with other organizations in matters relating to library/information science education.

The purpose of the Association for Library and Information Science Education is "to promote excellence in education for library and information services." It promotes research related to teaching and to library and information science, encourages the interchange of ideas and information among library educators, and cooperates with other organizations in matters of mutual interest. Membership is made up of ALA-accredited schools and persons employed full-time in those programs. Institutions and persons from institutions offering a graduate degree in librarianship or cognate fields may hold associate memberships.

The Office of Educational Research and Improvement in the U. S. Department of Education administers all library grant programs, including HEA Title II-B, which provides fellowships for master's, postmaster's, and doctoral degree candidates.

In 1984, the U. S. Department of Education funded a project to identify and describe competencies needed by information professionals within several areas of specialization and to recommend educational requirements that would ensure that information professionals would achieve the recommended level of competence. Competencies cover knowledge, skills, and attitudes; type of work setting, functions performed, professional level; prevailing trends in the information profession; types of users; techniques used; and types of materials handled. The report, *New Directions in Library and Information Science Education*—published in 1986 and called the King Report—is expected to be useful in designing or restructuring library and information science programs and in the administration of libraries and information centers.[18]

It is the responsibility of state departments of education to formulate the basic program for the education of professional personnel in the field of education as a prerequisite for certification, and since school librarians are part of the public school's professional personnel and are certified as both teachers and librarians, their professional preparation is closely related to the professional preparation of teachers. State departments of education may assist in developing programs for the education of school librarians in state institutions of higher education, set standards for these programs, and accredit them.

Some state library extension agencies have the responsibility for certifying librarians for positions in public libraries and have worked with library schools in developing programs to satisfy the certification requirements for both professional and nonprofessional library positions. As a part of their program for the continuing education of public library personnel, the state library extension agencies conduct conferences, workshops, institutes, and short courses.

Several federal programs have contributed to professional library education. The National Defense Education Act of 1958, as amended in 1964, provided for short-term or regular-session institutes for advanced study by library personnel in elementary or secondary schools or by the supervisors of such personnel. Beginning July 1, 1967, institutes for school librarians became a part of the library training program authorized by the Higher Education Act of 1965.

In addition to the contributions of the Carnegie Corporation, which have been discussed earlier,[19] contributions to library education have been made by the Knapp Foundation, for education in school media librarianship,[20] and by the H. W. Wilson Foundation, for the study of the problems and needs of library education.

The H. W. Wilson Foundation aided in the establishment of ALA's Office for Library Education in 1966. A major contribution of this office, under the direction of Dr. Lester Asheim, was the statement of policy, "Library Education and Manpower,"[21] adopted by ALA in 1970. This statement "recommends categories of library personnel and levels of training and education appropriate to the preparation of personnel for these categories." Categories of professional library personnel and categories of supportive library personnel are described by title, basic requirements, and nature of responsibility.

PRESENT STATUS

The structure of library education includes 1) undergraduate programs, the majority of which are designed to enable school librarians to meet certification requirements; and 2) graduate programs, primarily the master's degree program, which is the basic professional program, post-master's, specialist, or certificate programs; and the doctoral program. Although there is not a prelibrary undergraduate curriculum comparable to premedicine, prelaw, or preengineering, there may be certain undergraduate prerequisites. In general, the student who is preparing for graduate study in librarianship is encouraged to emphasize broad general education in the humanities, social sciences, and natural sciences. Some schools require a foreign language. Library education is concerned in varying degrees with the whole range of human knowledge, but there is a certain body of knowledge which all professional librarians are assumed to possess. The majority of accredited library schools include in their basic professional curriculum a core of courses which includes a general introduction to librarianship, selection of materials, cataloging and classification, and reference materials and services. In a number of schools, an introductory course in information science[22] and a course in research methods are required.

Admission to the graduate library program is based on graduation from an approved college or university with an adequate background in general education and some subject specialization; scholarship as required for graduate study in the institution; and personal characteristics indicating aptitude and suitability for library service. Types of library curricula include college and university librarianship, public librarianship, school librarianship, special librarianship, and information science. Within these broad areas of specialization by types of agencies, further specialization by functions may be possible, such as cataloging and classification, administration, reference, subject bibliography, children's services, adult education, audiovisual materials and services, and some area of technology.

The undergraduate library science program is an instructional unit within a college or university which is approved by the appropriate accrediting association. The undergraduate program offers introductory preparation for library personnel for positions on the level of their preparation and provides a foundation for graduate study in the field of librarianship. It may also provide in-service training opportunities for librarians. There are more than 300 undergraduate programs.

Graduate programs include 61 accredited by the ALA and 90 not accredited. Of the ALA-accredited programs, some offer only the master's degree; others offer the post-master's, specialist, or certificate program; and some offer either the doctoral program or both the doctoral and the post-master's, specialist, or certificate programs.

PROBLEMS AND NEEDS

Some of the library education programs at the undergraduate level which have been established to meet the increasing demand for librarians—particularly school librarians—have given rise to concern among library educators. Lacking adequate financial support, a sizable number of these programs are substandard in staff, facilities, and learning resources.

Some critics of library education charge that the admission standards of some library schools as well as of undergraduate library programs are too low; that their faculties do not have the high level of leadership, scholarship, and experience which characterizes the faculties of certain other professional schools; and that much of the library school curriculum is less rigorous in its intellectual demands than in other graduate departments. Other critics complain of the wide gap which exists between what students are given the opportunity to learn and what they actually do as practitioners of librarianship. In other words, there is too much emphasis on the acquisition of techniques and skills and not enough on broad education or—at the other extreme—there is too much emphasis on the more intellectual and professional aspects of librarianship and not enough on the practical aspects. Students are sent out poorly prepared to deal intelligently with such important realities as management; budget making; planning quarters; evaluating objectives, materials, equipment, and services; public relations; local, state, federal legislation, and the merits of the various new technologies.

Some critics feel that library schools have not yet identified the kind of student they want to produce and appear to be more concerned with meeting current needs than with preparing for future change. Curriculum changes are often made without long-range planning, and *titles* of courses are modernized without changing the *content*.

Critics of doctoral programs charge that in some cases programs have been established before the institutions had the resources to support them, and that few have enough students or adequate graduate faculty to carry on significant doctoral study and research activities.

Decline in financial support, especially from the federal government, the high cost of the M.L.S., and declining enrollments make survival a major problem. Ten library school have closed during the past decade for these and other reasons.

Some important needs of library education are:

1. Budgets which will provide the salaries that will attract qualified faculties and provide the facilities, equipment, and resources necessary in carrying on a program of quality education;
2. Preparation of students to participate in and plan for changing patterns in librarianship and in library and information use, such as the system concept of library service, computerized access to knowledge and information materials, and utilization of all the newer technologies in library and information operations and services;
3. Provision not only of broad general education and education for specific kinds of library and information careers, but more exposure to the kinds of activities which the practitioner will have to perform and in settings where they will take place;
4. A clear definition of the boundaries of professional, subprofessional, and clerical work, and a determination of the levels of training needed for each category, who should offer these kinds of training, and what the several curricula should be;
5. Research into the problems and needs of library education and development of new teaching materials and new methods of teaching based on research findings;
6. More opportunities for the continuing education of librarians in new materials, new areas, new services, and new technologies;
7. Acceptance by educators, students, and practitioners of technological change and a willingness on their part to make advantageous use of technology in library/information operations;

8. Cooperation rather than competition with disciplines in related fields, such as business, computer science, and communication in the education of library/information professionals;
9. A broader and deeper understanding of the information field in order to develop programs—in both name and content—that will prepare graduates for careers in various information settings, not just in a traditional library;
10. A determination of the kind of students needed to fill positions in library and information settings now and in the coming decades and stronger recruitment efforts to attract them.

TRENDS

1. *The broader view*: The most easily recognized trend in library education programs is a change in name: 51 of the 61 ALA-accredited library schools have added the word information to the name of the school. Library education is becoming library/information science education and this broadened view is seen in various additions to the curriculum to include courses about the new technologies: computers, systems analysis, online searching, telecommunications, database management, etc. Some courses are directed to professionals in nontraditional information fields, such as information brokers, information managers, and online search specialists. Some schools now offer a dual master's degree, e.g. library science and information science, library science in various combinations with business, computer science, journalism, communication, or management.
There is a greater use in some programs of new techniques and tools: audio, visual, television, computers, videocassettes, teleconferences, electronic mail, etc.
2. *Extended programs*: Some library/information science programs have extended their master's programs to two years; some schools offer a postmaster's degree or specialist degree; and a number of schools offer a doctoral program.
3. *Research methods*: Research is now seen as vital in the practice of librarianship as well as in educating for the library/information professions. Most schools now offer—some require—one or more courses in research methods.
4. *"Distance" education*: Library/information science programs are providing "distance" education, that is, off-campus or extension courses, by telephone, radio, television, facsimile, videotext, electronic mail service, and other electronic means.
5. *Continuing ed:* Programs of continuing education have become necessary in order to keep the profession abreast of the changing social, educational, technological, and cultural needs of its varied clienteles, new developments within the profession, and the need for new kinds of skills in today's libraries. Workshops, seminars, short courses, teleconferences, and self-directed study are made available by library schools, state agencies, and professional associations. The Continuing Library Education Net-

work and Exchange Round Table of the American Library Association initiates and supports programs to make available quality continuing education.

6. *Comparative libarianship*: There is a growing interest in librarianship as it is practiced in other countries and a number of schools offer a course in international comparative librarianship. Library education and library activities in foreign countries are reported regularly in the literature. Study tours of libraries and library schools in foreign countries are offered for credit by some library schools; and fellowships and scholarships for study in foreign countries are also available.

7. *Financial assistance*: Scholarships, fellowships, assistantships, and internships for students preparing to begin or to continue their work in library schools are offered by state and other library associations, library schools, state library agencies, and philanthropic foundations.

NOTES

1. Justin Winsor, "A Word to Starters of Libraries," *The American Library Journal*, 1 (September 30, 1876): 1.
2. C.C. Jewett, "Second Annual Report of the Assistant Secretary of the Smithsonian Institution, Relative to the Library—Presented Jan. 2, 1850," *Fourth Annual Report to the Board of Regents of the Smithsonian Institution . . .* (Washington, D.C.: Printed by the Printers to the Senate, 1850), p. 38.
3. *The American Library Journal*, 1 (September 30, 1876): 12, 13.
4. *See* Sara K. Vann, *Training for Librarianship Before 1923, Education for Librarianship Prior to the Publication of Williamson's Report on Training for Library Service* (Chicago: American Library Association, 1961).
5. Charles Clarence Williamson, *Training for Library Service* (New York: Carnegie Corporation of New York, 1923), p. 21.
6. *Ibid.*, p. 6.
7. *Ibid.*, pp. 136-144, *passim.*
8. *Ibid.*, p. 140. Williamson noted that only four schools had a total expenditure in 1920-1921 of more than $10,000.
9. Florence Anderson, *Carnegie Corporation Library Programs, 1911–1961* (New York: Carnegie Corporation of New York, 1963), p. 7.
10. *Ibid.*, p. 10.
11. "The Second Annual Report of the Board of Education for Librarianship," *ALA Bulletin*, 20 (1926): 405-473.
12. ALA *Bulletin*, 27 (December 15, 1933): 610-613.
13. In 1956 the Board of Education for Librarianship was replaced by the ALA Committee on Accreditation.
14. American Library Association, Committee on Accreditation, "Standards for Accreditation 1972."
15. American Library Association, Committee on Accreditation, "Standards and Guide for Undergraduate Library Science Programs," *ALA Bulletin*, 42 (October 1958): 696-700. ALA does not accredit undergraduate library education programs. These standards are used only as general guidelines. The accreditation of a graduate or undergraduate library education program is

included in the accreditation of the parent institution by national, state, or regional accrediting agencies. *See*   p. 164 for a discussion of recent standards regarding education of school media specialists.

16. "Criteria for Programs to Prepare Library Technical Assistants," *ALA Bulletin*, 68 (June 1969): 787-793. Revised in 1979.

17. Formerly the Association of American Library Schools.

18. José-Marie Griffiths and David W. King, *New Directions in Library and Information Science Education* (Westport, Conn.: Greenwood Press, Inc. for American Society for Information Science, 1986).

19. *See* p. 94.

20. *See* pp. 162-163.

21. *See* p. 3, 4 n. "Library Education and Manpower, A Statement of Policy Adopted by the Council of the American Library Association, June 30, 1970." The title was changed in 1976 to "Library Education and Personnel Utilization."

22. See Chapter 19.

PART THREE

Types of Libraries and Library Services

No single plan can describe all libraries since the purposes, form, collection, and program of each library are determined by the specific needs of its clientele, influenced by the availability of funds, facilities, equipment, and number and quality of personnel. Over the years, however, libraries with the same general types of objectives and functions have come to be identified as a group or as a kind of library service, such as national, state, municipal, public, county, school, academic, research, and special.

In the following chapters, each major type of library service is considered, along with the kinds of activities and programs which, in general, are developed by a particular *type* of library to serve the needs of a particular *type* of clientele. Attention is also given to certain specific types of libraries within the large categories, such as elementary, junior high, and high school libraries in the school library category; junior college, college, and university libraries in the academic group; and various types of library and information facilities in the special libraries group.

It is important to remember that individual libraries within any given category differ in terms of their specific objectives and programs, which grow out of the specific needs of their users.

11

Library Activities

Libraries of all kinds have developed numerous activities and programs to meet the needs of their users. Some of these activities and programs are peculiar to a given type of library, while others are performed in all libraries and are considered to be basic to the operation of any library. Activities common to all libraries are concerned with 1) administering the library; 2) building the collection; 3) making the collection accessible for use; and 4) serving the users. The number and variety of these activities and the ways of performing them will vary according to the size, purposes, and clientele of the library, the adequacy of financial support, and the availability of personnel.

ADMINISTERING THE LIBRARY

The administrator is responsible for defining the objectives of the library, developing the policies and programs needed to achieve them, providing the organization, staff, and facilities needed to execute them, and exercising direction and control over them. Administrative activities include formulating and administering policies, rules, and regulations; preparing and administering the budget; planning and maintaining buildings and equipment; providing salary schedules; making recommendations regarding appointments, promotions, transfers, and dismissal of personnel; assigning activities and delegating responsibility; supervising the work of the staff; making surveys and studies, preparing and analyzing reports, statistics, and records; and engaging in public relations activities.

BUILDING THE COLLECTION

The size, nature, and content of the library collection depend upon the objectives of the library and the needs of the clientele. With these factors in mind, the librarian selects and acquires the materials required to carry on the library's program in keeping with established policies and procedures. Materials selection depends upon wide knowledge of available materials and the ability to evaluate them and to choose those which will contribute most effectively to the achievement of the library's purposes. Aid in performing this function is found in published bibliographies and lists of books, such as *Cumulative Book Index, Books in Print, Book Review Digest, Book Review Index,* and *Technical Book Review Index*; in book-review sections of professional journals such as *Library Journal* and newspapers; in evaluative book-reviewing media prepared for all libraries, such as *Booklist*; and in the publications prepared specifically for a given type of library, such as *Choice, Children's Catalog, Junior High School Library Catalog, Senior High School Library Catalog,* and *Public Library Catalog.*[1]

Selection means maintaining a live, balanced, up-to-date collection both in subject content and in kinds of materials. It involves withdrawing materials which are little used or obsolete as well as adding new materials.

The acquisition of materials requires a knowledge of publishers; the sources of hard-to-find and out-of-print materials; the comparative advantages of buying directly from publishers or through a dealer; and an understanding of ordering policies and procedures and of practices and policies regarding gifts and exchanges. It includes setting up and maintaining accounts and records and corresponding with publishers and/or dealers.

COLLECTION ACCESSIBILITY:
CLASSIFICATION AND CATALOGING

Throughout the history of libraries, the most satisfactory basis for organizing materials for quick and easy accessibility has been subject classification. In addition to providing a basis for organizing materials so that they can be found quickly and easily by the library user, classification provides a means of bringing books on the same subject together in one place—an additional aid to ease of use.

The most commonly used system of classification is the Dewey Decimal Classification. Devised by Melvil Dewey and first published in 1876, it is now in its twentieth edition and is used in libraries throughout the world. The basic plan of this system is to assign into ten decimal classes the whole of recorded human knowledge. The ten classes are divided into ten divisions and each division into ten sections; Arabic numbers are used decimally to signify the various classes of subjects.

A book is classified according to its subject matter and is given the number in the classification schedule which stands for that subject. It is further identified by an author number, using the first letter of the author's last name plus Arabic numerals. The table from which the author number is taken was developed by Charles A. Cutter about the time that Dewey was devising his classification system. The Cutter Table assigns certain numerals, used decimally, to letters of the alphabet in the order of the alphabet. Symbols may be added to indicate that the book is a certain kind of material, as Ref for reference. Classification number, author number, and symbol, if any, make the call number of the book, which indicates its subject matter and physical location in the library.[2]

The Library of Congress Classification System combines the letters of the alphabet and Arabic numerals. It provides 26 main classes compared to ten main classes in the Dewey Decimal Classification System. Main classes are designated by capital letters, subclasses (except Z and E-F) by two capital letters, and further divisions and subdivisions by integral numbers in ordinary sequence. Further expansion is possible through the use of decimal numbers and letters. The letters I, O, W, X, and Y are not used at the present time, but are reserved for future expansion of the system. The use of letters, numbers, and decimal numbers and letters makes possible the most minute classification.

Other systems of classification are *Bibliographic Classification*, edited by Henry E. Bliss; *Colon Classification* by S. R. Ranganathan; and the *Universal Decimal Classification*, which is an expansion of the Dewey

Decimal Classification. Other systems or adaptations are in use; in general, they are all based on classifying by subject.

The purpose of cataloging is to make all library resources completely accessible to users. The library catalog points out the location of each item it includes by giving the location symbol or call number. It provides several ways of finding materials: by author, title, and subject; by coauthor, editor, or translator; and by series, if the book is part of a series. All library catalogs provide the same kinds of information about the item cataloged; they differ in the format in which the information is presented. The library catalog may be a book catalog, a card catalog, an online catalog, a computer Output Microform Catalog (Com-Cat), or a CD-Rom (Compact Disk Read Only Memory) Catalog. There may be an author catalog and a subject catalog, but in general, all kinds of cards or entries are in one alphabet and constitute a dictionary catalog.[3]

The process of cataloging involves the systematic description of a publication by author, title, place of publication, publisher, date, collation, and subject matter. Notes concerning bibliography, series, and other points may be included and the call number is given. The subject matter of an item is indicated by the subject headings.

In 1901, the Library of Congress, as a service to libraries, began the practice of selling them copies of the printed cards which are used in the LC catalogs. Many libraries buy these cards, but through the MARC program, cataloging information is now available on magnetic tape and many libraries have access to it through such computer facilities as the Ohio Computer Library Center (OCLC).[4]

In addition to the library catalog, supplementary resources such as indexes to periodical and other literature, bibliographies, and catalogs of special materials provide access to all holdings in the library.

SERVICE TO USERS

All activities of the library are performed for the purpose of serving the clientele, but the circulation and reference departments serve the public most directly.

The activities of the circulation department involve issuing and receiving books; maintaining borrowers' records; keeping records and statistics; making studies of the use of library materials; collecting fines; and formulating policies and procedures for these activities.

The purpose of reference service varies by type of library. Reference work in the public library emphasizes facts, information, ideas, interpretation, and personal aid. It provides, in person and by telephone, practical information to be used immediately, as well as resources and aid in study and research. In the school library, reference work is closely allied to the curriculum, and students are encouraged and guided to learn to do the work themselves. In the college or university library, the object of reference service is to help students understand the usefulness of basic reference works and develop a facility for using all library resources independently. It has been said that "reference service is the special library's mode of existence" and that the desired information must be provided regardless of where and in what form it may be available.

The reference function, depending upon the type of library, includes giving information and answering factual questions; answering complex reference questions by literature searching, compiling bibliographies, and making annotations or abstracts when necessary; maintaining information and other files as required; borrowing and lending materials on interlibrary loan; and giving instruction in the use of the library by conducting formal classes and by giving instruction to individuals or groups on one or more kinds of materials.

NOTES

1. *Cumulative Book Index*, (New York: The H. W. Wilson Company, 1898-. Monthly); *Books in Print* (New York: R. R. Bowker Company, 1948-. Annual); *Book Review Digest* (New York: The H. W. Wilson Company, 1905-. Monthly); *Book Review Index* (Detroit: Gale Research Company, 1965-. Bimonthly); *Technical Book Review Index* (New York: Special Libraries Association, 1935-. Monthly); *Booklist* (Chicago: The American Library Association, 1905-. Semimonthly); *Choice* (Chicago: American Library Association, 1964-. Monthly); *Children's Catalog* (15th ed.; New York: The H. W. Wilson Company 1986); *Junior High School Library Catalog* (5th ed.; New York: The H. W. Wilson Company, 1985); *Senior High School Library Catalog* (13th ed.; New York: The H. W. Wilson Company, 1987); *Public Library Catalog* (8th ed.; New York: The H. W. Wilson Company, 1986).
2. In the Library of Congress Classification System, the call number for *Introduction to Librarianship* would be: Z721 (class number), G33 (author number). In the Dewey Decimal System, the call number would be: 021 (class number), G259 (author number).
3. For a discussion of all these kinds of catalogs, see Jean Key Gates, *Guide to the Use of Libraries and Information Sources*, 6th ed. (New York: McGraw-Hill Book Company, 1989). pp. 62-81.
4. *See*   p. 116 for a discussion of MARC (Machine Readable Cataloging).

12

Federal Government
Libraries and Services

When the government was located in Philadelphia, government officials and members of Congress made use of the available proprietary libraries. In 1800, a specific library for the federal government, the Library of Congress, was established in Washington. As the business of the new government grew and expanded, departments were formed and functional divisions and offices were organized within the departments. A library was authorized for each department and, in general, for each major functional part of the department. A variety of independent agencies, offices, commissions, and institutions have been established in the course of time, and almost without exception, library and information resources and personnel have been authorized for them. Today all libraries of the federal government, except the Library of Congress and the National Archives, are integral parts of the agencies they serve and their legal basis is in the congressional act which creates the agency.

Currently, the federal government owns and operates hundreds of libraries in this country and abroad—more, in fact, than any other body in the Western Hemisphere. They include government agency, institutional, military, college, university, school, special, and highly specialized technical and scientific research libraries. Specific examples are college and university libraries at West Point, the Air Force Academy, the Naval Academy, the National War College, the Industrial College of the Armed Forces, and the Air University, as well as school libraries on military posts and bases.

Of the many and varied types of libraries, those which serve the nation as a whole, as well as specific clienteles, are the National Archives; the National Libraries: the Library of Congress, the National Library of Medicine, and the National Agricultural Library; and the libraries operated by the United States Information Agency.

THE NATIONAL ARCHIVES

According to the exterior inscription on its Washington, DC building, the National Archives "holds in trust the records of our national life and symbolizes our faith in the permanency of our national institutions."

Records include textual documents, maps, photographs, video and sound recordings, and cover all the military and diplomatic as well as domestic activities of the federal government from around 1770 to the present time. The National Archives arranges, describes, and preserves these records; prepares and publishes guides to their use; provides reference service concerning them in person and through correspondence; furnishes authentic copies of records to appropriate persons, agencies, institutions, and libraries; sells facsimiles of historic documents and thousands of microfilms; and keeps on public display the original copies of the Declaration of Independence, the Constitution of the United States, and the Bill of Rights.

On April 1, 1985, the National Archives was made an independent agency in the Executive Branch with the name National Archives and Records Administration. There are 14 records centers in the United States, and 11 field branches. The Presidential Libraries are a part of the National Archives and Records Administration.

THE LIBRARY OF CONGRESS

The Library of Congress, created in 1800 for the purpose of serving the Congress, is supported by congressional appropriations and by the gifts of individuals and foundations. The Librarian of Congress is appointed by the President with the consent of the Senate.

In 1876, Ainsworth R. Spofford, Librarian of Congress, wrote: "As the library of the American people, supported and constantly enlarged by taxation, it is eminently fitting that this library should not only be freely accessible to the whole people, but that it should furnish the fullest possible stores of information in every department of human knowledge."[1] Spofford served as Librarian of Congress from 1864 to 1897 and under his administration, the Library began a period of spectacular growth. Beginning in 1865 the Library received a copy of each publication copyrighted in the United States. Acquisition of the Smithsonian Institution's scientific collection in 1866 laid the foundation for its now unsurpassed scientific collection; and the Peter Force historical library, acquired in 1867, added to both the size and importance of the library. Herbert Putnam, Librarian from 1899 to 1939, continued to enlarge its holdings, developed better ways of access to these collections through cataloging and classification, and provided many new and special services, such as printed catalog cards and interlibrary loan.

In size, the collections today are perhaps the largest in the world; in scope, they are definitely universal. The total collection, numbering more than 83 million items, includes federal and state documents; books and pamphlets in many languages; professional journals, periodicals, newspapers, and broadsides; manuscripts relating to American history and civilization, including the personal papers of most of the Presidents; maps and views; sheet music, music scores, and phonographic recordings of music, speeches, poetry, and readings; photographic negatives, photostats, prints, slides, films, filmstrips, and microforms; optical disks; and art prints and reproductions. Although it does not serve children, the library has an extensive children's collection for the use of teachers and other interested adults.

The Library of Congress serves members of Congress, agencies of the executive and judicial branches of the federal structure, scholars, researchers, students, libraries throughout the world, and the general public. Although it is not considered a public library, it is open to the adult public and provides service within the library. Materials are loaned to members of Congress, their staffs, high officers of the federal government, diplomatic representatives of other governments, and to other libraries on interlibrary loan.

The Library of Congress provides photocopies of materials for research; compiles and maintains the *National Union Catalog*, which gives information about the location of books in more than 1200 libraries in the United States and Canada; provides reading materials for the blind; operates the copyright office and registers all claims to copyright protection; produces catalog cards and cataloging data on machine-readable magnetic tape and sells these cards and tapes to libraries; maintains a catalog of newspapers in microform; and publishes bibliographies, guides, catalogs, and other materials of interest to libraries.[2] It sponsors such cultural events as chamber-music concerts, literary readings, and lectures; and offers cultural, educational, and informational exhibits. It also edits the Dewey Decimal Classification; provides cataloging information to publishers (Cataloging in Publication); maintains the American Folklore Center; and sponsors the Center for the Book.[3]

Under a grant from the Council on Library Resources, the Library of Congress made studies leading to the inauguration, in the fall of 1966, of a pilot program for the distribution of cataloging data in machine-readable form to 16 participating libraries—university, research, public, government, and school. These libraries received the equivalent of catalog cards in machine-readable form, that is, on magnetic tape. Catalog cards, book catalogs, reading lists, and other bibliographical materials could be produced automatically from the magnetic tape at a local computer facility.

The Machine-Readable Cataloging Project (MARC) has now been extended to all English-language monographs cataloged at the Library of Congress. MARC formats cover serials, maps, films, music, sound recordings, and manuscripts. MARC was the first development of its kind and magnitude in the world. It has been termed "the single most important contribution to date in the pursuit of national (or universal) bibliographic control."[4]

THE NATIONAL LIBRARY OF MEDICINE

The National Library of Medicine dates from 1836, when its predecessor, the Library of the Surgeon General's Office, was established. Under the direction of John Shaw Billings, who served as librarian from 1855 to 1895, the collection grew from fewer than 3000 volumes to more than 300,000 books and pamphlets. Billings also developed a system for large-scale indexing of current medical-journal literature, which resulted in the first issue of *Index Medicus* in 1879.

Now the world's largest research library in a single scientific and professional field, the National Library of Medicine collects materials exhaustively in all major areas of the health sciences and in chemistry, physics, botany, and zoology. Its collection numbers more than 3.8 million items in all major languages.

In order to provide more rapid and efficient bibliographical access to the great volume of medical literature, NLM adopted the Medical Literature Analysis and Retrieval System (MEDLARS), a high-speed data-processing facility, to perform various functions of literature analysis and retrieval, including the preparation of the monthly *Index Medicus*, the annual *Cumulated Index Medicus*, and other similar compilations, as well as for servicing requests for special bibliographies on demand. Today, MEDLARS search services are available to individuals and institutions throughout the world.

In October 1971, the library initiated a new service for physicians and other health professionals—an electronic network which links major libraries in the United States. This online bibliographic retrieval system, MEDLINE (MEDLARS On-Line) makes possible almost instant searches of more than five million citations from current journals on biomedical subjects. Besides MEDLINE, the library has about 20 databases, all of which are available through an online network of more than 13,000 institutions and individuals in the United States. Access to MEDLINE is also available through four commercial networks and on CD-ROM.

THE NATIONAL AGRICULTURAL LIBRARY

The National Agricultural Library, founded as a part of the Department of Agriculture in 1862 "to acquire and diffuse among the people of the United States useful information on subjects connected with agriculture in the most general and comprehensive sense of the word," was designated a national library in 1962. NAL was a pioneer in many library activities: it printed library catalog cards in 1899; made the first use of photographic copies for interlibrary loan in 1911; and developed a photocopying machine for the purpose of providing quick and inexpensive copies. It carried on the first library experimentation with automated storage and retrieval of information, and in 1934, established the first major United States Documentation Center, *Bibliofilm*, in cooperation with the American Documentation Institute and Science Service.

The collection of the National Agricultural Library exceeds 1.5 million items, including journals, books, pamphlets, maps, newspapers, microforms, and reports in all major languages, many of which are on highly technical and scientific aspects of agricultural and allied sciences. Bibliographical access is gained through the card catalog, bibliographies, published catalogs, online databases, and various computer-produced printouts. The principal database is AGRICOLA (Agricultural Online Access), which is made up of several databases. AGRICOLA is available through DIALOG, SYSTEM DEVELOPMENT CORPORATION, and BIBLIOGRAPHIC RETRIEVAL SERVICE. It is also available on CD-ROM.

The library provides individual loan, reference, photocopying, and bibliographical service to employees of the Department of Agriculture and gives interlibrary loan service to government and other libraries. In addition, it serves colleges and universities, research institutions, agricultural associations, industry, and other government agencies.

NAL compiles and publishes monthly the *Bibliography of Agriculture*, an index to the world's agricultural literature received in the library, and compiles bibliographies on special subjects for the use of the department and for public use.

THE UNITED STATES INFORMATION AGENCY

The United States Information Agency, in carrying out its basic purpose of "increasing mutual understanding between the people of the United States and the people of other countries," makes use of all the techniques and tools of modern mass communication, including libraries. The United States Information Service (the name it carries overseas) maintains and/or supports 156 libraries and reading rooms in 95 countries and supports libraries in 111 binational centers. USIS libraries contain more than 950,000 books, films, and periodicals.[5]

The library collections focus on materials that will help people in foreign countries learn about the United States—its people, history and culture. Considerable emphasis is placed on publications in the sciences and social sciences, but attention is also given to the classics which have influenced American life and thought, especially those which are not easily available locally.

Attracting millions of visitors annually, USIS libraries provide, in addition to reference and other library services, such programs as lectures, concerts, seminars, exhibits, documentary film showings, and special activities for children.

USIS libraries do not replace local or national libraries; they supplement them. In many instances, they have served as a demonstration of the value of public library service to a community and have introduced into the community such library practices as free use of books and openshelf access to materials. They encourage and assist local librarians who are trying to improve their own library service by providing useful study and reference materials in library science; giving advice on problems related to cataloging, reference work, and book selection; and often by sponsoring library workshops and short courses. They also give information and advice to the large number of librarians who annually come to the United States to study library methods and practices on State Department grants, under the auspices of foreign governments, or at their own expense.

OTHER FEDERAL LIBRARIES

Of the thousands of libraries supported by the government in this country and around the world, most are parts of systems, such as those in the hospitals of the Veterans Administration; those maintained on the research installations of the National Aeronautics and Space Administration; and those operated by the armed services on shipboard and Naval stations, and on Army posts and Air Force bases. Wherever armed forces personnel are stationed, in this country and throughout the world, collections of general materials are maintained. Usually they are under the management of professional civilian librarians when outside of combat zones and where the size of the collection makes the use of a professional staff feasible.

Beginning primarily as a service to provide recreational reading materials, the library programs of the Army, the Navy, and the Air Force have added general nonfiction works and various kinds of reference materials along with current periodicals, professional journals, and special materials on international relations, world political affairs, area economics, and foreign languages. In most instances, there is a close coordination of effort between the library staff and those who manage the off-duty education program, particularly in cases where a degree-granting local college or university offers credit courses for military personnel, on the installation or in convenient nearby facilities.

In 1895, Congress enacted legislation which provided for the designation of 637 libraries, both academic and public, as depositories to receive free-of-charge publications issued by the federal government.

This legislation also required that the designated libraries make their depository materials available to anyone who might want to see them. The Depository Library Act of 1962 permits the designation of additional depository libraries and extends the kinds of publications to be distributed to include those printed by the executive departments as well as those printed by the U.S. Government Printing Office. There are more than 1,370 Federal Depository Libraries in the United States and its territories and possessions: Guam, the Canal Zone, Puerto Rico, and the Virgin Islands.

FEDERAL ASSISTANCE TO LIBRARIES

In addition to those library activities of the federal government already covered in the section on the Library of Congress, assistance to libraries is provided by other government offices and agencies as a regular part of their program. For example, the Smithsonian Institution in Washington receives the official publications of foreign governments and distributes them to libraries in the United States. The Smithsonian also maintains a Science Information Exchange, which receives notices of current research projects from scientists supported by the federal government and invites privately employed scientists to submit similar reports. These notices are classified, duplicated, filed, and placed on computer tape. When a scientist makes an inquiry, the exchange's resident scientists retrieve relevant notices and send them to the inquirer.

Throughout the years the U. S. Office of Education has made statistical studies and reports on libraries. Creation of the Library Services Branch in the U. S. Office of Education in 1937 represented the first action to assign to an agency of the federal government specific responsibilities in the field of libraries and librarianship, beyond the making of statistical studies and reports. Since 1937, the office has had several names and functions. Now called the Department of Education, it administers through its Library Programs Divisions all programs for libraries, information centers, and educational technology. The National Center for Education Statistics collects data and from time to time reports on the conditions of education in the United States, including libraries.

The year 1956 was a turning point in federal assistance to libraries bringing both new legislation and increased services. The Library Services Act of 1956 was followed by new depository library legislation in 1962 (Public Law 87-579), the Higher Education Facilities Act of 1963, the Library Services and Construction Act of 1964, the Elementary and

Secondary Education Act of 1965, the Higher Education Act of 1965, and a number of programs in other areas which gave indirect aid to libraries. Much of this legislation included specific provisions for the improvement and expansion of library facilities and services; other measures aided libraries indirectly by providing funds, personnel, or materials for institutions which libraries serve; and still other measures offered aid to libraries which choose to participate voluntarily in numerous programs for social, educational, and economic betterment.[6]

In 1970, the National Commission on Libraries and Information Science was established. A permanent and independent agency within the Executive Branch, it is charged with the responsibility for developing and recommending overall plans for libraries and information services adequate to meet the needs of the people of the United States.

The commission conducts studies, surveys, and analyses of the library and information needs of the Nation, including the special needs of rural areas, and socially, educationally, and culturally deprived areas and groups, and the elderly; develops an overall plan for meeting these needs and advises the President and Congress on the implementation of the plan; promotes research and development activities to improve library and information needs of all groups; sponsors continuing education programs; supports the literacy efforts of libraries and other agencies; and plans and directs conferences, including the White House Conference on Library and Information Services in 1978 and the White House Conference on Library and Information Services scheduled for July 1991.

NOTES

1. A. R. Spofford, "The Library of Congress or National Library," U.S. Bureau of Education, *op. cit.*, p. 258.
2. Current publications are announced in its weekly *Information Bulletin*, its *Annual Report*, and in the Superintendent of Documents' *Monthly Catalog of United States Government Publications*. LC's exchange program covers every nation in the world, centering on official and semiofficial agencies and educational and research institutions of all types.
3. For a detailed account of each year's activities, see the *Annual Report of the Librarian of Congress*.
4. Council on Library Resources, *Seventeenth Annual Report* (Washington, D.C.: Council on Library Resources, 1974), p. 11.
5. "U. S. Information Agency Fact Sheet, September 1988" (Washington, D.C.: United States Information Agency, 1988), p. 10.
6. Specific legislative acts are discussed in appropriate chapters.

13

State Responsibility For Library Service

In the first quarter of the nineteenth century, there was a general trend toward establishing libraries as a part of the state government.[1] By 1876 every state and territory had a library, located at the seat of government and maintained at public expense primarily for the use of the legislature, state officers, and the courts.

From the beginning of the establishment of state-supported colleges and universities, the states had recognized their responsibility to provide some library services in these institutions. This responsibility assumed greater proportions and received stronger emphasis in the first decade of the twentieth century when accrediting agencies included the library as an area to be evaluated in granting accreditation to an institution.[2] The state's responsibility for library service in the public schools is a part of its total obligation for providing public education since the public school library is part of the public school system; and this responsibility is carried out by its central educational agency, the state department of education.[3]

Toward the end of the nineteenth century, the concept of state responsibility for library service was broadened to include free public library service for the people of the state as well as for its officials. In 1890 a specific agency, called the state library commission, was established by the state of Massachusetts for the purpose of extending library service within the state. By the close of the century, many states had established or designated specific agencies—referred to as library extension agencies—to be responsible for developing and extending library services throughout the state.[4]

Thus, historically, the state's responsibility for library services includes:

1. The provision of library service for the state government;
2. The provision of library service in state-supported educational institutions: the public schools, colleges, and universities;
3. The improvement and extension of public library service throughout the state.

LIBRARY SERVICE TO THE STATE GOVERNMENT

Library service to the state government[5] must provide the best possible resources, legal and otherwise, for the operation of the government and the administration of justice. It may be organized into separate units such as the historical collection, archives, legislative and reference service, law collections, or combinations of these. It may be provided by a unit in the executive, legislative, or judicial department, or by the State Library Agency.

The complete body of laws and official papers constitute the basic collection needed for service to the state government. The collection also includes books; research and information reports; trade, industrial, and professional journals; files of state newspapers and major newspapers from other states; maps; statements of public policies; a complete collection of the documents of the state government and those of other states; extensive collections of both local and federal documents; and means of access to legal materials available only through computerized databases. The library contains, or has access to, regional, state, and local historical materials, such as biographies and papers of the state's eminent citizens, local histories, directories, guides, and archives of the state's own records and those of local governments.

Library services performed for the state government include providing information and reference service for the governmental agencies and the courts; supplying legislative reference and information service to the legislative branch of government; furnishing information on laws and government to the supreme court and other state officials; setting up libraries in some of the divisions and agencies of state government; and maintaining bibliographical and interlibrary loan services for its own clientele and other libraries.

The professional staff of the library serving the state government should meet the professional requirements of education, training, and specific qualifications established by the appropriate state agencies; and they should have a background of education and experience in the specialized areas in which they will work.

THE STATE LIBRARY AGENCY

The state library agency may be an independent agency governed by a board or commission; it may be a division of a larger department: education, state, or other department; it may report directly to the governor or it may be under the legislature.[6] Whatever its title and control, "the state library agency . . . shall ensure that library functions essential to meeting a majority of the information needs of its citizens are defined and provided for by an appropriate agency . . . ."[7]

The acts creating state library extension agencies have not always included the funds for providing the staff, quarters, and central collection of books and other materials required for planning and carrying out a program designed to improve and extend library service statewide. In the early twenties, some assistance came in the form of books from the World War I libraries collected by the American Library Association and made available to the public at the close of the war. During this period, individuals, clubs, associations, book publishers, and such philanthropic foundations as the Rosenwald Foundation provided funds for salaries, services, and additional materials for the central collection. When state aid was provided, it was often for books only; funds for personnel, quarters, and services had to be supplied by the counties in which library services were provided.

Early efforts of state library extension agencies to carry out their responsibility for improving and extending library service statewide included shipping traveling libraries to communities without library service; lending collections of books to public libraries; making loans of books by mail to individuals who did not have access to free public library service; answering reference questions by mail; and visiting schools, communities, and institutions of higher education to give instruction and advice on library matters. Other services to schools included providing schools with collections of books for long periods; classifying books in school libraries; and compiling booklists for the use of school librarians and teachers. These efforts were designed to meet the immediate need for books and to create library-minded communities which would want to organize their own libraries.

During the Depression of the 1930s, state library extension service was sometimes the first state program to be reduced. However, under the Works Progress Administration, federal funds were made available for the establishment of libraries operated and supervised by certified workers on the federal relief rolls. Some of these libraries, which were established to provide employment, later were absorbed into county libraries. Clerks, bookbinders, and menders were employed in the state agency's central library headquarters and in libraries in the counties. Without these workers, library services during this decade would have been severely curtailed and many libraries would have been forced to close.

In the late thirties, the state's contribution to library service was said to be "the weakest link in the chain of library development,"[8] but indications of improvement could be seen in new library legislation enacted in some states; in new programs of state aid to libraries for salaries, books, and equipment; in the increased number of states requiring certification; and in the development of stronger state library extension agencies. In some states, financial aid was granted for multicounty demonstrations to show the advantage of larger units of service.

The transition from a peacetime to a war economy in the early forties brought many new problems and duties to the state library extension agency. Withdrawal of WPA funds in 1943 and the subsequent decrease in personnel led to the curtailment of a number of local public library services. In some states, civic-minded citizens and educational and cultural organizations helped to keep the libraries open. Library extension was greatly hampered by wartime restrictions, which resulted in a shortage of books and other library materials, staff, and transportation facilities. The state library agency was called upon to extend new and additional services to government, hospitals, and military camps and installations, and to disseminate informational and educational materials relating to the war. At the close of the war, interest in the expansion and improvement of library services was revived; and national, state, and local library associations and groups renewed their efforts to secure adequate financial support on all levels.

In 1948, under the sponsorship of the American Library Association and supported by many state and national organizations, the Public Library Demonstration Bill was introduced in Congress to provide for the demonstration of public library service in areas without such service or with inadequate facilities. The program, under the supervision of the state library extension agency, was designed to aid the estimated 33 million people in the United States without access to free public library service, about 90 percent of whom lived in rural areas.[9] The bill, reintroduced in 1949 and 1950, failed to pass by three votes.

Although the Public Library Demonstration Bill failed to pass, it pointed up the great inadequacy of public library service, gave to the state library extension agencies a stronger awareness of their responsibility for providing library service for all the people, encouraged them to study their needs and to begin statewide planning, and called attention to the advantage of larger units of library service.

In 1956, federal aid for libraries became a reality in the Library Services Act. At that time, in spite of more than a half century of effort on the part of state library extension agencies, national and state organizations, civic leaders, and private organizations, some 25 million people were still without local public library service and another 87 million had inadequate library service as measured by state standards. Twenty-nine states had a total of 319 counties without local public library service— slightly over ten percent of all counties in the United States.[10]

The purpose of the Library Services Act was to promote the further extension by the states of public library services to rural areas without such services or with inadequate services.[11] Funds, allocated on the basis of the per capita income, were to be spent for books and other library materials, library equipment, salaries, and other operating expenses, but not to erect buildings or purchase land. The state library agency was designated as the administrative unit for the act at the state level, with responsibility for preparing and submitting to the U. S. Commissioner of Education a plan for using the funds to maximum advantage in extending and developing public library service to rural areas and for administering the approved plan.

Congress extended federal aid to urban as well as to rural public libraries in the Library Services and Construction Act of 1964 (LSCA),[12] which provided funds for grants to states on a matching basis to extend public library service to all areas either without service or with inadequate service, and to construct public library buildings. This law, like the Library Services Act, is administered by the state library agency in accordance with the state plan which it submits to the U. S. Department of Education.

LSCA has been extended through 1994. It includes Title I, public library improvement and service to special groups—the disabled, handicapped, persons with limited English speaking ability; and strengthening the state library agencies; Title II, public library construction; Title III, interlibrary cooperation among all libraries and across local and state boundaries; Title IV, special project grants to eligible Indians and Hawaiian natives; Title V, foreign language materials; Title VI, grants for library literacy programs developed by state, public, and local libraries.[13]

The state library agency has thus risen to a new position of importance and leadership in planning, administering, and coordinating the state's program of library services. With this stronger status have come new duties as a part of the agency's new legal responsibilities as well as increased demands for the services it traditionally performed.

The state library agency has responsibility for keeping state library laws up to date; gathering and publishing annual statistics of all libraries in the state; conducting research to determine public library needs; and certifying personnel when required. Other functions include providing reference, bibliographical and interlibrary loan services to supplement local libraries through technology and networks; providing consultants to give guidance on all aspects of library service; offering programs of continuing education; interpreting library service to all units of government within the state and to the public; and providing leadership in maintaining freedom to read and freedom of access to information. Through its extension program, it provides direct library service to sparsely settled areas; encourages and facilitates cooperative library services; makes resources available through machine-readable files, interlibrary loans, and rapid communication among libraries such as teletype, electronic mail, and telefacsimile. It also formulates standards; issues newsletters, journals, and other publications; administers the Library of Congress program for the blind and physically handicapped; handles state and federal grants-in-aid to individual libraries, public library systems, multitype systems, and to nonpublic libraries, such as hospital or academic libraries; and does some book processing.

In order to carry out its programs, the state library agency maintains a central collection of materials for the use of both government and citizens of sufficient size and scope to reinforce the resources of other libraries.[14]

To the basic collections of books, periodicals, pamphlets, newspapers, and audiovisual materials are added microforms and materials in electronic formats; research and information reports; the laws and official documents of the state, and a collection of those of other states, the federal government, and local governments; historical and archival materials; and reading materials for the blind and visually handicapped, the disadvantaged, and minority groups. The collection should be large enough in number of copies to supply the needs of individuals, organizations and agencies, and libraries which it serves.

The professional staff should have a degree from an ALA-accredited library school; they must have strong leadership, organizational, and management ability; political know-how; experience and skill in working with groups—both governmental and civic—and with individuals; general and specialized backgrounds; and training and experience in all the highly specialized areas of the state agency's program.

COUNTY, MULTICOUNTY, AND REGIONAL LIBRARIES

State library agencies early extended library service to small communities, and rural areas without such service, by means of boxes of books and traveling libraries. It was not until the county was seen as the unit of support and service that rural communities were able to have libraries of their own; and not until the states passed legislation permitting a county to establish libraries that the county library could become a reality.

The first county library was established in Van Wert County, Ohio in 1898, followed seven months later by a county library in Washington County, Maryland.[15] During the first decade of the twentieth century, Wisconsin, Oregon, and Minnesota passed legislation providing for the support of library service. However, it was not until California passed a county library law that the county library movement began to make noticeable gains.

In 1909, under the leadership of James L. Gillis, a county library law was passed in California. It was revised in 1911 to enable counties to create and maintain their own independent libraries. By 1916, county libraries had been established in 37 of California's 58 counties. By 1920, a total of 26 other states had enacted similar legislation, and a decade later, a multicounty unit was established in Vermont. At the present time (1990) all states permit the establishment of county or multicounty libraries voluntarily or on petition of a required number of citizens.

In spite of the long tradition of county library service, however, development of county libraries was slow, and in 1956, just prior to the passage of the Library Services Act, 319 counties in 29 states did not have local public library service[16] and only 29 percent of the state grants-in-aid to libraries went to county or multicounty libraries. Three decades later, 187 counties still do not have local public library service. More than

6.5 million people in 23 states are not serviced by a public library; and in two states, a sizable portion of the population receives library service from the state library by mail or other direct service.[17]

The county library may be 1) a department of the county government with or without its own board; 2) a library service provided by contract with an existing public library, i.e. an established library in a city is paid by the county to provide library service for the remainder of the county; or 3) a joint city-county system which serves both city and county under the county government. A county library may serve an entire county or only the part which does not already have library service.

The Board of Trustees of a county library may be appointed by county officials; it may be legally responsible for the operation of the library, or may be only advisory; the library may be responsible to some officer in the county government. The operation of the county library and the determination of its services and policies is at the county level. County libraries are financed by taxes voted by the county, general revenue funds, long-term bonds, and state and federal aid.[18]

A multicounty library is formed because one county does not have adequate human and/or financial resources to support library service or because the counties want to give expanded service. A multicounty library is established by vote of the participating counties, is supported by local taxes voted by each of the counties for that purpose, and is supervised by a library board composed of members from each of the participating counties.

The terms multicounty and regional are often used interchangeably. While a multicounty library is always made up of several counties and a regional library is sometimes made up of parts of one county, the term regional refers to multijurisdictional units formed 1) by several counties or parts of counties or other governmental units which cooperate to maintain library service; or 2) by areas defined by geographical, sociological, cultural, economic, or other factors within the same county. They are supported by public funds from the different governmental or geographic units which they serve, and their boards are made up of members who represent these units.

The objective of the county, the multicounty, and the regional library is to provide free library service to their constituencies on equal terms. Each kind of library maintains a central collection and extends service through branch collections, deposit stations, and bookmobile service. Multicounty and regional libraries maintain their central collections in one place and establish branches in the other counties or areas.

To the traditional services of reference, circulation, and reader guidance, the county, multicounty, and regional libraries, add: 1) special services to children and youth through bookmobile service to schools, book talks, story hours, and reading lists; 2) services to government employees of the counties and other governmental units served; 3) services to welfare institutions, hospitals, and penal institutions; 4) services to adults in the form of adult education; and 5) special services to the aged, the handicapped, the disadvantaged, and minority groups.

The passage of the Library Services Act in 1956 greatly accelerated the organization of county, multicounty, and regional libraries; the early efforts of the state library extension agencies under this act were directed to demonstrating the value of larger units of service by developing pilot projects of county or regional library service. These projects were organized to provide efficient and economical service to all residents of the area. Cooperative activities such as centralized processing, cooperative use of audiovisual materials, and centralized reference services were features of these projects. In 1971, the largest single category of LSCA expenditures was for statewide library projects, most of which encouraged or supported county or multicounty (regional) library development.

Other types of cooperation as well as of methods of extending and improving services are 1) voluntary arrangements by libraries to provide cooperative services in certain specialized areas, such as making union catalogs and lists or sharing certain resources; 2) contract service, in which one governmental unit contracts with another to provide certain kinds of library service for pay; and 3) public library systems, in which libraries cooperate with the state library extension agency on a voluntary basis in grouping themselves into regional systems in order to make available a wider range of resources to their users.

SYSTEMS, NETWORKS, AND OTHER COOPERATIVES

As early as 1923, C. C. Williamson recommended the extension and improvement of the county library system.[19] Recommendations for the organization of larger units, serving more people and able to provide greater financial support, were made in *A National Plan for Library Service in 1948*[20] and the Public Library Inquiry, in 1950, broadened the concept to one of library systems and called for "the organization of larger units of public library service by consolidation, federation, or confederation of smaller units into library systems serving cities, counties, multicounty or other districts of 100,000 or more people, with total expenditures within each system of $100,000 or more."[21]

During the past decade several factors have strongly influenced larger units of service, or systems. (The word "system" is used to describe either a single large library—municipal, county, or regional—with its branches, or a group of independent member libraries working cooperatively.) Standards for public libraries, adopted by the American Library Association in 1956, defined the areas of responsibility of the state agency in providing a program of supplementary services to back up individual libraries and library systems within the state; all standards were based on the systems idea of library service.[22] In 1963, *Standards for Library Functions at the State Level*[23] gave further stress to the necessity for larger units of service and the revised *Standards for Library Functions at the State Level* (1970 and 1985)[24] give primary emphasis to the development of networks of all types of libraries.

LIBRARY SYSTEMS

ALA's Public Library Association describes three main types of systems and the ways in which they are organized.[25]

1. A consolidated system: a single library board and administrator direct all libraries in an area as a single autonomous unit, usually a municipal public library system with a central library and branch libraries.
2. A federated system: one or more county boards of trustees appoint a system board of trustees to direct and control the activities of the system library. Local libraries within each county retain their autonomy and contract with the system for services and other assistance.
3. A cooperative system: the trustees of a group of local libraries establish a system by electing a board to have jurisdiction over the system and to represent them in directing the activities of the system. This system board establishes a headquarters unit, designates a central library to house the interlibrary loan collection, and determines what services the system will provide to its users. The member libraries continue to have complete autonomy and local library boards function as usual, operating their own libraries within the system.

Of these types, the cooperative system is the most common. The boundaries of such a system include an area large enough to ensure adequate financial resources for the needed materials and services. The state assumes a share of the financial responsibility through a program of state aid administered under state agency regulations. The resources of all the libraries in the system are available to member libraries through interlibrary loan, and a union catalog aids them in locating needed materials; an extensive reference collection is maintained, and each system designates a central library to provide interlibrary reference for all members. In addition, quick reference service is provided to users by means of teletypewriter, photocopy, telefacsimile, computer, and other electronic devices; rotating collections of books and other materials supplement the collections of individual libraries; service is extended to residents of the system area by means of bookmobiles; and a system-wide card is honored at any local library in the system. Central purchasing and processing and other cooperative practices result in substantial savings for member libraries.

Networks

A network is a combination of diverse information agencies linked together in a formal relationship and utilizing such electronic technologies as computers, telefacsimile, electronic mail, and other forms of communication technology. Networks, begun chiefly for purposes of shared cataloging, have now added such services as bibliographic retrieval, database searching, resource sharing, interlibrary loan, document delivery, and coordinated collection development. They may be self-supporting through member fees or partially supported by state and/or federal funds.[26] Some examples of networks are: Ohio Computer Library Center; Washington Library Information Network; New York State Interlibrary Loan Network, Southeastern Library Network (SOLINET), and New England Library Information Network (NELINET).

A consortium is a voluntary cooperative arrangement of a number of groups and/or libraries for such specific undertakings as resource sharing, interlibrary loan, collection development, union lists, etc. Consortia are numerous among special and academic libraries.[27]

Interstate Library Compact

The interstate library compact provides for an interstate library district governed by its own board, made up of representatives of participating libraries. The rights, duties, and obligations of each member are set forth in "an interlocking series of agreements." The first interstate library compact was enacted by Wisconsin in 1955.[28] In 1962, the Council of State Governments, at the request of the state librarians in New England, formulated an interstate library compact for that area, authorizing two different kinds of cooperation: 1) cooperation by communities on either side of a state boundary in creating a joint library or in sharing certain library resources or services; and 2) cooperative activities among the state libraries. Maine, New Hampshire, Vermont, Massachusetts, and New York joined the compact as soon as it was enacted.[29]

Current library literature offers many examples of cooperative library arrangements and activities. The *ALA Directory* lists more than 800 library systems in 46 states. Three states have one system and only one state does not have a system. Also listed are more than 400 networks, consortia, and other cooperative library organizations.[30]

SIGNIFICANT DEVELOPMENTS

1. All state library agencies prepare annual and long range programs for library development and extension.
2. More than 40 states have developed standards for public libraries relating to staff, qualifications, hours of service, and facilities.
3. Some states have developed standards for the accreditation of public libraries based on materials and facilities, number of persons served, programs, organization and administration, public relations, accessibility, reference services, and personnel.
4. Growing emphasis is placed on continuing education programs for trustees and personnel.
5. Database searching and other reference services are performed for the public.
6. Many state libraries operate the Library of Congress services for the blind and physically handicapped.
7. County, multicounty, and regional libraries have been greatly strengthened and improved and many new ones have been established. The Center for the Study of Rural Librarianship estimates that rural libraries account for 82 percent of all libraries in America.
8. Cooperative undertakings, such as centralized purchasing, processing and pooling of certain types of materials have been put into operation. State agencies have encouraged the development of machine-readable bibliographic databases and automation of various library operations.
9. State library agencies have participated in developing literacy programs conducted by the state, the public library and other libraries.

PROBLEMS

1. *Insufficient funds to support adequate library programs.* The state must provide a sound foundation of financial support to make up for declining federal assistance and to supplement local funds.
2. *Difficulties in serving large, sparsely settled areas.* Small population means inadequate local tax support as well as too few users to justify more than a

minimum program of resources and services. More large units of service and cooperative activities are essential.

3. *Indifference toward library improvement.* In some situations, both library boards and citizens are complacent about the inadequacy of library service. This attitude indicates a lack of understanding and appreciation of the importance of library service, which is itself a problem and must be met through education, public relations, and demonstrations of the value of library service.

4. *Lack of influence and visibility* in the state governmental structure. The state library agency must have appropriate legal authority commensurate with its responsibility if it is to assume leadership in planning and coordinating a plan for total service; and it must have a status comparable to other state agencies.

5. *Standards.* Strong standards are needed as guides in building a program of services which will carry out the purposes of the state program and enlist public support for it.

6. *Research.* In order to determine needs and to plan ahead, research must be conducted and resources must be available to implement the findings.

7. *Change.* Greater attention must be given to changing patterns of use, changing audiences, changes in societal conditions, in information needs of patrons, and in ways of serving these needs.

8. *Inadequate salaries.* The position of leadership in which the state library agency now finds itself calls for the most talented and the best qualified personnel which the profession can offer. Salaries commensurate with the responsibilities of the position must be offered in order to attract this kind of personnel.

9. *Suspicion and/or hostility* toward cooperative activities which seem to threaten local autonomy. This problem, involving personal attitudes and prejudices, is not an easy one to overcome. It requires careful explanations, effective public relations, and skillful leadership. In addition, the rising cost of materials and equipment needed for automating library operations discourages such cooperative activities as systems and networks.

NOTES

1. *See* pp. 68-69.
2. *See* p. 172.
3. *See* pp. 153-154.
4. Oliver Garceau, *The Public Library in the Political Process,* op. cit., p. 39.
5. *Standards for Library Functions at the State Level,* Prepared by the Subcommittee for Library Functions at the State Level, Association of Specialized and Cooperative Agencies, American Library Association (Chicago: American Library Association, 1985), Chapter 5, *passim.*
6. *The Book of the States, 1988-89* (Lexington, KY: The Council of State Governments, 1988), pp. 323-324.
7. Standards for Library Functions at the State Level, *op. cit.,* p. 1.

8. Carleton Bruns Joeckel, *Library Service* ("Staff Study, Number 11"; Washington, D.C.: U.S. Government Printing Office, 1938), p. 20.
9. U.S. *Congressional Record*, 81st Cong. 2d Sess., 1950, XCVI, Part 3, 3119.
10. Wilfred L. Morin and Nathan M. Cohen, *State Library Extension Services* ("Misc. No. 37, OE-15009"; Washington, D.C.: U.S. Department of Health, Education, and Welfare, 1960), pp. 4, 23.
11. In the Library Services Act, "rural area" refers to any place of 10,000 population or less, according to the latest United States census.
12. *See also* pp. 144-145.
13. Consult the state library agency for information regarding the titles which are funded each fiscal year and regarding changes in the law.
14. *See also Standards for Library Functions at the State Level, op. cit.*, Chapter 5.
15. There are variations in library literature regarding these dates. This information comes from Mary Lemist Titcomb, *Story of the Washington County Free Library* (Hagerstown, Md.: n.d.), pp. 7, 14. According to Titcomb, librarian of the Washington County Library, boxes of books were first transported by wagon between branch stations in her county by the janitor, and the first book wagon—designed for that specific purpose—started its run in April 1907.
16. Morin and Cohen, *op. cit.*, p. 4.
17. *American Library Directory 1988-1989* (New York: R. R. Bowker Company, 1988).
18. Under the Library Services Act and the Library Services and Construction Act, grants are made by the federal government to the states for the extension and improvement of rural public library service.
19. Williamson, *op. cit.*, p. 146.
20. American Library Association, Committee on Postwar Planning, *A National Plan for Library Service* (Chicago: American Library Association, 1948).
21. Alice Bryan, *The Public Librarian* (New York: Columbia University Press, 1952), pp. 445, 446.
22. American Library Association, Public Libraries Division, Coordinating Committee on Revision of Public Library Standards, *Public Library Service, A Guide to Evaluation with Minimum Standards* (Chicago: American Library Association, 1956), pp. 9, 17-18.
23. *Standards for Library Functions at the State Level* (Chicago: American Library Association, 1963).
24. American Association of State Libraries, *Standards for Library Functions at the State Level* (Revision of the 1963 edition; Chicago: American Library Association, 1970) and *Standards for Library Functions at the State Level* (1985), *op. cit.*
25. American Library Association, Public Library Association, *A Primer About Library Systems* (Chicago: American Library Association, n.d.), unpaged.
26. *See also* pp. 144-145.
27. *See* pp. 184, 194, 199.
28. Michelle R. Vale, "The Interstate Library Compact," *Library Journal* 91 (May 15, 1966): 2420.

29. Mitchell Wendell, "An Interstate Compact for Libraries," *Proceedings of the Third Assembly on the Library Functions of the States Held November 13-15,* ed. Mary A. McKenzie (Washington, D.C.: Library of Congress, 1964), p. 44.

30. *ALA Directory 1988-1989, op. cit.,* pp. 2147-2168.

14

Municipal Public Libraries

As a public agency, the public library is authorized by state law; supported by general public funds or special taxes voted for the purpose; and administered on the basis of equal access to all citizens of the city, town, county, or region which maintains it. Voluntary gifts may supplement public financial support. Public library service is not mandatory in any state, but all states have a general permissive legal authorization for the establishment and maintenance of public libraries.[1]

Other kinds of state laws relating to public libraries are:[2]

1. General laws relating to municipalities, which may include sections relating to the establishment of libraries;
2. Separate acts for each kind of public library—municipal, county, regional, or multicounty;
3. Special legislation concerning particular cities, which may include sections relating to libraries if a commission or city-manager form of government is established;
4. Special state legislation concerning a particular library, such as that which established the Boston Public Library.

In the preceding chapter, state, county, multicounty, and regional public libraries were discussed. This chapter is devoted to the municipal public library, which is supported and controlled by the people who reside within the geographical boundaries of the municipality.

In terms of their control, municipal public libraries fall into several categories:[3]

1. Those administered by a board appointed by the mayor, the city council, the city manager, or the city commission or elected by the people;
2. Those administered as a department of the city government by the city government;
3. Those attached to the school district as the legal entity and administered either by separate boards or by the board of education.

Most public libraries are administered by a board which determines the policies of the library; employs a librarian; gives advice in the preparation of the budget and works for the necessary funds; provides buildings and facilities; develops and works for needed new library legislation; stimulates interest in, use of, and support for the library; and works with public officials, other libraries, library associations, and citizens in providing quality library service.

Perhaps the most significant feature of the free public library throughout its history is that it has been financed from local tax revenues or by a local tax for the specific purpose of maintaining it. This has been its weakness as well as its civic strength. As competition for local tax dollars has increased, many municipal libraries have not been able to maintain a program of services adequate to the demand made upon them by their users.

DEVELOPMENT SINCE 1876

The tax-supported free public library, which came into being with the establishment of the Boston Public Library in 1852, had its most vigorous growth in Massachusetts, where there was "wealth and a concentrated urban population that inherited the habit of communal cultural activity."[4] These same conditions—wealth, a concentrated urban population, and cultural activity—have continued to be vital forces in the development and growth of public libraries.

During the last decade of the nineteenth century and the first two decades of the twentieth, constructive efforts were made to expand services in the public library. Such activities as children's departments, open shelves, cooperation with public schools, extended hours of service, subject departmentalization, and the establishment of branches—resulting from the work of such pioneering leaders as Caroline M. Hewins, William Brett, Arthur Bostwick, Samuel S. Green, William

Foster, and John Shaw Billings—enabled the public library to extend its services and increase the accessibility of its resources.

Branch libraries date from 1870, when the East Boston Branch of the Boston Public Library was established.[5] During the last decade of the nineteenth century, the trend toward branches was well established, aided by the Carnegie program which covered branches as well as the central library, offering most of the same services on a limited scale, or as distribution centers for the circulation of popular books at the neighborhood level.

World War I gave the public library the opportunity to make a significant contribution to the community and the nation, and it responded by serving as an agency of war publicity for the government; aiding in the Americanization of aliens; and providing library facilities for soldier's hospitals, the handicapped, and the blind. The emphasis on democracy during and immediately following the war focused attention again upon the essentiality of an informed electorate in a democratic society and gave new importance to the educational role of the public library. This role assumed greater proportions in the face of the educational and informational requirements of the great numbers of foreign born in the population. Early efforts to meet these needs included reading guidance and the provision of special materials and services to factory workers and to immigrants. These services grew gradually into a planned program of adult education offering advisory service in terms of reading programs and reading lists designed to encourage purposeful use of the library's materials by both individuals and groups; informational and educational services to business, community organizations and agencies, and special groups, such as labor, immigrants, and migratory workers; and library-sponsored group programs on books or films, forums, lectures, and the "Great Books." For more than 30 years, emphasis on adult education was a major factor in planning the program of the public library; and by 1955, the adult education activities developed during that 30-year period were accepted parts of the public library's service to adults.[6]

The Depression of the 1930s called for additional public library resources and services. In response, vocational and occupational readjustment and guidance as well as adult training classes were added to the program. The public library participated in the Federal Emergency Programs of the times—the Works Progress Administration and the National Youth Administration—by providing the unemployed with jobs and training in clerical work, bookbinding and repair, and other nonprofessional activities. The library benefited, in turn, because these workers, performing routine tasks, released professional librarians for other duties. In many instances, library services which otherwise would have been curtailed or dropped completely were maintained because of these emergency programs of the federal government. In addition to providing funds for training and employing clerical and other nonprofessional workers in existing libraries, the federal government aided in extending free public library service to sections of the country lacking such service by making funds available for the establishment of branch libraries in towns. Donations from the local community, civic organizations, and individuals supplemented federal funds and helped to provide books and other library materials.

The public library's program of service to the public schools, begun before the end of the nineteenth century, was greatly expanded during the late 1930s and 1940s.[7] In addition to opening its own collections and facilities for the use of students and teachers, the many services to the public schools have included lending boxes of books; setting up school libraries wholly by the public library and the public librarian; instructing students in the use of library materials; giving book talks and holding story hours for children; and assisting teachers in the evaluation and selection of materials to supplement the curriculum.

During World War II, the public library planned programs and disseminated materials to inform and educate citizens on the issues involved; extended new services to government, business, and industry; sponsored programs for both recreational and cultural growth; provided services to transient groups of workers; and served as a clearinghouse of information relating to the war effort.

The interest in science and technology, stimulated by the Russian Sputnik in 1957, created a need for new library materials—both popular and technical—for all levels of readers and attracted many new readers to the library.

INFLUENCES ON THE PUBLIC LIBRARY

Called "an organ of social democracy and an instrument of personal self-realization,"[8] the American public library has been characterized, from the beginning, by its commitment to the goals of promoting an enlightened citizenry; providing the opportunity, materials, encouragement, and stimulation for continuing self-education; and serving the community inside and outside the library walls. These basic goals distinguish the free public library from all other types of libraries and have determined the nature and extent of its program.

A number of factors outside the community have influenced the public library in developing programs and services to meet these objectives. Some of these influences have been noted: philanthropy,[9] the adult education movement, war, economic depression, and scientific and technical advances. Some other factors which influence the municipal public library are the state library extension agencies, surveys and studies, the federal government through federal legislation, and professional associations.

STATE LIBRARY EXTENSION AGENCIES

State library agencies, created to stimulate and aid in establishing public libraries on the local level, have aided their development by supplementing the local library's resources with loans of special collections of books and other materials; making grants-in-aid from federal and state funds for salaries and/or materials or other purposes; giving advice and technical assistance; providing consultative services in planning local programs and expanding services; giving reference service; making studies and reports and preparing statistics relating to public library programs and resources; providing supervision in states where it is required; and certifying personnel when it is required.[10]

SURVEYS

An effective public library program grows out of an understanding of the community it serves: the educational and cultural level of the people; their occupational, avocational, and recreational interests; the governmental organization; the economic, social, and geographical characteristics of the area involved; and the nature and number of educational, social, and cultural institutions supported by the community. These kinds of information can be obtained by community surveys, which have become necessary aids in planning library service to a given community. On national and state levels, the survey has been used frequently and successfully to determine the strengths and weaknesses of public library service in given areas and to guide in planning national or state programs.

Among the most significant and far-reaching of many studies was the Public Library Inquiry, which resulted from the proposal of the

American Library Association in 1946 that the Social Science Research Council conduct a sociological rather than a professional study of the American public library to determine its potential and actual contribution to American society. In 1947, under a grant of $200,000 from the Carnegie Corporation of New York and with Dr. Robert D. Leigh as director, the study was begun "to make an appraisal in sociological, cultural, and human terms of the extent to which libraries are achieving their objectives and an assessment of the public library's actual and potential contribution to American society."[11] Many aspects of the public library were studied and analyzed and reports were published.[12] The results, proposals, and recommendations of the Public Library Inquiry and the goals which it set played a major role in shaping the program of the public library in the fifties and continue to influence public library thinking and planning at all levels. Some of these recommendations were: larger units of service; increased funds including federal grants; emphasis on service to known users; acquisition of quality materials rather than popular ones, and informational and educational materials rather than recreational ones.[13]

Following the Public Library Inquiry numerous studies have been made of libraries in a state or an area, of various aspects of library service, and of library service to specific groups such as the disadvantaged.[14] In 1972, *A Strategy for Public Library Change: Proposed Library Goals-Feasibility Study*,[15] measured the public library then against the institution at the time of the Public Library Inquiry. It studied the societal factors affecting the public library; examined public library development between 1950-1970; and made recommendations for additional study.

THE FEDERAL GOVERNMENT

With the exception of the legislation relating to depository libraries in 1895, which included some public libraries, federal legislation of benefit to public libraries did not begin until 1956 with the Library Services Act which provided library services to rural areas only, including funds for materials and services. This act, amended in 1964 and called the Library Services and Construction Act (LSCA),[16] provides federal funds on a matching basis for both urban and rural areas which lack public libraries or have inadequate facilities and services. LSCA has been extended through 1994 and provides federal funds to improve services to the disadvantaged, the handicapped, and native Americans; to provide increased information and referral services to patrons; to make effective use of technology; to develop and expand state, regional, and interstate cooperative arrangements; and for construction, alteration, or renovation of library buildings.

Under this legislative act, during the 25-year-period from 1956-1981, federal funds brought public library service for the first time to more than 17 million people and improved service to 100 million. Some 2000 public library buildings were built, remodeled, or expanded, and 171 million books were purchased with a combination of LSCA, state, and local funds.[17] Public library building has continued; 111 new buildings and 124 additions or renovations were completed in 1989,[18] and 799 projects are in progress in 1990.[19]

PROFESSIONAL ASSOCIATIONS

The mission of the Public Library Association, a division of the American Library Association, is "to advance the development and effectiveness of public library service and public librarians."[20] Among its concerns and priorities are: free and equal access to information for all persons; continuing education; research; public relations; planning and evaluation of public library service; funding; literacy programs; and service to special groups.

General standards for public libraries were drawn up in 1933, describing the purposes and setting forth standards for reasonably adequate service in terms of buildings, staff, collection, and special services. *Postwar Standards for Public Libraries* followed in 1943. Both the *National Plan for Public Library Service,* 1948, and *The Public Library Inquiry,* 1950, made recommendations concerning standards for public libraries. In 1956, *Public Library Service: A Guide to Evaluation with Minimum Standards,* covering all major aspects of the public library program, was published by the American Library Association. *Interim Standards for Public Libraries* (1963)[21] and *Minimum Standards for Public Library Systems, 1966* (1967)[22] followed. Standards and/or guidelines for most of the services provided by the public library have been formulated by ALA and PLA.

In the late 1970s, the Public Library Association moved away from quantitative standards and recommended community-based planning and evaluation of public library services. PLA's planning tool, the Public Library Development Project, which was presented to the membership in 1987, includes: *A Planning Process for Public Libraries* (1980),[23] which gives guidance for step-by-step planning and role-setting; *Output Measures for Public Libraries* (1982, 2d ed., 1987),[24] which provides guidance on using measurement to evaluate library service, such as circulation per capita, reference transactions per capita; on choosing measures; and on interpreting data; and the Public Library Data Service which will be developed to provide selected data from public libraries regarding output measures, role choices, holdings, staff, expenditures, and community characteristics.

THE PUBLIC LIBRARY PROGRAM

Function

It is the function of the municipal public library to provide the printed and nonprinted materials to meet the individual and group needs of its constituency for information, education, self-realization, recreation, and cultural growth and for assistance in carrying out their duties as citizens and members of the community. The library organizes, interprets, and guides citizens in the use of these materials and makes them easily, freely, and equally available to all citizens.

Collection

The collection of materials, selected on the basis of the needs and interests of the constituency, should include books, periodicals, pamphlets, newspapers, pictures, slides, films, music scores, maps, disc and tape recordings, the various microforms, and archival materials which relate to the local community. In addition to these materials, the public library should provide the equipment for using audiovisual materials, microreproductions, and recordings.

Services

The services of the public library are designed to facilitate and invite use of resources and satisfy the reading goals of individuals of all ages and groups. These services include organizing materials for ease of access and convenient use through cataloging, classification, and shelf arrangement; lending procedures that provide an equal opportunity for all patrons to use the materials; guidance to the user in finding materials and using library resources; and stimulation of use of materials through publicity, display, reading lists, story hours, book and film discussions, and planned reading programs. Other services include providing information service, both to persons who come to the library and to those who telephone; giving assistance to cultural, civic, and educational organizations in finding and using materials; sponsoring cultural programs in the library for children, young people, and adults; collecting special materials of interest to the community; borrowing materials on interlibrary loan; making computer searches; extending library services to all points of the community through branches, deposit stations, and bookmobiles; organizing the library for easier access and specialized service into subject departments and departments for age levels; and coordinating the library program with other educational and cultural services in the community.

The variety and number of library services to meet the needs and demands of its supporting community are, in fact, limited only by the budget of the library and the initiative and imagination of the staff. Services range from the basic types named above to such services as providing equipment for photographic reproduction of materials; short-term loans of paintings and other art forms, audio- and videocassettes, and computer software; and books by mail. Large public libraries issue publications, annotated bibliographies, and reading lists.

Staff

The staff of the public library should be "comparable in intellectual caliber, education, and personal qualifications with other social and educational leaders in the community."[25] This statement, apt when it was made more than three decades ago, becomes more appropriate as the public library's functions call for increasing cooperation in library planning and library activities in which all leaders of the community must participate and for which the public librarian must provide leadership. A broad general education, some subject specialization, and professional education in library and information science should be combined with an understanding of the public library's objectives; ability to study the community and determine what is required in terms of buildings, personnel, and materials to develop a program to meet its needs; political acumen; and ability to work with people.

Organization

The organization of the public library varies according to the size of the library; the nature of the community and the needs of the residents; the objectives and purposes of the library; and the availability of physical facilities, staff, and financial support. In general, the public library—regardless of size—will have, in addition to the traditional departments of acquisition, technical processing, circulation, reference, and administration, a department which serves children and young people with collections especially selected for them. The large public library will be organized into departments which serve highly specialized purposes: subject departments, such as humanities, science and technology, and business; an extension department, including bookmobiles and deposit stations; departments serving special groups, such as the foreign born or the disadvantaged; departments concerned with a particular kind of material, such as audiovisual materials or government documents; and branch libraries.

PROBLEMS

Perhaps the most critical problems facing the public library are declining financial support and limited use. Declining financial support from federal and other sources comes at a time when all costs are rising; when new and diversified programs are needed to provide services to formerly inadequately served or unserved publics, such as the disadvantaged, minority groups, the aging, the handicapped, and ethnic groups; and when computerized library operations are becoming more and more essential to efficient service, but are not within reach of many libraries because of their prohibitive cost.

The limited use of the public library by the publics it proposes to serve has been seen in various studies beginning with the Public Library Inquiry. Some findings are: three out of every ten adults use the library; women use the library more than men; the young more than the old; the educated more than the uneducated; single persons more than married persons; urban dwellers more than rural; and professional and white-collar workers more than nonprofessionals and blue-collar workers.[26]

Major problems derive from the growth of large metropolitan areas. The shift in population from rural areas to the cities has brought demands for more materials and services to meet the needs of the new and unpracticed library user as well as those of the habitual user. At the same time, the shift of population from the inner city to the suburbs has created the need for more and better branch services.

Other problems facing the public library:

1. *Automation.* Among the many questions to be answered in planning for automation are: What library operations should be automated? What retraining can be done? What funding is required and who will provide it? These are still major questions for many libraries.

2. *Mass of publications and rising costs.* The public library, like all other libraries, has the problem of knowing what to select, what to keep, what to microfilm, what to store, and how and where to store it. The high cost of new types of materials—audio- and videocassettes, compact discs, computer software, etc.—diminishes the funds formerly used for books, serials, and newspapers. Added to the original high cost of these materials, is the high cost of maintenance—replacing torn, mutilated, or stolen items, etc.

3. *Censorship.* Censorship may be practiced by individuals and/or groups who attempt to remove books from libraries, to prevent libraries from acquiring certain titles, and in some cases, to force libraries to acquire specific publications. Censorship may relate to so-called immoral or obscene subjects, to the contents of textbooks and other materials used in the public schools, to religious problems, to political questions, or to racial matters.[27]

4. *Problem patrons.* Disruptive, destructive, violent, and/or threatening patrons are a growing problem in public libraries. Additional staff, stronger security measures, and cooperation with community officials are needed. "Latchkey children" (children who are unattended and unsupervised at home because both parents work or for other reasons) are requiring much attention from public library staff, either to maintain discipline or to provide programs that will help the children benefit from the time spent in the library. The homeless are also problem patrons because they feel they can use the library, which is a publicly-supported institution, as they would a home—for shelter, warmth, etc. All of these patrons put an extra burden on staff, facilities, and resources.

5. *Preservation of resources.* Fires and natural disasters, destruction of property, theft, and mutilation, in addition to the great number of "brittle books," are a constant threat to the safety of library resources and facilities.

6. *Inadequate facilities.* Added to already inadequate space for resources, staff, and readers is the need for space and facilities to accommodate new types of materials such as computers, CD-Roms, etc.

7. *Fees.* When, how, how much—or whether—to charge user fees, especially for the new types of materials and services such as audio- and videocassettes, computer searches and software, as well as interlibrary loan, information and referral service, telefacsimile transmission, etc., are recurring problems.

8. *Qualified staff.* In many libraries, especially small ones, there is no staff member with a master's degree in library or information science. Many do not even have a college degree. Recruiting and retaining qualified staff is a major problem in public libraries.

9. *Bilingual/bicultural materials.* Inadequate collections of bilingual and bicultural materials to serve the needs of the non-English speaking population and to aid them in learning how to use the same materials other citizens use is a growing problem, especially in areas where large numbers of immigrants are settling.

10. *Statement of mission.* Often a clear statement of the library's mission is lacking. What are the roles of the public library: information provider, recre-

ation center, people's university—a combination of all of these? If so, how much attention should be given to each role?[28]

TRENDS

Some trends in public library services and operations, based on a large number of examples, are:

1. Increased efforts are being made to bring information directly to people through outreach programs, service by mail, interlibrary loan, and additional bookmobile stops. Of some 70,000 library outlets which served the public in 1982, about 70 percent were bookmobile stops.[29]
2. Cable television is being used for educational programs, story hours, and staff training.
3. Expanded service is given to business and industry and to the community in the form of quick information and referral service.
4. Information centers for citizens have been opened in public libraries to provide information and referral service on such problems as voting, and jobs; and guidance is given on finding and using various kinds of information.
5. Provision for continuing education for library staff is being made through scholarships, independent study projects, workshops, leave arrangements, and so forth.
6. Public libraries are cooperating with each other and in multitype ventures in the form of systems, networks, and consortia.
7. Public libraries are using technology in numerous library operations: word processing, database searching, interlibrary loan, public access catalogs, union catalogs, electronic mail, desktop publishing,[30] telefacsimile transmission of data, and electronic bulletin boards.
8. Public libraries are participating actively in the political process in their observation of Legislative Day, or Library Day, lobbying on the state and national levels for legislation favorable to libraries.
9. Collections are being expanded to include increasing numbers of nonprint materials: audio- and videocassettes, computer software, compact disks, and the equipment for their use.

NOTES

1. With the exception of the state of Michigan, where the constitution provides for the establishment and support of a library in each township, the legal provision for municipal libraries is found in the library laws enacted by the state legislature.
2. Joeckel, *op. cit.*, pp. 53-59, *passim.*
3. Libraries not controlled by the public but which are called public libraries because they are free to all residents of the community may be corporation, association, or privately endowed libraries.

4. Oliver Garceau, *The Public Library in the Political Process: A Report of the Public Library Inquiry...* (New York: Columbia University Press, 1949), p. 38. *See also* p. 72.

5. Walter Muir Whitehill, *Boston Public Library: A Centennial History* (Cambridge, Mass.: Harvard University Press, 1956), p. 85.

6. Margaret Ellen Monroe, *Library Adult Education, the Biography of an Idea* (New York: Scarecrow Press, Inc., 1963), pp. 10, 12.

7. *See also* p. 157, 160.

8. Lowell Martin, "Potential Role of the American Public Library," *A National Plan for Public Library Service*, ed. Carleton B. Joeckel and Amy Winslow ("Planning for Libraries," No. 3; Chicago: American Library Association, 1948), pp. 1-2.

9. *See* pp. 74-75.

10. *See also* pp. 125, 134.

11. Lester Asheim, ed., *A Forum on the Public Library Inquiry* . . . (New York: Columbia University Press, 1950), p. 242.

12. Bernard Berelson, *The Library's Public* (New York: Columbia University Press, 1950); Alice Bryan, *The Public Librarian* (New York: Columbia University Press, 1952); Oliver Garceau, *The Public Library in the Political Process* (New York: Columbia University Press, 1949); Robert D. Leigh, *The Public Library in the United States* (New York: Columbia University Press, 1950); James L. McCamy, *Government Publications for the Citizen* (New York: Columbia University Press, 1950); William Miller, *The Book Industry* (New York: Columbia University Press, 1949); Watson Pierce, *Work Measurements in Public Libraries* (New York: Social Science Research Council, 1949); Gloria Waldron, *The Information Film* (New York: Columbia University Press, 1949).

13. *See also* pp. 150.

14. Examples are: Douglas M. Knight and E. Shepley Nourse, *Libraries at Large: Tradition, Innovation, and the National Interest* (New York: R.R. Bowker Co., 1969); Lowell A. Martin, *Baltimore Reaches Out: Library Service to the Disadvantaged* (Baltimore: Enoch Pratt Free Library, 1967); Virginia Mathews and Dan Lacy, *Response to Change: American Libraries in the Seventies* (Indiana Library Studies, Report 1, 1970; ERIC (ED 044131)). "The Access to Public Libraries Study," *ALA Bulletin*, 57 (September, 1963): 742-745. The Center for Statistics in the United Stated Department of Education collects statistics of libraries and publishes reports. The Office for Research of the American Library Association makes statistical and other studies of public libraries. Surveys are made by the National Commission on Library and Information Science, by private research firms under contract to a library, a professional organization, or the federal government. Reports of these studies and surveys are carried in the current literature.

15. Public Library Association, *A Strategy for Public Library Change: Proposed Public Library Goals-Feasibility Study* (Chicago: American Library Association, 1972).

16. *See also* p. 127.

17. "25 Years of Achievement with the Library Services Act and the Library Services and Construction Act, 1956-1981" (Washington, D.C.: ALA Washington Office, 1981), *passim*.

18. Bette-Lee Fox, *et al.*, "Ruins Among the Splendor: Library Buildings 1989," *Library Journal* 114 (December 1989): 49.
19. *Ibid.*, p. 65.
20. *ALA Handbook of Organization 1987/1988, op. cit.*, p. 107.
21. *Interim Standards for Small Public Libraries* was designed to provide interim goals for libraries which serve populations under 50,000 until they can meet the goals of *Public Library Service* and/or *Minimum Standards for Public Library Systems, 1966.*
22. *See* pp. 88-89.
23. Vernon Palmour, *et al. A Planning Process for Public Libraries* (Chicago: American Library Association, 1980).
24. Douglas L. Zwezig and Eleanor Jo Rodger, *Output Measures for Public Libraries: A Manual of Standardized Procedures* (Chicago: American Library Association, 1982); Nancy Van House and others, *Output Measures for Public Libraries: A Manual of Standardized Procedures*, 2d ed., prepared for the Public Library Development Project (Chicago: American Library Association, 1987). *See also* Charles R. McClure and others, *Planning and Role Setting for Public Libraries: A Manual of Options and Procedures*, prepared for the Public Library Development Project (Chicago: American Library Association, 1987).
25. Alice Bryan, *The Public Librarian* (New York: Columbia University Press, 1952), p. 6.
26. *See* Knight, *op. cit.*, pp. 72-73.
27. The importance of the problem of censorship is evidenced by the wide coverage it is given in library and other literature. Recent information relating to this problem can be found in current issues of *American Libraries, Library Journal, School Library Journal, Wilson Library Bulletin,* and other professional journals.
28. *See* pp. 145-146.
29. "The NCES Survey of Public Libraries, 1982: Final Report," in *Bowker Annual of Library and Book Trade Information,* 31st ed. 1986 (New York: R. R. Bowker Company, 1986), p. 346.
30. Desktop publishing is the process of creating documents by using a microcomputer and software which allows the operator to control all page design elements of the document, including text, graphics, and printout. It is used for brochures, newsletters, bookmarks, reports, and other in-house publishing.

15

School Library Media Centers

EDUCATIONAL OVERVIEW

A national system of education in the sense of a unified system with an official of the federal government as director does not exist in the United States. Under Article I, Section 8 of the Constitution—the general welfare section—the federal government expresses its interest in education in a number of ways: Congress enacts laws which provide financial support for various educational programs; the Supreme Court protects against unconstitutional laws and practices relating to education; the United States Department of Education, representing the executive branch of the federal government, renders important advisory, consultative, and research services.

Although the Constitution does not mention education, Article X, which provides that "powers not delegated to the United States by the Constitution, nor prohibited by it to the states, are reserved to the states respectively or to the people," implies that control of education shall be in the hands of the states. The states have created local administrative units called school districts, delegating to them the authority to organize and operate public elementary and secondary schools. Certain important regulatory and leadership functions, however, have been retained by the state.

Each state has made constitutional and statutory provisions for a system of public education, although these provisions vary from state to state. In general, however, each state constitution provides for the creation of a central educational agency and gives to the legislature the power to establish the agency, describe its functions, and assign its responsibilities in carrying out the provisions of the constitution. The central educational agency usually consists of a state board of education and a chief state school officer, who, with a staff under his direction, comprise the state department of education.

In addition to its regulatory and leadership responsibilities, the state department of education has a major responsibility for the development and improvement of the instructional program of the schools, and school library services are a part of instruction.[1] In all the state departments of education, some services are performed for school libraries and librarians. In several states, the state library extension agency, in addition to the state department of education, has certain responsibilities for school libraries, such as providing loans of library materials.[2]

In addition to providing consultative services on library equipment, quarters, and materials; compiling statistics; and making reports on school libraries, the state department of education establishes standards for evaluating the effectiveness of the school library; formulates requirements and programs for the education and certification of school librarians; provides for the supervision of school libraries; and may provide state aid for books, equipment, and salaries.

STANDARDS

Standards are criteria which are formulated by the state department of education to be used in judging the quality of a school. They may be minimum standards, which must be met before a school can be accredited; or they may be guides to be used in a school's self-study or its long-range planning. They may be both quantitative and qualitative. Some standards are applicable to both secondary and elementary schools; however, some states have separate standards for each type of school library.

In addition to the state departments of education, there are regional, national, and professional organizations which formulate standards for school library programs.[3]

CERTIFICATION

Certification requirements are closely coordinated with the educational program for school librarians, which is planned under the leadership of the state department of education. In general, states require a minimum of a bachelor's degree, including specific courses in library science and a specific number of semester hours, ranging from ten to 30 semester hours in different states. The educational requirement may vary depending on the school enrollment, and certification is usually given for grade levels—elementary or secondary—or it is based on the amount of service which the librarian gives, either part-time or full-time. School librarians are required to meet teacher certification requirements in all states.

SUPERVISION

The primary concern of state school library supervision is to develop, improve, expand, and interpret the program of school library service. The state school library supervisor works with the chief state school officer and with several divisions of the state department of education in planning the state's program for developing school library services, cooperating closely with divisions in the areas of certification, curriculum development, school plant, research, and teacher education. The supervisor also advises on needed legislation and legislative changes; recommends changes in standards when needed; and assists in developing programs of library education in state institutions.

STATE AID

All states provide financial aid for the schools under their jurisdiction. This aid, granted on the basis of formulas fixed by law or by regulation, may be given for a specific purpose, such as transportation, or it may be given to strengthen the entire school program, allowing the local board to determine where it is most needed. Such aid may be used to improve the school library program. Some states provide direct state aid to school libraries for materials, salaries, or both.

Local Responsibility for Education

Through the local school districts, created by the state as the governmental units for educational purposes and governed by boards of citizens chosen by the people for the purpose of managing their schools, the American people have been able to keep the schools close to the community, fashioning them according to community desires and interests. The only limitations are those imposed by the federal Constitution, which must not be contradicted; by the constitutional, statutory, and regulatory mandates of the state; and by the amount of local financial and moral support which can be mustered. The actual administration of the school is delegated to the chief local school officer—usually the superintendent of schools—who is employed to carry out the policies and regulations of the board.

In the financing of public schools, state and federal funds supplement local funds; the amount of money required for schools each year is determined by the school board of each district. The financial plan of a school district, showing the services, activities, and materials of the school program in dollars and cents, is the budget, which is submitted annually to the board by the superintendent. When it is adopted in its final form by the board, the budget reflects the areas of a school program which the board has chosen to support and the relative importance it has given to each area, such as buildings, equipment, teachers' salaries, transportation, and libraries. Thus, the school library, a vital part of that program, is dependent upon the local board of education, which authorizes it, provides for it, controls it, and administers it through its duly constituted agent, the chief local school officer, who delegates immediate responsibility to the librarian.

SCHOOL LIBRARY DEVELOPMENT TO 1960

In the nineteenth century and the early part of the twentieth, the mastery of subject matter was the primary goal and the textbook and recitation were the tools used to achieve it. Library materials were not considered essential to the process. The first school libraries to appear were used little, and their contribution to the teaching-learning process was minimal. Even when the demand for free schools and the resulting compulsory school-attendance legislation led to curriculum changes—both in the revision of content and the addition of such new subjects as chemistry, physics, and physical geography—increased library services were not considered necessary. But in the 1920s and 1930s, the emphasis in education shifted from the subject matter to the learner, and in the child-centered schools which resulted, the ambitious goal was to provide the opportunity for the development of each child's potentialities. Materials to meet the differences in each child's learning ability, interests, and needs were required in order to organize the activities and experiences that would provide this opportunity. Libraries were organized in some high schools; in some elementary schools a room was set aside as the library with a teacher serving as part-time librarian. The holdings of schools libraries increased impressively during this period. In the late thirties, the U. S. Office of Education reported a total of 27,800 centralized school libraries with a total of 28,300,000 volumes, but more than 33,000 schools were still served by classroom collections usually supplied by the public library.[4]

Specific requirements concerning high school library facilities were included in state standards for accrediting schools, but a school could operate without being accredited. Regional accrediting associations also included the library in evaluating the secondary school, but membership in these associations was voluntary then as it now, and the accreditation of a high school was not dependent upon accrediting the elementary school in the system. The existence of standards and criteria for the accreditation of schools encouraged but did not guarantee the development of school libraries.

In the 1940s, enrichment of the curriculum and the project method of teaching called for a greater number and diversity of library materials than were then available. Much of this need for books was filled by two public library agencies: the state library extension agency with traveling libraries and boxes of books and local public libraries with materials and services which they provided for both the school and public library.[5]

Often the only available funds for the school library were provided by such organizations as the Parent Teacher Association. In some schools, enterprising teachers raised funds for libraries by holding school festivals and other programs, using the proceeds to buy books.

However, library service to schools by public libraries and state agencies did not constitute *school library service*. In 1941, a statement of principles developed by the Joint Committee of the National Education Association and the American Library Association, *Schools and Public Libraries Working Together in Library Service*, emphasized the belief that the local board of education is basically responsible for providing a school library in every school. When, in 1945, the American Library Association published the first compilation of national standards for school libraries, *School Libraries for Today and Tomorrow*,[6] it reiterated this belief in the board of education's responsibility for providing school library service. These standards, both quantitative and qualitative, covered services to students and faculty, library personnel, and book collections.

The American Library Association had early shown its interest in school libraries by forming the School Library Section in 1914. The School and Children's Library Division was established in 1936, and the American Association of School Librarians was formed as an ALA division in 1951.

The Library Services Branch of the U. S. Office of Education was established in 1937, with a school library specialist on its staff. This federal agency contributed to the development of school libraries through statistical and research studies, conferences, and institutes emphasizing the needs of school libraries and serving as guides to those who were endeavoring to develop and improve school library service.

In the mid-1950s, the program of the public school was severely criticized; the objectives of education were questioned and a return to the idea of subject mastery and intellectual achievement was demanded. Reading ability, individual instruction, independent study, and the necessity for developing all students to the maximum of their ability were emphasized. Science, mathematics, and modern foreign languages received precedence in the curriculum, and increased efforts were made to identify and educate the gifted student. New instructional materials, media, and services were urgently needed. The school library was the logical source to fill these needs, but in too many instances, either a library did not exist or was unable to provide these materials and services. In 1960, there were libraries in 94.2 percent of high schools, but in only 31.2 percent of elementary schools.[7]

Secondary School Libraries

Several important factors contributed to the development of the high school library, but for one reason or another did not aid the growth of elementary school libraries. Two major factors were 1) college admission requirements and 2) the insistence on higher standards of secondary school library service by regional accrediting associations, national professional organizations, and state departments of education.

In 1900, the Middle States Association organized the College Entrance Examination Board to secure uniformity in the requirements and examinations for college admission, and the first examinations were given in 1901. That same year, the North Central Association established a Commission on Accredited Schools and began to work on standards for secondary schools. The standards, agreed upon in 1902, included the statement that "library facilities should be adequate to the needs of instruction."[8] Since that time the library has been included in the areas to be evaluated in the accrediting of a secondary school for admission to membership in the association.[9]

The Southern Association began the accrediting of secondary schools in 1912, the Northwest Association in 1918, the Middle States Association in 1921, and the New England Association in 1952.[10] The Western College Association does not admit secondary schools to membership.

Other educational agencies became interested in high school libraries, and in 1915 the Library Committee of the Department of Secondary Education of the National Education Association was formed to investigate actual conditions of high school libraries. The committee's final report, "Standard Library Organization and Equipment for Secondary Schools of Different Sizes,"[11] giving practical working standards for both junior high schools and high schools, was presented by the chairman, C. C. Certain, to the National Education Association at its annual meeting in 1918 and adopted at that time as its official standards for high school library development. It was approved also by the education committee of the American Library Association. The Certain Report—or the Certain Standards, as they were called—included recommendations regarding quarters, staff, collection, budget, and supervision. They continued to influence all school library standards for more than 20 years.[12]

In 1945, the American Library Association's standards for school libraries, *School Libraries for Today and Tomorrow*,[13] were added to those of the state departments of education and the regional associations in an effort to further improve the quality of school library resources and services.

Additional aid to high schools in studying their programs and in long-range planning was given by a self-study instrument, *A Planning Guide for the High School Library*,[14] published in 1951 by ALA, which provided a means of measuring the adequacy of each area of the school library program.

The Elementary School Library

Efforts on behalf of elementary school libraries have always been fewer and less successful than those for secondary school libraries. Even though the state departments of education included library materials and services in their criteria for a quality elementary school, it was the responsibility of the local board of education to provide them. Lacking a motivation of comparable urgency to that of meeting college admission requirements, local school boards too often failed to find a place in the budget for the elementary school library. The services provided by the traveling libraries or the boxes of books sent out by the state library agency or the public libraries were, in too many instances, considered adequate to the needs of the elementary school.

Interest in libraries for elementary schools grew, however, in spite of limited local funds and support. In 1925, a Joint Committee of the Department of Elementary School Principals of the National Education Association and the School Libraries Section of ALA, under the chairmanship of C. C. Certain, made a study of the conditions of elementary school libraries and drew up standards for them. The "Report of the Joint Committee on Elementary School Library Standards"[15] defined the purposes of, and established standards for, the organization and maintenance of a library in elementary schools with minimum enrollments of 500 or maximum enrollments of 2000. These standards, relating to the aim, scope, collection, staff, use, organization, and supervision of elementary school libraries, were circulated widely and were very helpful in arousing interest and support for elementary school libraries and in providing guidance for those who were planning to establish them. The ALA standards, *School Libraries for Today and Tomorrow*, recognized the importance of the elementary school library by presenting both quantitative and qualitative standards for elementary as well as secondary school library programs.

The regional accrediting associations had only an indirect influence on the elementary school library. Some associations required that a high school have the highest accreditation granted by the state agency before it could apply for membership in the regional association, but this condition benefited the elementary school and its library only if the state agency required the same accreditation for both the elementary and the high school. In 1952, the Southern Association of Colleges and Secondary Schools provided for the affiliation of elementary schools with the association through membership in the cooperative program.[16]

In spite of the efforts of many educators, librarians, and professional organizations to improve the conditions of the elementary school library, the beginning of the 1960s found it still the most neglected part of the educational program, with more than 9,860,000 elementary school children attending schools which did not have centralized libraries.[17]

The Junior High School Library

The strictly localized approach to school development in the various states resulted in greatly varying forms of school organization. In general, grades one to six have belonged to the elementary school and grades nine to 12 to the high school; but grades seven and eight, not having a fixed place in the administrative organization, sometimes have been a part of the elementary school and sometimes a part of the high school. Library facilities for these grades have been those of the school to which they are attached.

In the first two decades of the twentieth century, the major functions of the junior high school were to keep pupils in school and to enable college-bound students to take courses earlier and thus qualify for college earlier. In the 1930s, the importance of the particular needs of the period of early adolescence for the junior high school program grew steadily, and by 1940, early adolescence became the focal point around which to develop the junior high school educational program.

State departments of education have evaluated and accredited the junior high school for many years, at first as a part of a six-year high school, but more recently as a separate unit. Of the regional accrediting associations, thus far only the Southern Association of Colleges and Schools accredits the separate junior high school. All the systems for judging the quality of junior high schools which have been developed by individual schools, state educational associations, and state departments of education include the library as an area to be evaluated.

School Libraries Since 1960

A new era for all school libraries opened in 1960 with the publication by the American Association of School Librarians of the *Standards for School Library Programs*.[18] These were followed in 1969 by *Standards for School Media Programs*[19] and in 1975 by *Media Programs: District and School*.[20] These standards show a progressive emphasis on the importance of media in all formats in the school library media center collection.

The Instructional Materials Center Concept

As early as 1956, the American Association of School Librarians set forth its philosophy of the school library as an instructional materials center: the concept that the school library should serve as a center for books, other printed forms, films, recordings and all newer media devoted to aid learning; and that it should locate, gather, and coordinate the materials for learning and the equipment for their use. This concept led to the designation of the school library as the instructional materials center (also called a materials center, learning resources center, instructional resources center, or media center). By whatever name, it became an integrated unit administering both the traditional functions and services of the school library and the newer functions and services of the audiovisual media. The instructional materials center concept has been of major importance in planning school library media centers during the past three decades.

Philanthropic Contributions

Philanthropic foundations have played a vital role in the development of school libraries in recent years. For example, in 1962 the School Library Development Project, under a grant of $100,000 from the Council on Library Resources,[21] began the task of implementing the *Standards for School Library Programs*. Direct grants were made to 21 states for intrastate training projects, consultant services were provided in these and other states, and materials were developed and produced to aid in planning school library development. In 1962 also, a grant of $1,130,000 was made by the Knapp Foundation, Inc. to the American Library Association to support a five-year project for the establishment of a given number of school libraries to serve as examples of the kind of library recommended in the *Standards for School Library Programs*. The Knapp School Libraries Project, as it was called, provided for two programs in elementary schools with "existing provisions for library service"; three programs in elementary schools in different geographical locations which had less adequate library service; and three programs in secondary schools which had average or above-average provisions for library service.[22]

In 1963, the Encyclopaedia Britannica School Library Awards were initiated to "highlight the importance of good elementary school libraries to quality education and to encourage citizen planning for their development." Now called the National School Library Media Program of the Year Award, it is sponsored by the Encyclopaedia Britannica Educational Corporation and the American Association of School Librarians. Cash awards are presented annually to school districts that have shown outstanding achievement in exemplary school library media programs.

National Library Week

National Library Week is the annual observance of a year-round program which calls attention to libraries, books, and reading. Launched by the National Book Committee in cooperation with the American Library Association in 1958, National Library Week has as its purpose the focusing of public attention on the importance of reading in our national life and as a source of personal fulfillment, and on libraries. The message of National Library Week is carried in numerous newspaper and magazine articles and editorials; radio and television programs and announcements; and programs sponsored by libraries, library associations, and civic groups. Among its tangible results are the Knapp School Libraries Project and the Encyclopaedia Britannica Awards.

Federal Legislation

The concerted efforts of librarians, educators, citizens groups, professional organizations, and news media in the mid-sixties resulted in alerting large blocks of the public to the important place of the school library in the educational program, to its deficiencies, and to what is needed to raise it to an adequate level of efficiency. One of the most far-reaching results of these efforts is the Elementary and Secondary Education Act of 1965. This act authorized a program of grants for the acquisition of school library resources, textbooks, and other instructional materials for the use of students and teachers in public and private elementary, junior high, and high schools; and financial assistance in establishing supplementary education centers, developing and establishing exemplary elementary and secondary school programs, expanding research in elementary school library problems and relationships, and strengthening state departments of education.

Succeeding legislative acts, the Educational Amendments of 1974 and the Education Consolidation and Improvement Act of 1981 have provided decreasing funding for the school library media center. The recently enacted School Improvement Act (1988) amends ECIA and other acts and provides continuing funding for library books and material, computer hardware and software for instructional use, and professional development of librarians.[23]

Other federal legislation affecting school libraries includes the National Defense Education Act of 1958, which was amended and extended in 1964, and the Vocational Education Act of 1963. These acts provided materials to support new programs in the school curriculum.

Public and private school libraries have improved dramatically with ESEA Title II funding. Since 1966, the proportion of public schools with libraries has risen from 52 percent to 93 percent; 75 percent of private schools have media centers compared with 44 percent in 1966.[24]

THE SCHOOL LIBRARY PROGRAM

New standards for school library media programs, *Information Power: Guidelines For School Library Media Programs*,[25] are designed to aid in preparing programs for the next decade and into the twenty-first century. These standards define three roles for the library media specialist: information specialist, teacher, and instructional consultant. According to the standards, "the mission of the library media center is to ensure that students and staff are effective users of ideas and information."[26] In carrying out this mission, the media specialists must provide intellectual and physical access to information, ensure freedom of access to information and ideas, promote literacy, provide leadership and experience in the use of information and instructional technologies, and participate in networks to provide access to resources outside the school. Included in the standards are guidelines covering school library program development; the role of the information specialist; leadership, planning and management; personnel; resources and equipment; facilities; and district, regional, and state leadership.

Collection

The nature and size of the library collection of a particular school will depend upon many factors of which one of the most basic will be the philosophy of education held by those responsible for the school and the consequent specific objectives and programs of that school.

Since no two schools will have the same philosophy, objectives, program of instruction, or pupil needs and interests, their library collections will not be the same. However, all media centers should provide materials for all areas included in the curriculum and the school program and for recreation. These materials should be in sufficient quantity to enable teachers to find the materials required in the teaching-learning process and to provide the student with resources adequate for class assignments, independent research and inquiry, reading, listening, viewing, and personal enjoyment. The collection, selected cooperatively by teacher and librarian in relation to school organization and classroom activity, should include books, magazines, newspapers, pamphlets, films, filmstrips, pictures, slides, transparencies, maps, globes, disc and tape recordings, displays, models, exhibits, microforms, new formats and delivery systems such as compact discs, CD-ROM, video discs, videotext, cable and other television systems, optical discs, etc., and the equipment needed to use them. The collection should be organized for efficient use and easy accessibility to students and teachers in the library and classroom and for home use.

The school library media center should also provide an extensive, up-to-date, and functional collection of professional books, magazines, pamphlets, curriculum guides, resource units, audiovisual, and other instructional and professional materials for the use of faculty members and administrators, both for reference and general professional reading.[27]

Guides in the selection of materials for the school library media center are the Library Bill of Rights, Access to Resources and Services in the School Library Media Program: An Interpretation of the Library Bill of Rights, and Statement on Labeling.[28]

Staff

The professional staff of the media center consists of a media specialist, technical assistants, other media professionals, and a support staff including technicians and clerks. The size of the staff is based on the number of users. Staff activities cover participation in curriculum development, working with students and teachers, providing sources and services appropriate to user needs, and planning physical facilities to provide an effective learning environment.

The media specialist must have a broad background of general education and graduate level training in both library and information science education and media; special training in school library organization and management; a wide knowledge of literature, with special emphasis on the level of library user to be served—children, adolescents, young adults, the gifted, or special groups—and on all topics of current interest to children and young people; and knowledge of the various technologies and types of communications. The media specialist must know the curriculum, modern methods of teaching, and educational psychology and keep up with developments in these areas as well as all areas of school librarianship, in order to be able to work with administrators, teachers, students, and citizens in the development and operation of an effective school media program.

The basic educational requirements for school librarian media specialists, including preparation in education and library science, are set by the certification agencies in the several states. Meeting the basic requirements, however, does not conclude the education of the school librarian. The necessity for keeping up to date in both education and librarianship calls for continuing education throughout one's library career, through conferences, workshops, and institutes as well as in advanced formal courses.

Problems

The problems facing education in general—and specifically elementary and secondary education—are shared by school media centers as integral parts of the educational program. Other problems are:

1. *Selection of materials and equipment.* What materials should be acquired? The rapid expansion of knowledge, which is recorded and transmitted in diverse forms, creates the serious problem of knowing what and how much to select out of the multitude of materials now available. Another serious selection problem grows out of the pressures exerted by the ever-present censors, who may demand the removal of materials to which they object or who may demand that certain materials be included in the collection.[29]
2. *Acceptance by administrators and teachers* as active participants in the instructional program. In spite of the fact that educators, when questioned, willingly acknowledge the essentiality of the school library to the school program at all grade levels, an examination of current books on modern American education will reveal few references to the school library or the school media specialist.
3. *Participation in cooperative arrangements.* When and under what conditions should the school media center become a part of a network?
4. *Providing adequate services* for the changing information needs of an increasingly diverse student population.
5. *Lack of staff* necessary to provide the services required by students and teachers. In 1985, for example, about 20 percent of the public and 54 percent of private school library media centers had less than one full-time equivalent (FTE) staff member.[30]
6. *Inadequate collections* of information materials—books, periodicals, newspapers. In 1985, over half of the public school book collections were smaller than the lowest level (8000) recommended by the 1975 standards.[31]
7. *Decrease in funds* available for purchase of print materials due to the shift in expenditures from print to audio, visual, video, computers, computer software, and other electronic materials and equipment, and the high cost of these materials and equipment.
8. *Rising cost* of books and periodicals and decrease in the numbers that can be bought with available funds. The average number of books added to collections in 1985 was 315, compared with 502 in 1974.[32] Collections are becoming outdated and, therefore, unused.

9. *Diminishing federal funds* in the 1980s resulting in cuts in needed purchases and services.
10. *Deterioration* of library materials from poor quality paper and from use.

Significant Developments

1. The use of microcomputers in the schools from 1981-1985 rose from 18 to 92 percent.[33] Use is also increasing rapidly in routine and administrative areas, online catalogs, and access to databases.
2. The number of cooperative arrangements among school libraries, such as a state cooperative or consortium, cooperation with several types of libraries in a multitype network, and school/public library cooperation is growing. Cooperative purchasing, processing, collection building, and resource sharing are among the activities.
3. Newer media in school media collections include microforms, microreaders, television equipment, computers, computer software, compact discs, videocassettes, etc.
4. Collections of materials and resources to aid in remedial teaching of the retarded or the disadvantaged and collections of ethnic and racial minority materials are being developed.
5. Innovative programs are being introduced into the school media center to meet the needs of special groups: slow readers, the disadvantaged, the handicapped.
6. Increased attention is being given to instruction in the use of library materials and equipment, and videocassettes and other visual aids are being used for this purpose.
7. Interlibrary loan services are provided to students and teachers.

NOTES

1. Council of Chief State School Officers, *Responsibilities of State Departments of Education for School Library Services* (Washington, D.C.: Council of Chief State School Officers, 1961), Foreword.
2. *See* pp. 125-126.
3. *See* pp. 158-159, 160-161.
4. Carleton Bruns Joeckel, *Library Service* ("Staff Study Number 11"; Washington, D.C.: U.S. Government Printing Office, 1938), p. 21.
5. *See* pp. 125-126, 142.
6. American Library Association, Committee on Postwar Planning, *School Libraries for Today and Tomorrow; Functions and Standards* (Chicago: American Library Association, 1945).
7. Mary Helen Mahar and Doris C. Holladay, eds., *Statistics of Public School Libraries, 1960-61*, Part I: Basic Tables (Washington, D.C.; U.S. Government Printing Office, 1964), p. 3.
8. William E. McVey, "Origin and Development of Criteria for the Accreditation of Secondary Schools in the North Central Territory," *The North Central Association Quarterly*, 17 (April 1944): 286.
9. *Ibid.*, p. 291.

10. John R. Mayor and Willis G. Swartz, *Accreditation in Teacher Education: Its Influence on Higher Education* (Washington, D.C.: National Commission on Accrediting, 1965), p. 36.
11. "Standard Library Organization and Equipment for Secondary School Libraries of Different Sizes, Report of the Certain Committee on Library Organization and Equipment," National Education Association of the United States, *Addresses and Proceedings of the 56th Annual Meeting* (Washington, D.C.: National Education Association, 1918), pp. 691-719.
12. Frances Lander Spain, "The Application of School Library Standards," National Society for the Study of Education, *Forty-Second Yearbook, Part II: The Library in General Education* (Chicago: The Department of Education, University of Chicago, 1943), pp. 269-292.
13. *See* pp. 157-158.
14. Frances Henne *et al.*, *A Planning Guide for the High School Library Program* (Chicago: American Library Association, 1951).
15. "Report of the Joint Committee on Elementary School Library Standards," National Education Association of the United States, Department of Elementary School Principals, *The Elementary School Principalship—A Study of Its Instructional and Administrative Aspects* ("Its Fourth Yearbook"; Washington, D.C.: National Education Association, 1922), pp. 326-359.
16. "Committee on Elementary Education, Cooperative Program in Elementary Education," *Proceedings of the Sixty-Ninth Annual Meeting of the Southern Association of Colleges and Schools, November 30-December 3, 1964* (Atlanta, Ga.: Southern Association of Colleges and Schools, 1965), p. 236.
17. Mahar and Holladay, *op.cit.*, p. 8. A total of 83.8 percent of all elementary schools—including those with centralized libraries—were not served by school librarians. *Ibid.*, p. 43.
18. American Association of School Librarians, *Standards for School Library Programs* (Chicago: American Library Association, 1960).
19. *Standards for School Media Programs*, Prepared by the American Association of School Librarians and the Department of Audiovisual Instruction of the National Education Association (Chicago: American Library Association, 1969).
20. *Media Programs: District and School.* Prepared by the American Association of School Librarians, American Library Association, and Association for Educational Communications and Technology (Chicago: American Library Association, 1975).
21. The Council on Library Resources was established by the Ford Foundation. *See also* p. 175.
22. *See* Peggy Sullivan, ed., *Realization: The Final Report of the Knapp School Libraries Project* (Chicago: American Library Association, 1968).
23. *See* pp. 100-297 for details.
24. Center for Education Statistics, Office of Educational Research and Improvement, *Contractor Report: Statistics of Public and Private School Library Media Centers 1985-86, With Historical Comparisons from 1958-1985* (Washington, D.C.: U.S. Department of Education, 1987), pp. iii, 3.
25. *Information Power: Guidelines for School Library Media Programs*, prepared by the American Association of School Librarians and Association for Educational Communications and Technology (Chicago: American Library Asso-

ciation and Washington, D.C.: Association for Educational Communications and Technology, 1987).

26. Ibid., p. 1.
27. These materials may be part of the collection of the district media center. *See Information Power, op. cit.,* pp. 96-101.
28. *See* Appendix II.
29. *See* current issues of professional journals in librarianship and the *Newsletter on Intellectual Freedom,* published bimonthly by the Intellectual Freedom Committee of the American Library Association.
30. *Statistics of Public and Private School Media Centers, 1985-86, op. cit.,* p. iii.
31. *Ibid.*
32. *Ibid.*
33. Center for Education Statistics, *Digest of Education Statistics* (Washington, D.C.: U.S. Government Printing Office, 1987), p. 305.

16

Academic Libraries

Libraries in institutions of higher learning are as varied and distinctive as the institutions which they serve. Under the umbrella heading of "academic libraries," they cover those libraries found in junior colleges; four-year liberal arts colleges; teachers colleges; agricultural and mechanical colleges; men's colleges; women's colleges; technical schools; schools of theology, religion, law, and other professions; and the central libraries in universities and the more specialized libraries in the colleges within the universities.

The legal basis for institutions of higher education is found in the charters granted by special acts of the state legislatures for the establishment of specific institutions or in the articles of incorporation granted under the educational or corporation laws of the states. Public institutions are controlled by state or local government; private institutions are usually governed by a corporation. Both public and private institutions of higher education are administered by a board. The legal status of the library in academic institutions may be determined by the charter or by the articles of incorporation, but, in general, it is established by the bylaws of the board.

DEVELOPMENT OF ACADEMIC LIBRARIES

Among the forces which have played vital roles in the development of institutions of higher learning and thus of the libraries in these institutions are the regional, state, and professional accrediting agencies; professional organizations; private philanthropy; Friends of the Library groups; and federal legislative programs.

Accrediting Agencies

Ever since there have been schools, there have been standards of some kind which were prescribed by or for a given institution. As early as 1784, the Board of Regents of the State of New York had responsibility for maintaining standards in institutions of higher education in the state. The state department of education, the state university, or some other state agency is usually given the responsibility by the state legislature for developing standards and criteria for evaluating junior colleges, four-year colleges, and colleges of teacher education. A number of state agencies either accept the accreditation of regional or national agencies as the basis for their approval of institutions or adapt the criteria developed by these agencies to their own use.[1]

A major influence in the development of higher education has been the nongovernmental accrediting agencies, the regional associations of schools and colleges. An accrediting association is "the cooperative venture of a large number of institutions who are earnestly seeking first to ascertain what are the best standards of college work and, second, effective ways and means of bringing these standards to the attention of the institutions within its constituency."[2]

To combat certain critical problems facing both secondary and higher education, regional associations of educational institutions began to appear during the last two decades of the nineteenth century. Standards were needed on the college level for admission, program, facilities, graduation requirements, transfer of students, and preparation of faculty.[3] These associations did not begin to accredit colleges immediately. The North Central Association initiated accrediting procedures for institutions of higher education in 1910, the Southern Association in 1917,[4] the Middle States Association in 1921, the Northwest Association in 1921, the Western Association in 1949, and the New England Association in 1952.[5]

Accreditation, "a phenomenon peculiar to the United States,"[6] is the recognition accorded to an educational institution that meets the standards or criteria established by a competent agency or association. The process of accreditation includes establishing minimum standards or criteria by the accrediting agency which an institution must meet in order to be accredited; examination of the institution by the agency to determine whether it has met the standards or criteria; publication of a list of institutions which meet the standards and are therefore accredited; and periodic reviews to ascertain whether the accredited institution continues to meet the standards or criteria.[7]

The influence of the regional associations upon the development of academic libraries has been of major importance, for they have always included the library as a major area to be considered in the accreditation of an institution.[8] Early criteria for evaluating the library were quantitative, measuring such aspects as the number of books in the library and the amount of reading space per student. Although these quantitative standards were opposed by many educators and librarians, they did succeed in drawing the attention of college administrators to the substandard condition of their libraries and forced them to provide financial support of at least minimum adequacy for improvement so that accreditation would be granted.

New criteria adopted in 1934 by the North Central Association, and later by other associations, stressed the importance of evaluating an institution in terms of its own objectives, with emphasis upon qualitative rather than quantitative standards.

Other accrediting agencies, in addition to state agencies and regional associations, include the national associations or councils made up of institutions and/or organizations which are related in purpose or interests, such as the National Council for Accreditation of Teacher Education; associations of schools which prepare for a particular profession, such as the Association of American Law Schools; and organizations of members of a profession, such as the American Library Association.

Professional Organizations

The Association of College and Research Libraries, representing research and special libraries and libraries in institutions of post-secondary education, including those of community and junior colleges, colleges, and universities, became a division of the American Library Association in 1938. The mission of the Association of College and Research Libraries (ACRL) is to "foster the profession of academic and research librarianship and enhance the ability of academic and research libraries to serve effectively the library and information needs of current and potential library users."[9] It contributes to the professional development of academic and research librarians, promotes and speaks for their interests, and encourages study, research, and publication relevant to academic and research librarianship. The association publishes *College and Research Libraries* and *College and Research Libraries News.*

In 1990, ACRL approved "Standards for Community, Junior, and Technical College Learning Resources Programs," which apply to two-year or three-year academic institutions that award an associate degree or certificate.[10] "Standards for College Libraries," adopted by ACRL in 1986, apply to libraries which serve academic programs at the bachelor's and master's degree levels.[11] "Standards for University Libraries," adopted in 1989, set out the role of the university library and include areas to be considered in the evaluation of a university library.[12]

Of the other professional organizations and groups which contribute directly or indirectly to the advancement of academic libraries, notable examples are the Association of Research Libraries,[13] an organization of the largest research libraries in the United States, the majority of which are university libraries; the Special Libraries Association,[14] which includes certain aspects of academic librarianship in its range of concerns; and the American Association of Community and Junior Colleges which provides leadership and services for community, technical, and junior colleges.

Private Philanthropy

At the same time that Andrew Carnegie and later the Carnegie Corporation were making grants for public library buildings,[15] they were also financing library buildings on college campuses. After 1917, the emphasis in the Carnegie Corporation's program for the development of academic libraries moved from buildings to the improvement of services, and between 1921 and 1935 endowment grants were made to 11 institutions for general library uses or for salaries for librarians. Eventually grants totaling $667,500 were made to 21 colleges and universities for library development.[16]

In addition to the Carnegie Corporation, other philanthropic organizations aided in the development of college libraries in the first half of the twentieth century, notably the Rosenwald Foundation, which contributed to the improvement of facilities in libraries of Black colleges in the South; and the General Education Board, which made grants to libraries of small colleges—especially in the South—for library materials, equipment, and personnel.

Funds given to academic institutions by philanthropic foundations for scholarships, fellowships, and research development contribute both directly and indirectly to the growth of libraries in those institutions. Outstanding contributions for these purposes have been made by the General Education Board of the Rockefeller Fund, the United States Steel Foundation, and the Ford Foundation.

A significant contribution of the Ford Foundation to all libraries was the establishment in 1956 of the Council on Library Resources to aid in the solution of library problems and to conduct research, develop, and demonstrate new techniques and methods for the improvement of library organization and service. The Council has supported the publication of selection aids for college libraries, such as *Choice* and *Books for College Libraries,* projects undertaken by individual libraries, and studies of specific library activities and functions.

Friends of the Library

Since the beginning of academic libraries, there have been individuals and groups who have aided them by giving money, books, and effort toward furthering the library's aims and programs. These Friends of the Library groups, as they are usually called, are made up of alumni and friends of the institution who continue to work on behalf of the academic library by making individual or group gifts and donations; bequests; memorials in the form of endowment, buildings, equipment, and special collections; and who influence interested individuals, organizations, and foundations to make contributions. Friends of the Library groups may be formally organized, and they may issue promotional and informational publications.

Federal Legislation[17]

The National Defense Education Act of 1958, amended in 1964, provided funds to improve the teaching of science, mathematics, and modern foreign languages; to train modern foreign language teachers and counseling and guidance personnel at summer or academic year institutes on college campuses; to operate short-term or regular-session institutes for teachers of English, reading, history, and geography; for school librarians and school library supervisors; for educational media specialists; and for teachers of disadvantaged youth. Academic libraries were strengthened to support these programs.

The Vocational Education Act of 1963 made available funds for salaries of librarians, library books and other materials, construction, and equipment for departments or divisions of a junior college or university which offered courses in vocational education.

The Higher Education Facilities Act of 1963 authorized federal grants and loans to institutions of higher education for construction of various facilities, including libraries. The Higher Education Act of 1965 provided financial aid to libraries for materials, special equipment, research projects and demonstrations relating to libraries and the training of librarians. Re-authorizations of the act have added various provisions. The five-year extension authorized by Congress in 1985 includes the following: funds for college library resources; library career training programs and re-training programs; fellowships for bachelor's, master's, post-master's and doctoral candidates; and research and demonstration.[18]

CHARACTERISTICS OF ACADEMIC LIBRARIES

In the past decade there has been a steady increase in the number of academic libraries and an enormous growth in library collections. In 1964-65, there were an estimated 2,175 libraries, with a total of 240 million volumes. By 1988, the number of academic libraries had grown to 4,824 (including college, university, and junior/community college libraries)[19] with collections ranging from under 50,000 volumes to one million and more.[20]

Function

The basic function of the academic library is to aid the institution in carrying out its program. Each kind of academic library—junior college, college, and university—in addition to the characteristics which it shares with all academic libraries, serves certain purposes and has certain features and problems peculiarly its own, which grow out of the particular character and scope of its parent institution.

THE JUNIOR COLLEGE LIBRARY

The American junior college had its beginnings in the small two-year private colleges, the two-year curricula of the normal schools and four-year colleges, the one- or two-year technical and business institutes, and the two-year extensions—the thirteenth and fourteenth grades—of the public secondary school. It has had various names: city college, technical institute, business school or college, junior college, and—more recently—community college. Some junior colleges are privately endowed and controlled, but more than two thirds are maintained and controlled by the public.

The number of community colleges has grown to more than 1,250 in 1988 with a total enrollment of more than eight million students. There are public junior colleges in each of the states.

Purposes and Programs of the Community College

Less expensive and more convenient than the four-year college or the university, the community college provides the first two years of college work for students who will transfer to a college or university at the junior level. It offers a liberal arts program, general education, vocational and technical education programs to update occupational skills or retrain for new jobs, and various continuing education opportunities. The community college library may be called the learning resources center, or it may be a part of a larger unit that includes a library, audiovisual center, computing center, and a telecommunications center. The role of the community college library (learning resources program)[21] must be consistent with the mission of the parent institution and must be related to its educational goals, curricula, size and complexity, and diversity of resources.

The learning resources program should make available a collection of materials including various forms of print and non-print media, computer software, optical storage technologies, and other formats.[22] It should provide books, periodical publications, pamphlets, and audiovisual and other educational resources and materials in each area of emphasis in the several curricula. It should include bibliographical aids; professional and other materials for faculty use; and recreational materials for reading, viewing, or listening by both students and faculty.

The community college library serves students and faculty by making materials available for assigned and voluntary reading and study in the library or at home; by giving formal and informal instruction in the use of the library; by encouraging wide reading through easy accessibility of materials, reader guidance, displays, and book discussions; and by providing bibliographical information and special materials for the faculty.

An adequate and effective program of library services for such a varied clientele and instructional program calls for a staff which understands and supports the purposes and objectives of the community college idea in general and those of their own institution in particular and is knowledgeable about all types and forms of materials and services. A broad educational background, an acquaintance with the literature of the subject fields, and an ability to identify and appraise resources for the diversity of course offerings and the varying abilities of the students are desirable qualifications for staff members. Professional staff should have degrees and/or experience appropriate to the position requirements.[23]

THE COLLEGE LIBRARY

In general, the name "college" is given to an institution of higher learning which offers a four-year curriculum leading to a bachelor's degree in arts and sciences; requires graduation from an accredited secondary school or its equivalent for admission; and is not divided into separate schools and faculties. This definition does not cover the wide variation among colleges as to control, purposes, programs, and size. There are liberal arts colleges, many of which emphasize specializations in given fields rather than liberal education; colleges for the preparation of teachers, and technical and agricultural colleges. Some colleges offer a fifth year leading to the master's degree; some call themselves universities before they have developed a sufficient number of professional schools or faculties with the quality of advanced teaching and study to merit the title. Colleges may be under state, municipal, or denominational control; or they may be privately endowed and controlled. Enrollments range from fewer than 500 students to more than 10,000.

At the turn of the century, college libraries entered upon a period of growth and expanded rapidly after World War I. In most cases, their major concern was to acquire and to preserve materials rather than to encourage and facilitate their use since at that time, the textbook was the chief method of instruction. As more general and specialized knowledge became available, dissatisfaction with the textbook as the core of the teaching process became widespread, and increasingly, in the thirties, the college library was given the requirement and the opportunity to select and evaluate learning materials to support the teaching program and to aid students in their use.

In the forties and fifties, such educational emphases as education for democratic living and for world affairs; subject specialization; the teaching of science, mathematics, and foreign languages; and the importance of using a variety of materials called for new courses and new methods of instruction. The library endeavored to support the new curricular and instructional programs by longer hours of service, larger collections, open stacks, flexible circulation policies, new attention to instruction in library use, acquisition of various kinds of print and nonprint materials, and the provision of carrels and listening and viewing facilities.

In the past two decades, public pressure for higher education for all, coupled with the enormous increase in high school graduates, has resulted in tremendous growth in college enrollments. New curricula, new areas of specialization, and new methods of instruction have been introduced in an effort to meet the needs of the great number of students. Advances in science and technology have called for additional specializations and additional innovations in curriculum and in methods of instruction.

Purposes and Programs of the College Library

The role of the library, as an essential part of the educational program of the parent institution, has included "collecting the records of civilization and documentation of scientific pursuit,"[24] and providing programs which teach users how to retrieve and interpret these records and documents.

The library's collection should include all types and forms of recorded information, including print materials in all formats, audio and visual materials, sound recordings, computer materials, graphics, microforms, machine-readable reports, government documents, archival materials, and the equipment needed to utilize these materials.[25] The collection should be selected and developed on the basis of the institution's educational philosophy and objectives, the extent and nature of the curriculum, the methods of instruction, the size and nature of the student body, the size of the faculty and their needs for research materials, and the range of services required by the library's users. The library should make materials easily accessible physically through open shelves or other efficient means, and bibliographically through catalogs, bibliographies, and indexes; give special assistance in the use of specific materials as well as formal instruction in library resources and use; borrow needed materials on interlibrary loan from other libraries; make database searching available; and provide adequate and comfortable physical facilities for study.

In order to be able to offer such a program of services, the staff of professional librarians must be educated in library and information science with a degree from an ALA-accredited program[26] and have some subject specialization as well as language proficiency. They must keep up with trends in higher education, curriculum developments, methods of teaching, and new materials and sources in order to be able to participate actively in the instructional program of the college.

The college library is organized and administered by the director or chief librarian. The organization should be suitable to the needs and programs of the institution and should encourage the fullest and most effective use of the library's resources.[27] Theoretically, the size of the professional staff will be determined by the type of organization within the library, the college enrollment, the size and character of the collection, the teaching methods in use, the number of hours the library is open, the arrangement of the building, the range of services, and the amount of funding.

THE UNIVERSITY LIBRARY

A university is an institution of higher education which has a liberal arts college; offers a program of graduate study; usually has two or more professional schools or faculties; and is empowered to confer degrees in various fields of study.[28]

Before the Revolution, all institutions of higher learning in America were called colleges. Following the Revolution, new state institutions called universities were organized and some of the private colleges were reorganized in order to assume the broadened university functions. The state university made its appearance in the late eighteenth century,[29] but these early institutions received little financial support from the state and the instruction given was hardly advanced enough to qualify under modern standards as university teaching. The University of Virginia, established by Thomas Jefferson in 1825, has been called America's first real state university.[30] Deliberately planned as a public enterprise and completely undenominational, it offered a broader selection of subjects and more advanced work than existing colleges and predecessor universities.[31]

In the course of westward expansion, universities were established under the leadership of educators from the Eastern states, and by the time of the Civil War, 21 state universities and several municipal universities had been founded. Most of the municipal universities, however, appeared after the war with the development of large urban centers; they were planned to provide publicly supported free higher education for the people who lived in the cities.

One of the major influences on American higher education in the nineteenth century was the German university. Great numbers of American students went to study in Germany, attracted first by the advanced level of teaching and later by the German idea of scholarly research. The first American university to be founded in the true German tradition was Johns Hopkins University in 1876. "Non-sectarian and dedicated to the unfettered search for truth," it did not attempt to duplicate existing colleges, but aimed to supply the needs of the United States in certain special learned fields.[32] Following the example of Johns Hopkins, certain of the firmly established private colleges such as Harvard, Yale, Columbia, and Princeton were reorganized and expanded into universities along the lines of the German tradition.

The German-educated scholars of the latter half of the nineteenth century brought back such new instructional techniques as the seminar, the laboratory method, and the lecture. These new methods influenced not only the development of university organization and program, but also the development and use of great university libraries.

In the twentieth century, the university has added many new fields of graduate education as well as research programs for the benefit of the university; the local, state, or federal government; and business and industry.

Purposes and Programs

"The mission of the university library is to provide information services in support of the teaching, research, and public service mission of the University."[33] Since the range of the total program of the university extends from the freshman to the doctoral candidate engaged in scholarly research,[34] the university library must try to offer resources and services of comparable range.

The university library will offer a general collection of materials in all formats as required to support the academic programs, including the most recent editions as well as those of historical value; general and specialized reference, curricular, and research materials in both English and foreign languages; rare materials, such as incunabula, first editions, manuscripts, papers, letters, museum objects, broadsides, and historical maps. Also, newspapers and periodicals in English and foreign languages; federal, state, local, and foreign government publications as well as those of the United Nations; special materials, such as results of research, theses, dissertations, archives, and microforms; and diverse forms of materials and equipment, such as disc and tape recordings, films, sound tracks, language laboratories, videotapes, listening and viewing apparatus, and, increasingly, computers and auxiliary machines.

The physical organization of the university library will be determined by its administrative organization and the costs involved. The library may be centralized in one building or divided into departmental or college libraries. Some universities provide a library for undergraduates in a separate building with all the materials, facilities, and service necessary to meet their basic needs.

Access to the collection within the library is gained through catalogs, indexes, and bibliographies. Needed materials outside the library are made available through online access to various databases, telefacsimile transmission, and other forms of information transfer.

Services and Staff

The university library provides ready access to materials, facilities for uninterrupted individual study, interlibrary loan, translation assistance, typing facilities, and photocopying devices; it participates in cooperative undertakings in bibliographical service.

The library director must have the training, ability, and skill to develop and administer this highly complex part of the institution's intellectual life; to interpret the library's program to society in general, to users, and to the staff; and to secure financial and other support. The professional librarians should have a broad general education and training in library and information science and in each specialized area of service offered by the library, such as specialists in subject fields, languages, materials of instruction and special types and forms of materials, reader guidance, research, and all forms of technology. They must be competent both as librarians and as educators. The size of the professional and support staff depends on the number of programs offered, the physical organization of the library, the number of services provided, and available funds.

Problems

Some of the problems of academic libraries grow out of developments within the institutions the libraries serve: increased total enrollment; the growing number of graduate and undergraduate programs; new comprehensive areas of study, such as non-Western countries and civilizations, and literature of ethnic and minority groups, which require resources that are expensive, scarce, and difficult to acquire; the trend toward providing more opportunities for independent study; and an expanding extension program. All these problems contribute to the need for additional facilities, staff, and resources, which in turn produce the urgent need for an appreciable increase in funds allocated on a reliable and continuing basis.

Major problems derive from the curricular changes in all institutions of higher education and particularly from the scholarly and research undertakings of university libraries, which require extensive and highly accessible collections of books, journals, and reports as well as other kinds of materials in a diversity of forms and languages. Pressing needs are for more space for the library's active collection and for storage of little-used materials; larger and better trained staffs—especially in more subject competencies—to explain resources, prepare bibliographies, and locate materials in other libraries.

The rapid expansion of knowledge in every field, which has resulted in a deluge of new publications in many forms, has brought another set of problems. Since one library can acquire only a small percent of these materials and some materials—though soon obsolete—must be kept by some institutions, the problems of what to acquire, what to keep, what to store, and how to store it are urgent. Other problems are: how to reduce the size of the collection; how to curb growth of the collection; how to reduce the time and cost of processing and cataloging each item; and how to describe accurately each item by word or number so that it can be retrieved and made more easily and quickly accessible to users.

There are problems within the library: centralization vs. decentralization—when, where, and whether to establish branch libraries; how to evaluate the effectiveness of the undergraduate library to determine whether the advantages outweigh the disadvantages; in a time of stable or declining budgets, how to meet the rising cost of all publications; how to answer the demand from outside the library for more accountability; how management can provide a working environment and adequate rewards for those who work in libraries and at the same time respond satisfactorily to the needs of users; what responsibility the library must assume regarding photocopying under the present copyright restrictions; in view of the high cost of automation, whether to automate, and if so, what functions; which of the newer technologies the library should offer; whether to charge fees for the newer services; and when, with whom, and to what extent the library should participate in cooperative arrangements.

Problems relating to library personnel involve the need for librarians with advanced preparation in a subject area; faculty status for librarians;

the changing tasks of professional librarians resulting from the new functions and services of the libraries; the movement toward unionization in libraries, which began with nonprofessionals and now includes the professional staff; and discrimination against women, minorities, and others.

Problems relating to the collection are the physical deterioration of library materials from theft, mutilation, fire, flood, and other disasters.

Overarching problems in all academic libraries are how to communicate more effectively with the clients and how to secure greater use of the library by the people for whom it was planned.

Trends

In spite of these problems, and in answer to some of them, there are encouraging trends in academic libraries. Some progress is being made in achieving full faculty status for academic librarians. Participative management is being tried in a number of libraries with representatives of the staff working in groups to recommend possible solutions of library problems to library administrators. Staff development activities in the form of seminars, staff exchanges, travel, performance evaluation, time off for courses, and so on are increasing. There is a strong recognition of the need for total integration of traditional library services and a wide range of new educational technology; this recognition is reflected in the standards for junior college libraries and in the college library standards. Interest in bibliographic instruction is evidenced by workshops, the development of new materials, and the attention paid to it in all standards for academic libraries. The use of nonprofessionals is both a trend and a problem since a tight job market gives rise to concern among professionals that nonprofessionals may be given their jobs. There is renewed interest in specialization—subject, function, and type of material.

Aid in solving some of the problems mentioned earlier is available through cooperative measures. Academic libraries participate in local, regional, and national cooperative arrangements, including multitype networks and consortia. Cooperative activities include: making union lists and catalogs; centralized purchasing and processing; interlibrary loans of unusual or out-of-print materials for graduate students, faculty, and other qualified researchers; reciprocal borrowing privileges; cooperative storage; cooperative reference service; photocopying services; and cooperation with other types of libraries—public, special, and research.

Unions are becoming stronger in academic libraries, and in some instances have brought substantial benefits to library personnel, such as higher pay, a shorter work year, and better working conditions.

For some time, the computer has been used in circulation, acquisition, and making book catalogs. Many libraries are providing access to their own and other library collections through online catalogs. Computer searching of various databases is available in many libraries by librarians or by patrons. The use of the newer electronic technologies, CD-ROMs, and others in library operations is increasing.

NOTES

1. Theresa Birch Wilkins, "Accreditation in the States," *Accreditation in Higher Education,* ed. Lloyd E. Blauch (Washington, D.C.: U.S. Government Printing Office, 1959), p. 41.
2. G. F. Zook and M. F. Haggerty, *The Evaluation of Higher Institutions,* Vol. I: *Principles of Accrediting Higher Institutions* (Chicago: The University of Chicago Press, 1936), p. 15.
3. *See* pp. 158-159.
4. The name was changed in 1963 to Southern Association of Colleges and Schools, when elementary schools were admitted to membership.
5. Mayor and Swartz, *op. cit.,* p. 36.
6. *Ibid.,* p. 11.
7. Wilkins, *op. cit.,* p. 3.
8. At the first annual meeting of the North Central Association in 1896, five "elements" needed by an institution in order to be recognized as a college were set forth, and among them was "a good library" (Richard J. Jesse, "What Constitutes a College," *Proceedings of the First Annual Meeting of the North Central Association,* p. 26).
9. *ALA Handbook of Organization 1987/1988,* p. 50.
10. "Standards for Community, Junior and Technical College Learning Resources Programs: Draft" (Chicago: Association of College and Research Libraries, 1990). These standards, adopted by the Association of College and Research Libraries in January 1990, will be submitted for approval to the American Library Association in June 1990.
11. "Standards for College Libraries, 1986," *College and Research Libraries News* 47 (March 1986): 189-200.
12. "Standards for University Libraries: Evaluation of Performance," *College and Research Libraries News* 50 (September 1989): 679-691.
13. *See* pp. 188-189.
14. *See* pp. 199-200.
15. *See* p. 75.
16. Anderson, *Carnegie Corporation Library Programs,* op. cit. pp. 5, 12..
17. *See* also p. 192.
18. Not all of these programs are funded. Information regarding these programs can be found in annual reports in the *Bowker Annual of Library and Book Trade Information,* reports from the Washington ALA Office, and re-

ports from the United States Department of Education, Library Programs Division.

19. Bowker Annual of Library and Book Trade Information 1988, *op. cit.*

20. Mary Jo Lynch, *Libraries in an Information Society: A Statistical Summary* (Chicago: American Library Association, 1987), p. 12.

21. "Standards for Community, Junior and Technical College Learning Resources Programs: Draft," *op. cit.*, pp. 1,2. This term is used in these standards.

22. "Standards for Community, Junior and Technical College Learning Resources Programs" *op. cit.*, p. 15.

23. *Ibid.*, p. 45.

24. "Standards for College Libraries," 1986, *op. cit.*, p. 189.

25. *Ibid.*, p. 191.

26. *Ibid.*, p. 194.

27. *Ibid.*, p. 198.

28. Carter V. Good, ed., *Dictionary of Education* (3d ed.; New York: McGraw-Hill Book Co., 1973), p. 632.

29. *See* p. 73.

30. John S. Brubacher and Willis Rudy, *Higher Education in Transition, An American History: 1635-1956* (New York: Harper & Row Publishers, Inc., 1958), p. 144.

31. Thomas Jefferson laid down strict rules for the library of the University of Virginia, specifying that only books of "great reputation and too expensive for purchase by private means, and authoritative expositions of science and translations of superior elegance" should be acquired. (Brubacher, *op. cit.*, p. 94.)

32. Brubacher, *op. cit.*, p. 176.

33. "Standards for University Libraries . . ., *op. cit.*, p. 680.

34. The research aspects of the university library are discussed further in the next chapter, Research Libraries.

17

Research Libraries

> Every man is a valuable member of society who, by his observations, researches, and experiments, procures knowledge for men . . . it is in his knowledge that man has found his greatness and his happiness, the high superiority which he holds over the other animals who inhabit the earth with him, and consequently no ignorance is probably without loss to him, no error without evil.[1]

Emphasis on research, not only in the sciences of nature but also in the behavioral and social sciences and the fields of humanistic study, has been increasing steadily for generations in technologically and industrially advanced countries. This emphasis has accelerated radically since World War II, largely as the result of a widespread judgment that information and knowledge issuing from research constitute the basic ingredient in economic growth and prosperity. The result has been a very great expansion of research facilities and resources in universities, with a marked shift of research responsibilities from specifically skilled and motivated individual scholars to faculty members at large; a growth of research resources in government agencies and in large public library systems; an increased development of independent private research libraries and centers; and an expansive development of library resources and services to support the research activities of private industrial and commercial companies.

In 1964, the president of the Council on Library Resources stated that "the essential function of the research library . . . is to provide access in bibliographic and in physical terms to the records of human communication."[2] In terms of this function, research libraries cut across standardized group classifications, such as school, academic, public, and special. Consequently, there is not a precise category into which research libraries can be placed; they may be classified as "specialized" or "general" according to the fields of knowledge covered by their collections and services. Moreover, there are not any published precise quantitative standards by which to evaluate all research libraries. The forms and the subject content of the collection of research materials will vary with the particular mission of a specific library. The quantity of materials will vary with a particular library's decision regarding the extent to which it will attempt to be locally self-sufficient; that is, the extent to which its own collection will provide all, or at least the most significant part of, the materials and resources which its users need as against depending on effective access to resources other than its own.

For example, the collection of an independent research library which specializes in science—such as the John Crerar Library in Chicago or the Linda Hall Library in Kansas City, Missouri—will differ from the research materials of a university in that the collection will be predominantly scientific, whereas the university will provide materials of research in the humanities and social sciences as well as in the pure and applied sciences. Also, the collections of the university's research library will be built upon the resources of the university's central library. The same type of difference applies in comparing the research collections of a university with the research materials of the Henry F. Huntington Library in San Marino, California, and the Newberry Library in Chicago—both of which are privately endowed libraries emphasizing literature and history.

Although quantitative comparisons of research collections are not feasible, quality and service standards for academic research libraries are promoted actively by two national professional organizations, the Association of College and Research Libraries, which was discussed in the preceding chapter, and the Association of Research Libraries.

The Association of Research Libraries (ARL) was formed in 1932 with 44 member libraries for the purpose of studying the common problems of scholarly libraries and improving cooperation among the group as a whole. The Association has 119 members; and although most of them are university libraries, also included are privately endowed research libraries, public, and national libraries. Membership in the association is by invitation and is limited to the largest research libraries in the country.

The member libraries of ARL are not the only ones in this country which fully merit being called "research libraries"; however, a general understanding of the basic purposes, functions, and cooperative activities of the association's members will be adequately indicative of all research libraries. In this chapter, therefore, the discussion will be limited to the *types* of research libraries represented in the association's membership. The numerous libraries and library services in business, industry, and government, which are maintained in support of technical and scientific inquiry, experimentation, and research, will be discussed in the next chapter, "Special Libraries."

AVAILABILITY OF RESOURCES

The resources of a university research library are available to the students, faculty, university research staff, and visiting scholars. The materials and services of a research library in a public library system are open to the public under the regulations and conditions established by the particular library. Use of some independent research libraries is restricted to advanced scholars and is permitted only by special arrangement; others are open to the public under regulations limiting the locale in which the materials can be used. The research resources and services of the three national libraries—the Library of Congress, the National Library of Medicine, and the National Agricultural Library—are available to scholars; to students; to the research staffs of government agencies, businesses, and industries; and to the general public under regulations regarding the form and nature of the materials, the time and place of their use, and the nature and importance of the particular project on which the user is working.

Functions

According to Title II, Part C of the Higher Education Act, "a research library is one that makes a significant contribution to education and research, is broadly based, and has national or international significance for research; and is in demand by researchers."

The common basic function of all research libraries is to provide the resources and services to meet the research requirements of their users in the form needed and at the time required. In light of this purpose, the research library has a special responsibility to keep its clientele up to date and intellectually stimulated by providing pertinent literature, not only in areas of immediate concern, but also in areas of emerging and developing importance within the scope of the particular library's mission; and by contributing to the preservation, transmission, and accessibility of new knowledge.

Collection

The collections of research libraries are comprehensive, ranging from clay tablets and papyrus scrolls to the latest technical reports and today's newspapers, and including materials in all forms of human communication on every conceivable subject.

The forms of the materials will vary with the fields of research interest included in the library's purpose. For example, a collection in the areas of science and technology will include reports of original research, monographs, abstracts, handbooks, tables of formulas, microforms, conference proceedings and reports, and certain types of laboratory material, as well as journals and materials in traditional book form. The production of information and knowledge materials in scientific and technical fields is currently so massive that most of the materials in the holdings of the science research library may be of very recent date. Collections of research libraries devoted to the humanities and social sciences will have many of the forms of materials which a science collection includes. In these fields, materials will not be as new as they are in science and technology, nor will they go out of date as rapidly. In all fields of research interest, there will be materials in several languages.

Cooperative arrangements are maintained with other research libraries and with academic, public, and special libraries to extend and supplement the resources of an individual collection.

Services

The research library will offer, in addition to many traditional services, such specialized services as: acquiring, organizing, and preparing for use needed and pertinent materials *without delay*; examining new materials and providing information about them to appropriate users, in the form of reviews, abstracts, tables of contents, and photocopies of excerpts; maintaining highly specialized reference files and indexes; conducting literature searches; translating publications wholly or in part; providing quick reference and referral service, person-to-person and by telephone; operating a delivery service, on occasion; and extending the limits of its own resources by interlibrary loan and through such methods of bibliographical cooperation as union lists and catalogs and the exchange of catalogs and bibliographies, and through the use of various electronic technologies such as telefacsimile.

Cooperative Activities[3]

Early attempts at cooperation among research libraries were the Farmington Plan and the Center for Research Libraries. The Farmington Plan, administered by the Association of Research Libraries, was initiated in 1947 to ensure that at least one copy of each new foreign book and pamphlet that might be of interest to a research worker in the United States would be acquired by an American library, promptly listed in the Union Catalog at the Library of Congress, and made available by interlibrary loan or photographic reproduction. Some 60 research libraries participated in the plan and each one accepted responsibility for collecting the literature of a given subject area from a particular country or region, using assigned book dealers in the country or region both for selection and distribution. Beginning with Western Europe, the plan was extended to Africa, Australia, Latin America, the Far East, South and Southeast Asia, and the Middle East. All fields of knowledge were covered. The Farmington Plan ended December 31, 1972.

The Midwest Inter-Library Center, incorporated in 1949 by ten universities, became the Center for Research Libraries in 1965. It now has 97 members. Its primary purpose is to increase the library research resources available to cooperating institutions. Its activities include housing for common use the infrequently used materials held by each participating institution and infrequently used research materials not already available to the participants, such as doctoral dissertations from foreign universities, new foreign scholarly journals and other scholarly periodicals; centralized acquisition and cataloging of materials acquired by the participants for their own collections; and coordination of acquisitions to avoid unnecessary duplication.

Cooperative projects developed by the Library of Congress include: the National Union Catalog, which is a record of publications held by LC and 1100 other libraries; the Cooperative Conversion of Serials Project (CONSER), a 500,000-title computer catalog describing the serials held by eight major North American libraries; Cataloging in Publication; and the National Program for Acquisitions and Cataloging.[4]

Federal Legislation

In preceding chapters, federal programs, legislation, and services of potential benefit—financial and otherwise—to practically all types of libraries have been pointed out. Provisions of legislative programs of value to research libraries include:

1. The National Endowment for the Humanities, a part of the National Foundation on the Arts and the Humanities Act of 1965, is authorized to provide nonmatching grants and loans for research, fellowships, training, the publication of scholarly works, and exchanges of information in the humanities.
2. Title II, Part C, of the Higher Education Act, Strengthening Research Library Resources Program, provides funds to strengthen research library collections and make their holdings available to other libraries and to independent researchers.
3. The National Program for Acquisitions and Cataloging (NPAC) became operational in mid-1966. Prompt cataloging of materials acquired from foreign countries is made possible through the cooperation of foreign national libraries, who make available to Library of Congress catalogers the entries for their national bibliographies. LC accepts the cataloging used in these entries as the basis for its own cataloging of these materials. More than 90 libraries in the United States are participating in this shared cataloging program.
4. In 1973, the Library Services and Construction Act was amended to include within the definition of "public library" certain independent research libraries, provided they make their services available to the public free of charge, have extensive collections not available through public libraries, engage in the dissemination of humanistic knowledge, and are not an integral part of an institution of higher education.

Staff

The qualifications of the professional staff of a particular research library are implicit in the specific purpose and functions of that library. Obviously, the subject specialists will vary with the areas emphasized and served. The size of the staff, both professional and nonprofessional, will depend upon the volume of work involved in serving a particular library's clientele; the methods, techniques, and organizational system employed in serving the library's users; the funds available for personnel; and the availability of qualified personnel.

Certain qualifications should be common to the professional staff of all research libraries, including thorough specialization in the areas of knowledge emphasized, and in some cases, especially in the pure and applied sciences, specialization in the subdisciplines; facility in the appropriate languages; sufficient training in scholarly investigation and in the most effective bibliographical methods to be adept in literature searching and, thus, capable of giving clear, accurate, and adequate information on demand; proficiency in selecting and evaluating materials; ability to work effectively with subject specialists and research teams; and an understanding of the interrelationships of the subject fields. They should have an understanding of the library's new services created by automation and the changes in quantity and forms of information. The director is the manager and planner of the research library and must have the education and training necessary for carrying out these duties.

PROBLEMS

Among the problems facing the research library are:[5]

1. How to provide bibliographical access to the vast and ever-increasing quantities of recorded materials in all areas of thought, knowledge, and experience in order to enable the inquirer to become aware of, to identify, and to locate a particular item of information in whatever format it appears.
2. How to shorten the period of time between the publication of research materials, their acquisition by the library, and the cataloging of these materials.
3. How to improve techniques for the description, organization, and maintenance of the research collection, including the storage of little-used materials.
4. How to increase and make more effective cooperative activities in the sharing of library resources.
5. How to conserve and preserve materials. This problem is shared by all libraries whose collections include books published since the mid-nineteenth century when acidic alum rosin sizing was introduced into the manufacture of paper. Preservation projects include development of deacidification of whole books and improved permanent/durable paper.
6. How and where to secure funds to cover the high cost of traditional materials, new materials and services accompanying automation, networking, and other increased costs.

TRENDS

Several trends are worthy of attention:

1. *Management.* In 1969, the Council on Library Resources made a grant to the Association of Research Libraries to support a study of the problems of research library management. As a result of this study, the Council on Li-

brary Resources continues to support studies of library economics, library management, unit costs in library operations, and the application of research and development to libraries.[6]

2. *Cataloging in Publication.* An important step in the effort to catalog materials *without delay* was the agreement made in July 1971 between the Library of Congress and the American publishing industry providing for standardized cataloging data on the copyright page of current titles, thus making possible immediate cataloging of materials. This cooperative arrangement continues.

3. *Automation.* The major changes in the character of the research library are caused by the new technologies. New computer and telecommunication technology are resulting in improved service to library users and in more efficient library operations. Integrated library systems handle circulation, cataloging, technical processes, bar coding, and the public access catalog. Other technologies in use in research libraries include computer networks, online database searching, optical disc data storage, telefacsimile transmission of documents, electronic publishing, telecommunications, and CD-Rom technology.

4. *Cooperation.* No single library can have all the materials for research. New computerized networks have widened access to library materials. Research libraries cooperate in various consortia and/or networks. Most research libraries belong to one of the bibliographic networks, OCLC, RLG, WLN, SOLINET, or others.[7]

5. *Preservation and conservation.* Major attention is being given to preservation and conservation of deteriorating library materials. Numerous organizations and agencies are giving time and funds to the solving of these problems. Among these groups are the American Library Association, the Library of Congress, the Council on Library Resources, the Special Libraries Association, individual libraries, professional associations, the federal government (HEA Title 2-C), and corporations.

NOTES

1. James Smithson, founder of the Smithsonian Institution, quoted in the exterior inscriptions, Museum of History and Technology, Smithsonian Institution, Washington, D.C.

2. Verner W. Clapp, *The Future of the Research Library* (Urbana, Ill.: The University of Illinois Press, 1964), pp. 49-50.

3. *See also* p. 133. Current issues of professional journals offer numerous recent examples of cooperation.

4. *See* p. 192.

5. *See also* pp. 182-184.

6. See also the *Annual Reports* of the Council on Library Resources and Martin M. Cummings, *The Economics of Research Libraries* (Washington, D.C.: The Council on Library Resources, 1986).

7. OCLC: Ohio Computer Library Center; RLG: Research Libraries Group; WLN: Washington Library Network; SOLINET: Southeastern Library Network.

18

Special Libraries

The term "special" as currently applied to libraries has various meanings. At times it is used as an omnibus term to apply to all libraries that are not school, academic, public, or research; at other times it is used more inclusively to cover certain privately endowed specialized collections such as the John Crerar Library. It is often applied to subject branches or departments of public or university library complexes, such as the business branch of a public library or the industrial relations library of a university library system. It is also used to designate certain types of agencies called "information centers."

Article II of the Bylaws of the Special Libraries Association defines a special library as "(a) a library or information center maintained by an individual corporation, association, government agency, or any other group; or (b) a specialized or departmental collection within a library, for the organization and dissemination of information, and primarily offering service to a specialized clientele through the use of varied media and methods."[1]

At the turn of the century, public libraries began to extend special service to business and industry. In 1909, a group of 26 librarians under the leadership of John Cotton Dana, a distinguished pioneer of library service to business, founded the Special Libraries Association, which had as its objective "to promote the interests of the commercial, industrial, technical, civic, municipal and legislative libraries, the special departments of public libraries, universities, welfare organizations and business organizations."[2]

Since that time, thousands of libraries which call themselves special, or are given that label by others in referring to them, have been established in the United States and Canada. The principal growth has taken place since World War II, stimulated by the tremendous increase in the number of scientific, technical, business, and industrial research and development organizations; the flood of technological and scientific materials being produced; and the accelerating widespread interest in the transfer of information and knowledge having an immediate utilitarian value.

GROWTH OF SPECIAL LIBRARIES

Technical innovation has become recognized in recent decades as a necessity, not an option, since every new advance in mechanization adds to the ability of inventors, engineers, and scientists to design and develop newer and more efficient machines, which in turn speed up the design and development of still further advances in mechanization.

Long ago, specialization proved its effectiveness as a method for producing new and usable information; with each generation, research and learning have become more specialized and fragmented, not only in the fields of science and technology, but in all major fields of human experience. Such parent sciences as chemistry, biology, and physics have been divided and subdivided, and within subdivisions, there emerge specialized "specialties" such as microelectronics as a subspecialty of miniature electronics. In other areas of knowledge and professional practice, there are also multiplying specialties and subspecialties.

Out of the research in these fragmented areas of knowledge, and particularly in science and technology, have come, in ever-increasing numbers in recent years, reports and monographs, as well as articles in journals and other periodicals, on highly precise topics and problems. Not only has the production of materials on very specific topics and problems accelerated to a dizzy pace, but the time between the production of these materials and their practical application has so markedly decreased that those who have need for the information want to know about its existence much earlier and want access to it much faster than at any time in the past.

In answer to this need, there has been a rapid and large growth of libraries and information services agencies dedicated to identifying, collecting, and providing the specific and accurate information and knowledge that specialized users require.[3] More than 18,000 special libraries and information centers are in operation at the present time.[4]

DISTINGUISHING CHARACTERISTICS

Among the thousands of special libraries are those which serve historical societies; newspapers; schools of law, law firms, and state bar associations; officials and agencies of federal, state, county, or municipal governments; airlines; medical schools, hospitals, and medical societies; divinity schools, churches, and religious organizations; museums; military installations; prisons; learned societies; music organizations; banks, insurance companies, advertising agencies, publishing firms, and other businesses; and industries, large and small.

Each library is a unit of an agency, organization, institution, business, or industry—private or governmental—with the sole purpose of providing the information and knowledge resources that are vital to the parent organization's clientele in the achievement of the organization's specific objective, product, or service.

Since the clientele is a limited one in terms of interest and work and since the objectives of the library are specific rather than general, the collection of books, periodicals, and other materials is relatively narrow in scope, with emphasis on a single specific subject area or a group of related subjects which meet the requirements of the supporting organization.

In addition to the fact that the people who use and are served by special libraries usually are specialized in their interests and skills, some special libraries are most easily distinguishable from other types of libraries by the highly specialized form of the materials assembled and made available for use, as in the case of map libraries and picture libraries.

Special libraries vary in form and size, and although some have collections numbering into many thousands of items, the majority tend to be small and employ only a few persons.

Other kinds of libraries may cover education, scholarly research, aesthetic appreciation, and recreation in their objectives. The distinctive purpose of special libraries, however, is to provide information for immediate utilitarian application and to bring together users and information—in whatever form available—in the most effective way possible, at the time when and in the place where it is needed. The emphasis, then, is on *information services*.

Collection

The special library acquires, organizes, and maintains informational materials in fields pertinent to the work of the organization, for use by or on behalf of its clientele. The collection includes all basic, frequently used, and potentially useful materials to meet both current and anticipated needs of users. Depending upon the nature of the supporting organization, the collection may contain a variety of forms: books, pamphlets, translations, dissertations, periodicals, newspapers, press releases, transactions, reports, archival materials, yearbooks, directories, research and laboratory notebooks, patents, trademark specifications and standards, audiovisual materials, sheet music, recordings, manuscripts, clippings, abstracts, maps, blueprints, punched cards, magnetic tapes, tables, photocopies, microforms, and computer hardware and software. The size of the collection is determined by the purposes of the library and the availability of materials in its special area; it may contain works of permanent or historical value or literature which is only currently useful.

The determining factor in the organization of the collection is the necessity for quick and efficient access. Traditional systems of cataloging and classification can sometimes be used, but modifications and adaptations of these systems are often necessary. Efforts may be made to devise an entirely new system of bibliographic access, including a new classification scheme, printed checklists, indexes, computer printout catalogs, and electronic data-processing equipment.

Services and Staff

The "special" librarian is called information specialist, information manager, or by some other title using "information" rather than librarian. This specialist serves a clientele of specialists by examining all new literature which comes into the library, evaluating it, and making certain that it reaches the right persons; providing quick reference service, using photocopies as needed; making literature searches and providing bibliographies, abstracts, summaries, and translations if necessary; using interlibrary loan to provide additionally needed materials; providing selective dissemination of information (SDI) and document delivery service; maintaining company archives; encouraging the use of the library through displays, lists of new materials, and liberal loan policies; and developing programs to retrieve information through the use of computers.

The information specialist must have an understanding of the structure and policy of the organization or agency the library serves; knowledge of the subject specialty of the library, the supporting literature, and the techniques of reference and information service; a familiarity with the entire collection and the particular interests of the clientele, and the ability to match literature and client; an understanding of the basic principles of classification in order to adapt or devise systems to meet the needs of the diverse materials and forms of materials; an acquaintance with outside sources useful in locating needed information; ability to perform such special services as indexing, editing, abstracting, translating, and database searching, or knowing where these services can be procured quickly. The information specialist must be able to work well with people and within an organization.

The staff of the typical special library is small, often consisting of one professional librarian together with clerical assistants. However, some special libraries have a number of specialists on the staff, such as a translator, an abstractor, an indexer, or an information systems specialist. The information specialist should have a degree from an ALA-accredited program in library and information science.

Special libraries engage in cooperative activities and participate in most forms of cooperation: storage of certain materials, including on microfilm, microfiche, or optical discs; interlibrary loans; directories; cooperative cataloging and acquisition; duplicates exchange; union lists; and shared resources. Larger special libraries are members of OCLC or another bibliographic network. In addition to computers, many special libraries utilize CD-ROM technology, telefacsimile transmission of documents, telecommunications, and other electronic technologies.

Professional Associations

The Special Libraries Association, which began in 1909 with 26 members, had a membership of 12,000 professional librarians and information specialists by 1988.[5] The objectives of SLA are to "provide an association of individuals and organizations having a professional, scientific or technical interest in library and information science, especially as they are applied in the recording, retrieval, and dissemination of knowledge and information in areas such as the physical, biological, technical and social sciences and the humanities; and to promote and improve the communication, dissemination and use of such information and knowledge for the benefit of libraries or other educational organizations."[6]

SLA is organized into 44 regional chapters which elect officers, issue bulletins or announcements, and hold program meetings during the year. It is further organized into 26 divisions representing broad subject fields or types of information-handling techniques. Membership status is granted on the basis of education and/or professional experience and provisions are made for student members.

In addition to its official organ, *Special Libraries*, publications include source books, bibliographies, periodicals, monographs, and directories.

NOTES

1. *Who's Who in Special Libraries 1988-89* (Washington, D.C.: Special Libraries Association, 1988), p. 14.
2. Bill M. Woods, "The Impolite Librarians," *Special Libraries*, 55 (July-August, 1964): 347.
3. One of the best summations of the factors and forces leading to the development of new techniques and agencies to serve the specialized information needs of special clienteles will be found in S. C. Bradford, *Documentation*, with Introduction by Jesse H. Shera and Margaret E. Egan (2d ed.: London: Crosby, Lockwood & Son, Ltd., 1953).
4. *See Directory of Special Libraries and Information Centers* (Detroit: Gale Research, Inc., 1988).
5. *Who's Who in Special Libraries 1988-89, op. cit.,* p. 7.
6. *Ibid.,* p. 14.

19

Librarianship And Information Science

From the preceding chapters it can be seen that libraries have always endeavored to serve the needs of the societies of which they were a part. As the needs of these societies increased and changed, libraries, too, changed—in the number and forms of materials acquired, the methods of organizing and making them accessible, the number and kinds of services offered, and the kinds of facilities and equipment provided.

Admittedly, change in library practices has often been slow, seldom—if ever—dramatic, reluctant in most instances, and too late in some cases, with the result that some other agency, institution, or professional group has taken over. Such was the case with audiovisual media now administered by professionals called media specialists.

THE ELECTRONIC DIGITAL COMPUTER

Since the early 1940s, the increasing value and use of information as a commodity demanded the development of faster and more efficient facilities and processes for identifying, collecting, analyzing, evaluating, and disseminating it. Beginning in government and industry, where the need first presented itself to organize more specifically and speedily the recorded information of a narrowly defined subject field in support of intensive scientific research, the need has now spread to all disciplines. During the past four decades, emphasis on the importance of information as vital to economic and national development has resulted in the proliferation of information services: databases, bibliographic utilities, information professionals (translators, indexers, abstractors, managers, etc.) utilizing an increasing number of electronic devices, notably the computer and computer-like technologies.

There is general agreement that the electronic digital computer is the most versatile and helpful of all the machines, instruments and devices which have been produced to assist humans in carrying out important tasks. The multiple demonstrated capacities of the computer and its assumed potentials are so highly regarded that the "age of automation" is usually thought of as dating from the time when the first of these electronic devices, ENIAC,[1] was switched on in 1946 at the Army Proving Grounds in Aberdeen, Maryland, for the purpose of providing high-speed computational assistance in the national defense program.

Discovery of new uses for the computer and auxiliary machines has continued steadily since that time and today few, if any, areas of life have been left untouched by these machines. Along with the development of new uses, there has come a steady improvement in the performance and capabilities of computers in their calculating speed, storage capacity or memory, compactness and flexibility, and economy of operation.

Over the years, various technologies have offered libraries more efficient ways of acquiring, organizing, storing, and/or transmitting information and knowledge, including the telephone, typewriter, paper tape, punched cards, copy machine, microforms, audio, visual, and audiovisual forms. Introduction of the computer into library operations has come slowly. The repetitive and routine library tasks have yielded most readily to mechanization. Computers have proved most useful in such traditional operations as the acquisition of materials; the performance of bookkeeping, payroll, and accounting work; maintaining inventories of supplies and equipment; developing and updating patron registration files; preparing catalogs; recording circulation; expediting serials work; and keeping track of faculty reading and research interests.

In the early 1960s, the Library of Congress began to study the possibility of using computer technology in the cataloging of library materials.[2] By 1966, a pilot program was initiated for the distribution of cataloging data in machine-readable form to selected libraries. From this pilot program, Machine Readable Cataloging (MARC), has come computerized cataloging, the establishment of cooperative cataloging databases, and bibliographic utilities such as OCLC and RLIN, and the online public access catalog now in widespread use.

Even with the success of MARC, utilization of the computer in the storage and retrieval of information did not come easily or quickly to libraries. Lack of trained staff, patron and staff resistance to machines, unwillingness to change from established and familiar practices and formats to something "new and strange," inadequate space, inconvenience, the time required for the change, and the high cost of electronic equipment encouraged opposition. However, many factors influenced the adoption of the computer in libraries: the attention given to the new technologies—notably the computer—in library schools and in library and information science literature during the past decade; increasing familiarity with the computer in daily life; the proven capabilities of the computer and other electronic devices in performing library functions; additional funding from state and federal governments and industry for advanced technological equipment and training; pressure from administrators, patrons, and staff; availability of more trained personnel; competition from nonlibrary agencies; development of more economical microcomputers; availability of integrated systems; and, perhaps lastly, acceptance of the inevitable. Now, more and more libraries are finding the computer a necessary tool with unlimited potential for performing library operations.

INFORMATION SCIENCE

A major function of librarianship has always been to organize whatever types of materials have been available at the time; to recover, find, or retrieve information and knowledge from these materials; and utilizing any and all available methods, to transmit them in some usable form to those needing or requesting them. However, when librarianship was not ready or able to satisfy *all* the additional needs involved in managing the tremendous volume of information, a new discipline began to emerge. First called information retrieval, then documentation, it is now known as information science.

There is no consensus regarding a definition of information science, but there is agreement about what it does. According to the American Society for Information Science (ASIS), information science brings together and uses the theories, principles, techniques, and technologies of a variety of disciplines in solving information problems including computer science, psychology, mathematics, logic, information theory, electronics, communication, linguistics, classification science, library science, management science, and economics.[3]

In the broadest sense, the basic objectives of librarianship and information science are the same. Both are concerned with the acquisition, storing, and retrieval of information for use. However, there are major differences of emphasis in the techniques employed, especially the emphasis of information science on the use of computers and other electronic devices and on the interdisciplinary foundations of information science. In addition, library science is associated with a specific institution, the library, while information science is concerned with the creation, storage, retrieval and dissemination of information independent of any specific environment.[4]

With the growing volume of information, librarians and library educators became increasingly aware of the need to find more efficient and rapid ways of managing it. In 1950, Ralph Shaw, head of the U.S. Department of Agriculture Library developed the Rapid Selector, a complex device designed for searching recorded information, using electronics, optics, and photography.[5]

The Center for Documentation and Communication Research was established at Case Western Reserve University in 1955—the first information science research organization to be located in a university library school. Emphasis was on bibliographic organization, information storage and retrieval, indexing, and abstracting as they related to librarianship.[6]

Various experiments in information transfer were undertaken during the 1960s. An example was INTREX (Information Transfer Experiment) at MIT, a project directed toward the development of new methods for handling technical and scientific information, utilizing an online computer-based complex of devices easily accessible to users.[7]

In 1966, the Library of Congress began the distribution of cataloging data in machine readable form to selected libraries.[8]

By the 1960s, library schools began to add the word information to their title[9] and offered courses in areas of information science, such as computer programming and library systems analysis. Then, as now, in many instances new courses were devoted chiefly to some aspect of the computer and its use in libraries with little, if any, attention given to the science of information.

Information science is not computer science. The focus of computer science is on computer programming, data processing, and mathematics. Information science, as stated above, is concerned with solving information problems using the technologies of various disciplines, computer science being only one. It is also concerned with the nature of information—its generation, organization, processing, and distribution,[10] and with all information activities.

Information activities include many traditional library functions: collecting, classifying, recording, storing, providing bibliographic and physical access to information through reference service and, more recently, online bibliographic and database searching. Other information activities, some of which are carried on in special, research, and large public and university libraries include interpreting, analyzing, evaluating, translating, abstracting, indexing, and creating information. Still others involve teaching information professionals and developing and marketing information products.

The emergence of many occupational groups[11] concerned with the organization and dissemination of information and knowledge has given rise to dire predictions about the future of the library, e.g., "the library as an institution housing a physical collection" will eventually become obsolete and print on paper will be replaced by electronic publications.[12] Some persons believe that the basic functions of the library will not change as we move into the electronic environment, but that the ways in which these functions are carried out will change.[13] Others feel that to date no technology has replaced the printed word, but suggest that the usefulness of the printed page may not last.[14]

In the preceding chapters, it has been shown that many libraries have adopted new technologies, such as the computer, videocassettes, CD-ROM, and various forms of telecommunications and are utilizing them in library operations in their efforts to provide better service for their clienteles. Most libraries are in various stages of introducing and/or adopting some of the electronic technologies for the same purpose.

In state, public, school, academic, special, and research libraries, the influences of the information age are apparent in their standards, operations, services, planning, and cooperative arrangements. Library schools are accepting the responsibility for preparing librarians/information professionals who can perform in many different information environments by designing curricular offerings which include such interdisciplinary offerings as library science/management, library science/communication, library science/business, and library science/computer science.

Education and Training

The volume and complexity of information and the continuing development of more and more sophisticated electronic means of managing it have created the need for persons devoted to studying and understanding all of the activities involved in producing, acquiring, processing, analyzing, evaluating, and distributing this information.

The education and training of information professionals is a growing concern of schools of library and information science education and considerable attention is given in the literature and in numerous conferences, meetings, and seminars to designing courses and model curricula. Attention is also being directed to identifying the skills and competencies which information professionals should have. Some of these competencies are considered basic in librarianship, such as subject specializations, ability to use materials and technology, and skills related to each specific activity performed in the library. Information workers should also have a knowledge of the structure and format of information; of the individuals, organizations, and institutions constituting the information environment;[15] of what is required to provide service and produce products; and of what services and products are needed. In addition to a thorough grounding in library science, the information professional should have a background of study in certain disciplines, such as philosophy, linguistics, mathematics, and/or the social and behavioral sciences.[16]

Education and training of information professionals are provided by library schools whose graduates are employed in numerous information environments other than libraries; by other schools and divisions in colleges and universities, such as colleges of business or engineering whose graduates work with computers; in accounting, and in various aspects of information management; and by government agencies and industry.

Professional Organizations

The professional organization for information professionals is the American Society for Information Science (ASIS). Founded in 1937 as the American Documentation Institute, its initial interest was in the development of microfilm. In 1968, the name was changed to American Society for Information Science emphasizing its members' concern with all aspects of the information-transfer process.

ASIS defines its purpose as "the provision of knowledge, leadership and development opportunities for information professionals and organizations to enhance and advance the state of the art of information science and its applications."[17]

It provides a variety of services to its members, including conferences, meetings, continuing education programs, and publications. Among its 4000 members are information specialists from such fields as computer science, engineering, management, linguistics, librarianship, and education.[18]

Other professional associations concerned with information activities are the American Library Association, Special Libraries Association, and Association for Library and Information Science Education.

The National Commission on Library and Information Science has the responsibility for developing and recommending plans for meeting the library and information needs of the people of the United States.[19]

Additional contributions to information science have been made by the federal government, the National Science Foundation, the Council on Library Resources,[20] and industry through grants and other financial support to further research in specific areas.

A growing body of materials—textbooks, monographs, journals, conference proceedings, dictionaries, encyclopedias, audio, visual, and audiovisual materials, research reports, etc.—produced, by the various groups concerned with information—keep the information professional up-to-date.

NOTES

1. ENIAC: Electronic Numerator, Integrator, Analyzer, and Computer. *See* Stan Augarten, *Bit by Bit: An Illustrated History of Computers* (London: George Allen & Unwin, 1985).
2. *See* p. 116.
3. Martha Williams, "Defining Information Science and the Rise of ASIS," *Bulletin of the American Society for Information Science* (December/January 1988): 17-18.
4. Cuadra Associates, *A Library and Information Science Research Agenda for the 1980s: Final Report* (Santa Barbara, Calif.: Cuadra Associates, 1982).
5. Norman D. Stevens, ed., *Essays for Ralph Shaw* (Metuchen, N.J.: The Scarecrow Press, 1975).
6. Jesse H. Shera, *Documentation and the Organization of Knowledge*, ed. D. J. Foskett (Hamden, Conn.: Archon Books, 1966).
7. *Intrex: The Report of a Planning Conference on Information Transfer Experiments*, ed. Carl F. J. Overhage (Cambridge, Mass.: The M. I. T. Press, 1965).
8. *See* p. 116.

9. In 1989, of the 61 ALA-accredited library schools, 51 have the word information in their titles. However, schools which do not have information as part of the title may emphasize information science.

10. Martha Williams, *op. cit.*

11. *The Online Database Search Service Directory, 1988* lists more than 1700 libraries, information firms, and other sources which provide computerized information retrieval services using publicly available online databases. Some 2800 databases—science, business, technology, medicine, law, social sciences, and humanities—are available to the public. *See* Doris Morris Maxfield, *et al.*, *Online Database Search Service Directory* (2d ed.: Detroit: Gale Research Company, 1988).

12. F. W. Lancaster, "The Paperless Society Revisited," *American Libraries* 16 (September 1985): 554.

13. Tom Surprenant, "Future Libraries: The Electronic Environment," *Wilson Library Bulletin* 56 (January 1982): 336.

14. Pat Holholt, "The Nature of Information and Its Influence on Libraries," *Special Libraries* 75 (July 1984): 247.

15. José-Marie Griffiths and David W. King, *New Directions in Library and Information Science Education* (Westport, Conn.: Greenwood Press, Inc., for American Society for Information Science, 1986).

16. Anthony Debons, *et al.*, *Information Science: An Integrated View* (Boston: G. K. Hall & Co., 1988), pp. 15 ff.

17. *ASIS 1989 Handbook and Directory* (Washington, D.C.: American Society for Information Science, 1989), p. 8.

18. *Ibid.*, pp. 8, 10.

19. *See* p. 121.

20. *See* p. 175.

APPENDIX I

Bibliography

In addition to the sources cited in the notes, the following references are suggested.

GENERAL

Advances in Librarianship. Edited by Melvin J. Voigt. New York: Academic Press, 1970- . (Annual.)

ALA Yearbook of Library and Information Science. Chicago: American Library Association, 1976- .

American Library Directory. 1923- . New York: R. R. Bowker Company, 1978- (Annual.)

American Library Laws. Edited by Alex Ladenson. 5th ed. Chicago: American Library Association, 1984.

The Bowker Annual of Library and Book Trade Information. New York: R. R. Bowker Company, 1956- .

Council on Library Resources. *Annual Report.* Washington, D.C.: Council on Library Resources, 1956/57- .

Encyclopedia of Library and Information Science. New York: Marcel Dekker, 1968- .

PART ONE

Barnes, Harry Elmer. *An Intellectual and Cultural History of the Western World*. 3d rev. ed. New York: Dover Publications, Inc., 1985.

Ditzion, Sidney. "Mechanics' and Mercantile Libraries," *Library Quarterly* 10 (April 1940): 192-216.

Harris, Michael H. *History of Libraries in the Western World*. Metuchen, N.J.: Scarecrow Press, 1984.

Haskins, Charles Homer. *The Renaissance of the Twelfth Century*. Cambridge, Mass.: Harvard University Press, 1927.

Jackson, Sidney L. *Libraries and Librarianship in the West: A Brief History*. (McGraw-Hill Series in Library Education.) New York: McGraw-Hill Book Company, 1974.

Kenyon, Sir Frederic George. *Books and Readers in Ancient Greece and Rome*. 2d ed. New York: Oxford University Press, 1951.

Pfeiffer, Rudolf. *History of Classical Scholarship from 1300 to 1850*. Oxford: Clarendon Press, 1976.

Parsons, Edward A. *The Alexandrian Library: Glory of the Hellenistic World, Its Rise, Antiquities, and Destruction*. Amsterdam: Elsevier Publishing Company, 1952.

Reynolds, L. D., and N.G. Wilson. *Scribes and Scholars: A Guide to the Transmission of Greek and Latin Literature*. London: Oxford University, 1968.

Vervliet, Hendrik D. L. (ed.). *The Book Through Five Thousand Years*. London: Phaidon Publications, Inc., 1972.

PART TWO

"Current and Future Trends in Library and Information Science Education," *Library Trends,* Spring 1986 Issue. Ed. by George Bobinski. Champaign, Ill.: University of Illinois Press, 1986.

Johnson, Debra Wilson, and Jennifer Soule. *Libraries and Literacy: A Planning Manual*. Chicago: American Library Association, 1987.

Office for Intellectual Freedom, ALA. *Intellectual Freedom Manual*. Chicago: American Library Association, 1989.

Ranganathan, Shijali Ramamrita. *The Five Laws of Library Science*. Bombay: Asia Publishing House, 1963.

Shera, Jesse H. *The Foundations of Education for Librarianship* (Hayes and Becker Information Sciences Series.) New York: John Wiley & Sons, 1972.

White, Herbert S. (ed.). *Education for Professional Librarians*. White Plains, N.Y.: Knowledge Industry Publications, 1986.

Winter, Michael. *The Culture and Control of Expertise: Toward a Sociological Understanding of Librarianship*. Westport, Conn.: Greenwood Press, 1988.

PART THREE: Chapter 12

Bobinski, George. "The Golden Age of Librarianship," *Wilson Library Bulletin* 58 (January 1984), 338-344.

Goodrum, Charles A., and Helen Dalrymple. *The Library of Congress*. 2d ed. New York: Praeger Publications, Inc. 1982.

Annual Reports of the Library of Congress, the National Library of Medicine, the National Agricultural Library, the National Archives, the USIA, the U. S. Department of Education, and other government agencies.

PART THREE: Chapters 13 and 14

Anthony, Carolyn A. "The Public Library Development Program: Options and Opportunities," *Public Libraries* 26 (Summer 1987): 55-57.

Bobinski, George S. *Carnegie Libraries: Their History and Impact on Public Library Development*. Chicago: American Library Association, 1969.

Ditzion, Sidney H. *Arsenals of a Democratic Culture*. Chicago: American Library Association, 1947.

Garceau, Oliver. *The Public Library in the Political Process*. New York: Columbia University Press, 1949.

McClure, Charles (ed.). *State Library Services and Issues: Facing Future Challenges*. Norwood, N.J.: Ablex Publishing Corporation, 1986.

Monypenny, Philip. *The Library Functions of the State*. Chicago: American Library Association, 1987.

"NCES Survey of Public Libraries 1982: Final Report." In *Bowker Annual of Library and Book Trade Information*. 31st. ed. New York: R. R. Bowker Company, 1986.

Schuman, Patricia. "Library Networks: A Means Not An End " *Library Journal* 112 (February 1, 1987): 33-37.

Young, Virginia G. *The Library Trustee: A Practical Guidebook*. 4th ed. New York: R. R. Bowker Company, 1988.

PART THREE: Chapter 15

Aaron, Shirley, and Pat R. Scales (eds.). *School Library Media Annual*. Littleton, Colo.: Libraries Unlimited, 1983-

Center for Education Statistics. *Education Statistics*. Washington, D.C.: Government Printing Office, 1987.

Council of Chief State School Officers. *Educational Governance in the States: A Status Report on State Boards of Education, Chief State School Officers, and State Agencies*. Washington, D.C.: United States Department of Education, 1983.

Eisenberg, Michael B., and Robert E. Berkowitz. *Curriculum Initiative: An Agenda and Strategy for Library Media Programs*. Norwood, N.J.: Ablex Publishing Corporation, 1988.

PART THREE: Chapters 16-18

Clapp, Verner W. *The Future of the Research Library*. Urbana, Ill.: The University of Illinois Press, 1964.

Cohen, Arthur, and Florence B. Brawer. *The American Community College*. San Francisco: Jossey-Bass Publishers, 1982.

Fischer, Russell. "Managing Research Libraries: An Interview with David Weber" *Wilson Library Bulletin* 59 (January 1985): 319-323.

Lyle, Guy R. *Administration of the College Library*. 4th ed. New York: The H. W. Wilson Company, 1974.

Metcalf, Keyes D. *Planning Academic and Research Libraries*. Rev. ed. by Philip D. Leighton and David C. Weber. Chicago: American Library Association, 1986.

Rider, Fremont. *The Scholar and the Future of the Research Library*. New York: Hadham Press, 1944.

Thompson, James, and Reg Carr. *An Introduction to University Library Administration*. Chicago: American Library Association, 1987.

Weber, David C. "Brittle Books in Our Nation's Libraries," *College and Research Libraries News* 48 (May 1987): 238-244.

Woodsworth, Ann, and Barbara Von Wahlde. *Leadership for Research Libraries: A Festschrift for Robert M. Hayes*. Metuchen, N.J.: Scarecrow Press, 1988.

PART THREE: Chapter 18

Kruzas, Anthony T. (ed.). *Directory of Special Libraries and Information Centers*. Detroit: Gale Research Company, 1963- . (Irregular.)

Lynch, Beverly P. *Management Strategies for Libraries: A Basic Reader*. New York: Neal-Schuman Publishers, Inc., 1985.

Mount, Ellis. *Special Libraries and Information Centers*. New York: Special Libraries Association, 1983.

PART THREE: Chapter 19

Annual Review of Information Science and Technology. New York: Interscience Publishers, 1966- .

Buckland, Michael K. *Library Services in Theory and Context*. 2d ed. New York: Pergamon Press, 1988.

Crawford, Walt. *Current Technologies in the Library: An Overview*. Boston: G. K. Hall & Co., 1988.

De Gennaro, Richard. *Libraries, Technology and the Information Market Place: Selected Papers*. Boston: G. K. Hall & Co., 1989.

Encyclopedia of Information Systems and Services. 9th ed. Detroit: Gale Research Company, 1989. 3 vols.

Estabrook, Leigh S. "Librarianship and Information Resources Management: Some Questions and Contradictions." *Journal of Education for Library and Information Science Education* 27 (Summer 1986): 2-11.

Flynn, Roger R. *An Introduction to Information Science*. New York: Marcel Dekker, Inc., 1987.

Grover, Robert J. "Libraries and Information Professional Education for the Learning Society: A Model Curriculum," *Journal of Education for Library and Information Science Education* 26 (Summer 1985): 33-45.

Heilprin, Lawrence. *Toward Foundations of Information Science*. White Plains, N.Y.: Knowledge Industry Publications, 1985.

Machlup, Fritz, and Una Mansfield. *The Study of Information*. New York: John Wiley and Sons, 1983.

Matthews, Joseph R. *Public Access to Online Catalogs*. 2d ed. New York: Neal-Schuman Publishers, Inc., 1985.

Nelson, Nancy Melin (ed.). *Connecting with Technology 1988: Microcomputers in Libraries*. Westport, Conn.: Meckler, 1988.

Ong, Walter J. "Writing Is a Technology That Restructures Thought." *The Written Word, Wolfson College Lectures, 1985*, ed. Gerd Baumann. Oxford: Clarendon Press, 1986, 23-50.

Plato's Phaedrus, trans. with intro. and commentary by R. Hackforth (Cambridge: At the University Press), p. 157.

Pemberton, J. Michael, and Ann E. Prentice (eds.). *Information Science: The Interdisciplinary Context*. New York: Neal-Schuman Publishers, Inc., 1989.

Saracevic, Tefko (ed.). *Introduction to Information Science*. New York: R. R. Bowker Company, 1970.

Shera, Jesse H. "The Quiet Stir of Thought or, What the Computer Cannot Do," *Library Journal* 94 (September 1, 1969): 2875-2880.

Wright, H. Curtis. *Jesse Shera, Librarianship, and Information Science* (Occasional Research Paper Number 5) Provo, Utah: School of Library and Information Sciences, Brigham Young University, 1988.

Current journals in each area of librarianship and information science are important sources of information.

APPENDIX II

Guides For Professional Performance

THE PROFESSION

by Melvil Dewey
in *The American Library Journal*
Vol 1, No. 1, September 30, 1876, p. 5-6.

The time has at last come when a librarian may, without assumption, speak of his occupation as a profession. And, more, a better time has come—perhaps we should say is coming, for it still has many fields to conquer. The best librarians are no longer men of merely negative virtues. They are positive, aggressive characters, standing in the front rank of the educators of their communities, side by side with the preachers and the teachers. The people are more and more getting their incentives and ideas from the printed page. There are more readers and fewer listeners, and men who move and lead the world are using the press more and the platform less. It needs no argument to prove that reading matter can be distributed better and more cheaply through lending libraries than in any other way, and we shall assume, what few will presume to dispute, that the largest influence over the people is the printed page and that this influence may be wielded most surely and strongly through our libraries.

From the first, libraries have commanded great respect, and much has been written of their priceless worth; but the opinion has been largely prevalent that a librarian was a keeper only, and had done his full duty if he preserved the books from loss, and to a reasonable extent from the worms. There have been noble exceptions to this rule, but still it is a modern idea that librarians should do more than this. It is not now enough that the books are cared for properly, are well arranged, are never lost. It is not enough if the librarian can readily produce any book asked for. It is not enough that he can, when asked, give advice as to the best books in his collection on any given subject. All these things are indispensable, but all these are not enough for our ideal. He must see that his library contains, as far as possible, the best books on the best subjects, regarding carefully the wants of his special community. Then, having the best books, he must create among his people, his pupils, a desire to read those books. He must put every facility in the way of readers, so that they shall be led on from good to better. He must teach them how, after studying their own wants, they may themselves select their reading wisely. Such a librarian will find enough who are ready to put themselves under his influence and direction, and, if competent and enthusiastic, he may soon largely shape the reading, and through it the thought, of his whole community.

The time is come when we are not astonished to find the ablest business talents engaged in the management of a public library. Not that we have less scholarship, but that we have more life. The passive has become active, and we look for a throng of people going in and out of library doors as in the markets and the stores. There was a time when libraries were opened only at intervals, and visitors came occasionally, as they come sometimes to a deserted castle or to a haunted house. Now many of our libraries are as accessible as our post offices, and the number of new libraries founded has been so great that in an ordinary town we no longer ask, "Have you a library?" but "Where is your library?" as we might ask where is your schoolhouse, or your post office, or your church?

And so our leading educators have come to recognize the library as sharing with the school the education of the people. The most that the schools can hope to do for the masses more than the schools are doing for them in many sections, is to teach them to read intelligently, to get ideas readily from the printed page. It may seem a strong statement, but many children leave the schools without this ability. They can repeat the words of the book, but this is simply pronunciation, as a beginner pronounces another language without getting any clear idea of the meaning. Could the schools really teach the masses to *read*, they would be doing a great work. The children of the lower classes have to commence work at a very early age, and it is impossible to keep them in the schools long enough to educate them to any degree. The school teaches them to read; the library must supply them with reading which shall serve to educate, and so it is that we are forced to divide popular education into two parts of almost equal importance and deserving equal attention: the free school and the free library.

It is in the interest of the modern library, and of those desiring to make its influence wider and greater, that this journal has been established. Its founders have an intense faith in the future of our libraries and believe that if the best methods can be applied by the best librarians, the public may soon be brought to recognize our claim that the free library ranks with the free school. We hold that there is no work reaching farther in its influence and deserving more honor than the work which a competent and earnest librarian can do for his community.

The time *was* when a library was very like a museum, and a librarian was a mouser in musty books, and visitors looked with curious eyes at ancient tomes and manuscripts. The time *is* when a library is a school, and the librarian is in the highest sense a teacher, and the visitor is a reader among the books as a workman among his tools. Will any man deny to the high calling of such a librarianship the title of profession?

STATEMENT ON PROFESSIONAL ETHICS, 1981

Introduction

Since 1939, the American Library Association has recognized the importance of codifying and making known to the public and the profession the principles which guide librarians in action. This latest revision of the Code of Ethics reflects changes in the nature of the profession and in its social and institutional environment. It should be revised and augmented as necessary.

Librarians significantly influence or control the selection, organization, preservation, and dissemination of information. In a political system grounded in an informed citizenry, librarians are members of a profession explicitly committed to intellectual freedom and the freedom of access to information. We have a special obligation to ensure the free flow of information and ideas to present and future generations.

Librarians are dependent upon one another for the bibliographical resources that enable us to provide information services, and have obligations for maintaining the highest level of personal integrity and competence.

Code of Ethics

I. Librarians must provide the highest level of service through appropriate and usefully organized collections, fair and equitable circulation and service policies, and skillful, accurate, unbiased, and courteous responses to all requests for assistance.

II. Librarians must resist all efforts by groups or individuals to censor library materials.

III. Librarians must protect each user's right to privacy with respect to information sought or received, and materials consulted, borrowed, or acquired.

IV. Librarians must adhere to the principles of due process and equality of opportunity in peer relationships and personnel actions.

V. Librarians must distinguish clearly in their actions and statements between their personal philosophies and attitudes and those of an institution or professional body.

VI. Librarians must avoid situations in which personal interests might be served or financial benefits gained at the expense of library users, colleagues, or the employing institution.

LIBRARY BILL OF RIGHTS

The American Library Association affirms that all libraries are forums for information and ideas, and that the following basic policies should guide their services.

1. Books and other library resources should be provided for the interest, information, and enlightenment of all people of the community the library serves. Materials should not be excluded because of the origin, background, or views of those contributing to their creation.
2. Libraries should provide materials and information presenting all points of view on current and historical issues. Materials should not be proscribed or removed because of partisan or doctrinal disapproval.
3. Libraries should challenge censorship in the fulfillment of their responsibility to provide information and enlightenment.
4. Libraries should cooperate with all persons and groups concerned with resisting abridgment of free expression and free access to ideas.
5. A person's right to use a library should not be denied or abridged because of origin, age, background, or views.
6. Libraries which make exhibit spaces and meeting rooms available to the public they serve should make such facilities available on an equitable basis, regardless of the beliefs or affiliations of individuals or groups requesting their use.

Adopted June 18, 1948.
Amended February 2, 1961, June 27, 1967,
and January 23, 1980, by the ALA Council.

ACCESS TO RESOURCES AND SERVICES
IN THE SCHOOL LIBRARY MEDIA PROGRAM:
AN INTERPRETATION OF THE ALA LIBRARY BILL OF RIGHTS

The school library media program plays a unique role in promoting intellectual freedom. It serves as a point of voluntary access to information and ideas and as a learning laboratory for students as they acquire critical thinking and problem solving skills needed in a pluralistic society. Although the educational level and program of the school necessarily shape the resources and services of a school library media program, the principles of the Library Bill of Rights apply equally to all libraries, including school library media programs.

School library media professionals assume a leadership role in promoting the principles of intellectual freedom within the school by providing resources and services that create and sustain an atmosphere of free inquiry. School library media professionals work closely with teachers to integrate instructional activities in classroom units designed to equip students to locate, evaluate, and use a broad range of ideas effectively. Through resources, programming, and educational processes, students and teachers experience the free and robust debate characteristic of a democratic society.

School library media professionals cooperate with other individuals in building collections of resources appropriate to the developmental and maturity levels of students. These collections provide resources which support the curriculum and are consistent with the philosophy, goals, and objectives of the school district. Resources in school library media collections represent diverse points of view and current as well as historic issues.

Members of the school community involved in the collection development process employ educational criteria to select resources unfettered by their personal, political, social, or religious views. Students and educators served by the school library media program have access to resources and services free of constraints resulting from personal, partisan, or doctrinal disapproval. School library media professionals resist efforts by individuals to define what is appropriate for all students or teachers to read, view, or hear.

Major barriers between students and resources include: imposing age or grade level restrictions on the use of resources, limiting the use of interlibrary loan and access to electronic information, charging fees for information in specific formats, requiring permissions from parents or teachers, establishing restricted shelves or closed collections, and labeling. Policies, procedures and rules related to the use of resources and services support free and open access to information.

The school board adopts policies that guarantee student access to a broad range of ideas. These include policies on collection development and procedures for the review of resources about which concerns have been raised. Such policies, developed by persons in the school community, provide for a timely and fair hearing and assure that procedures are applied equitably to all expressions of concern. School library media professionals implement district policies and procedures in the school.

Adopted July 2, 1986, by the ALA Council.

STATEMENT ON LABELING:
AN INTERPRETATION OF THE LIBRARY BILL OF RIGHTS

Labeling is the practice of describing or designating certain library materials by affixing a prejudicial label to them or segregating them by a prejudicial system. The American Library Association opposes this as a means of predisposing people's attitudes towards library materials for the following reasons:

1. Labeling is an attempt to prejudice attitudes and as such, it is a censor's tool.
2. Some find it easy and even proper, according to their ethics, to establish criteria for judging publications as objectionable. However, injustice and ignorance rather than justice and enlightenment result from such practices, and the American Library Association opposes the establishment of such criteria.
3. Libraries do not advocate the ideas found in their collections. The presence of books and other resources in a library does not indicate endorsement of their contents by the library.

The American Library Association opposes efforts which aim at closing any path to knowledge. This statement does not, however, exclude the adoption of organizational schemes designed as directional aids or to facilitate access to materials.

Adopted July 13, 1951.
Amended June 25, 1971; July 1, 1981,
by the ALA Council.

Index